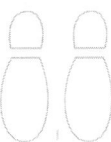

HTML
STUDIO
SKILLS

Ian Bell

Marcus Eby

Hayden
Books

President	Richard Swadley
Associate Publisher	John Pierce
Publishing Manager	Laurie Petrycki
Managing Editor	Lisa Wilson
Director of Marketing	Kelli S. Spencer
Acquisitions Editor	Michelle Reed
Development Editor	Robyn Holtzman
Production Editor	Kevin Laseau
Copy Editor	Meshell Dinn
Technical Editor	George Pytlik
Publishing Coordinator	Karen Flowers
Cover Illustration	Aren Howell
Book/Cover Designer	Sandra Schroeder
Manufacturing Coordinator	Brook Farling
Production Team Supervisors	Laurie Casey, Joe Millay
Production Team	Aleata Howard, Christopher Morris, Scott Tullis, Pamela Woolf
Indexer	Tim Tate

HTML Studio Skills

©1997 Hayden Books

All rights reserved. Printed in the United States of America. No part of this book may be used or reproduced in any form or by any means, or stored in a database or retrieval system, without prior written permission of the publisher except in the case of brief quotations embodied in critical articles and reviews. Making copies of any part of this book for any purpose other than your own personal use is a violation of United States copyright laws. For information, address Hayden Books, 201 W. 103rd Street, Indianapolis, Indiana 46290.

Library of Congress Catalog Number: 96-080341
ISBN: 1-56830-355-6

Printed in the United States of America 1 2 3 4 5 6 7 8 9 0

Warning and Disclaimer

This book is sold as is, without warranty of any kind, either express or implied. While every precaution has been taken in the preparation of this book, the authors and Hayden Books assume no responsibility for errors or omissions. Neither is any liability assumed for damages resulting from the use of the information or instructions contained herein. It is further stated that the publisher and authors are not responsible for any damage or loss to your data or your equipment that results directly or indirectly from your use of this book.

About the Authors

Marcus Eby has been working in graphic design for over five years and Web design for more than two. He has a background in film (editing, casting, foley), television (writing, directing) and animation (inbetween and cel painting). Each of these jobs and skills has molded his reputation as a Web designer.

Marcus has mastered many of todays graphics packages, including 2D and 3D packages. He is versed in HTML 3.2, Netscape 3, and MSIE 3, Java, CGI scripting, C and C++. With over 20 Web sites to his credit, and numerous graphic contracts, Marcus' skills in graphics, animation, and Web design have made him a leader in his field.

Ian is currently an Internet systems analyst and writer in beautiful Vancouver, Canada. Ian has eight email addresses, 798 CDs, and 423 empty Pepsi cans. He can most frequently be found in the crease, where every good Canadian goalie outta stay. You can always visit him at http://ian.cafe.net.

Trademark Acknowledgments

We would like to thank and acknowledge these companies, for either their trademark, support, and software:

Adobe, Microsoft, Netscape Communications, and Alchemy Mindworks.

All terms mentioned in this book that are known to be trademarks or services marks have been appropriately capitalized. Hayden Books cannot attest to the accuracy of this information. Use of a term in this book should not be regarded as affecting the validity of any trademark or service mark.

Dedication

I'd like to dedicate this book in two parts, first and foremost, I'm dedicating this book to my Mother, who was always there for me, and who taught me the meaning of giving, caring, and understanding, all in the face of insurmountable odds.

And second, unlike many people who seem to tread through life with only a friend or two, I've been blessed with many. To those who are on the path to their careers, Colin, Mark, Darren, Josh, Aquila, Lil, Eileen and Dwayne, (whew!) and to those who have already found their calling,

Charm, Gary, Glen, Charlene, Dána and whoever else I can't remember, I dedicate this to you guys (and gals), without whose support and friendship over the last few years (and in some cases, many more), I wouldn't have achieved close to what I have today. Thank you.

—Marcus Erby

Acknowledgments

I would like very much at this time to acknowledge the support of my newest friend, Ian Bell. Three months ago, we were complete strangers, and now we know way too much about each other. Also to Hayden Books who helped me from the very beginning by putting complete trust in me, allowing me to choose a coauthor (Ian), and letting us develop a book that takes the right blend of HTML and graphics and throws in a bit of humor, a whole heck of a lot of examples, and just a smidge of things to come, we thank you.

—Marcus Erby

Ian would like to thank the School of Communication at SFU, Mark and the Hairy One, Mom and Dad, Danara, and Stan the Man.

—Ian Bell

Hayden Books

The staff of Hayden Books is committed to bringing you the best computer books. What our readers think of Hayden is important to our ability to serve our customers. If you have any comments, no matter how great or how small, we'd appreciate your taking the time to send us a note.

You can reach Hayden Books at the following:

Hayden Books
201 West 103rd Street
Indianapolis, IN 46290
317-581-3833

Email addresses:

America Online: Hayden Bks
Internet: hayden@hayden.com

Visit the Hayden Books Web site at http://www.hayden.com

Contents at a Glance

Chapter 1: Understanding the Project 1
Chapter 2: Site Mapping and Blocking 13
Chapter 3: The <HEAD> and <BODY> Elements 25
Chapter 4: Text Elements 45
Chapter 5: Images and Multimedia 69
Chapter 6: The Fine Art of Tables 91
Chapter 7: Getting Interactive with Forms 133
Chapter 8: Working with Frames 157
Chapter 9: Advanced Graphics 175
Chapter 10: Animations 229
Chapter 11: Beyond HTML: Making Web Sites That Think .. 257
Chapter 12: Working with Your Web Server 277
Index 295

Table of Contents

1 Understanding the Project — 1
Determining the Site's Objective 2
   Informative 2
   Interactive 3
Determining the Site's Audience 5
   Bandwidth: How Fast Is Their Connection? 5
   Platform 6
   Demographics 9
Surveying the Content 10
   Examine Current Communication Practices 10
   Size Up Web Competition 11
Conclusion 11

2 Site Mapping and Blocking — 13
Site Mapping 13
   Flow of Interactivity 16
   Points of Entry and Exit 17
   Identifying Resource Points 18
Page Blocking 18
   Laying It Out on Paper 20
   Doing It in Style 20
   Designing the HTML Template 21
Conclusion 23

3 The <HEAD> and <BODY> Elements — 25
The Head Section 26
   <TITLE> 27
   <META> 28
The Body Section 31
   BACKGROUND 31
   BGCOLOR 39
   BGPROPERTIES (Explorer Only) 42
   LEFTMARGIN and TOPMARGIN
    (Explorer Only) 42
   LINK, VLINK, ALINK, and TEXT 43
Conclusion 44

4 Text Elements — 45
Fun with <FONT> 45
   SIZE 46
   COLOR 47
   FACE 51

  Pagination 52
    <P> or Paragraph Tag 52

 or Line Break Tag 53
    <HR> or Horizontal Rule Tag 56
    <I> Italic, <U> Underlined, and <B> Bold Tags 58
  Lists 59
    <UL> Unordered Lists and <OL> Ordered Lists 59
    <DL> Definition Lists 62
  Links and Anchors 63
    <A HREF> Links 64
    <A NAME> Anchors 66
  Conclusion 68

5 Images and Multimedia 69

  Placing Inline Images 70
  <IMAGE> Tag Attributes 71
    ALIGN 71
    BORDER, HSPACE, and VSPACE 72
    HEIGHT and WIDTH 73
    LOWSRC and ALT 74
  Adding Imagemaps to Pages 75
    How Imagemaps Work 75
    Comparing Map Formats 76
    ISMAP 77
    USEMAP 77
    Creating Map Coordinates 80
  Adding Audio and Video to Web Pages 83
    <BGSOUND> and <EMBED> 83
    Adding Inline Video/VRML 85
  Conclusion 89

6 The Fine Art of Tables 91

  <TABLE> Tag 92
    ALIGN Attribute 93
    VALIGN Attribute 94
    BGCOLOR Attribute 94
    BORDER Attribute 95
    CELLPADDING Attribute 96
    CELLSPACING Attribute 97
    FRAME Attribute (Explorer Only) 97
    RULES Attribute (Explorer Only) 99
    WIDTH and HEIGHT Attributes 101
    BORDERCOLOR Attributes (Explorer Only) 104
    BACKGROUND Attribute (Explorer Only) 105

	`<TR>` Tag	106
	ALIGN Attribute	108
	VALIGN Attribute	109
	BGCOLOR Attribute	110
	NOWRAP Attribute	111
	BORDERCOLOR Attributes (Explorer Only)	112
	`<TD>` Tag	113
	ALIGN Attribute	113
	VALIGN Attribute	114
	BGCOLOR Attribute	115
	COLSPAN and ROWSPAN Attributes	116
	NOWRAP Attribute	119
	WIDTH and HEIGHT Attributes	120
	BORDERCOLOR Attributes (Explorer Only)	123
	BACKGROUND Attribute (Explorer Only)	124
	`<THEAD>`, `<TBODY>`, and `<TFOOT>` Tags	125
	RULES="GROUPS" Attribute	127
	`<COLGROUP>` and `<COL>` Tags	127
	`<COLGROUP>` Tag	128
	SPAN Attribute	129
	`<COL>` Tag	130
	Conclusion	132
7	**Getting Interactive with Forms**	**133**
	Getting Started	135
	`<FORM>`	135
	Understanding `<INPUT>` and Its Attributes	138
	NAME Attribute	139
	VALUE Attribute	139
	TYPE Attribute	140
	`<SELECT>` and Its Attributes	152
	`<OPTION>` and Its Attributes	153
	`<TEXTAREA>`	154
	Conclusion	156
8	**Working with Frames**	**157**
	`<FRAMESET>` Tag	160
	COLS Attribute	162
	ROWS Attribute	162
	FRAMEBORDER Attribute	164
	FRAMESPACING Attribute	164
	SCROLLING Attribute	165
	`<FRAME>` Tag	166
	SRC Attribute	166
	NAME Attribute	167
	FRAMEBORDER Attribute	167

Table of Contents

       `MARGINHEIGHT` Attribute 167
       `MARGINWIDTH` Attribute 168
       `ALIGN` Attribute 168
       `SCROLLING` Attribute 169
       `NORESIZE` Attribute 169
   `<NOFRAMES>` Tag 170
   `TARGET` Attribute 170
   `<IFRAME>` Tag 171
       `HEIGHT` and `WIDTH` 172
   Conclusion 172

9 Advanced Graphics   175

   Creating Backgrounds 175
       Before You Start 176
       Setting Up Some Preferences 176
       Vertical Tiling 176
       Preparing the Image for the Web 182
   Working with Transparent GIFs 185
       Anti-aliasing 185
       Alpha Channel Mapping 186
       GIF89a (Transparent GIFs) 186
   Icons 191
       The Bullet Icon 191
       Sizing and Spacing 194
   Graphical Text, Tables, and Lists 195
       Using Graphical Text 195
       Using Graphical Tables and Borders Instead of Tags 202
       Spacing with Transparent GIFs 208
   Adobe Photoshop Techniques 211
       Working with Actions 211
       Working with Layers 215
       Shadowing Effects 218
       Resizing and Reducing the Palette 220
   Using Photographs 223
   Conclusion 226

10 Animations   229

   Creating Animations 230
   Importing Images into the Animation Programs 231
       GifBuilder (Mac Application) 232
       Microsoft's GIF Animator, GIF Construction
          Set (Windows Applications) 234
   Size Reduction Issues 237
       Working with Palettes 240
       Creating a Global Palette 240
       Timing, Frame Rates, and Clear Background Options 242

Animation Effects and Techniques 243
    The Fading Animation 243
    The Glowing Animation 250
    The Flashing Animation 254
    The Moving Animation 255
Conclusion 256

11 Beyond HTML: Making Web Sites That Think 257

CGIs and Server-Side Scripting 258
    Why Use CGIs? 258
    Working with CGIs 259
    Creating Forms with CGIs 261
The Jabber about Java 263
    Why Use Java? 263
    Working with Java 265
JavaScript and JScript 267
    Why Use JavaScript and JScript? 267
    Working with JavaScript and JScript 268
ActiveX 270
    Why Use ActiveX? 272
    Working with ActiveX 272
Conclusion 274

12 Working with Your Web Server 277

Comparing Platforms 278
    Performance 279
    Accessibility 279
    Extensibility 279
    Survivability 279
    Security 279
    Manageability 280
    Cost 280
Microsoft Internet Information Server
    for Windows NT 281
    Features of IIS 281
    Connecting to the Server 282
    Resources for IIS Administrators 284
WebSTAR for MacOS 285
    Features of WebSTAR 285
    Connecting to the Server 287
    Resources for WebSTAR Administrators 288
Apache for Unix 288
    Features of Apache for Unix 289
    Connecting to Your Unix HTTP Server 290
    Resources for Unix/Apache Administrators 292
Conclusion 292

Index 295

chapter 1

Understanding the Project

When developing Web sites of more than a few pages, it's important that the proper planning is incorporated. We can save ourselves a great deal of time and confusion by going through just a few simple processes to determine what is needed for a site and how to best put it together. If you're working as a consultant, or even in a company's MIS department, these exercises help you determine the cost of the project and the length of time necessary for you to complete the site.

Figure 1.1 is an example of a site designed using the planning processes outlined in the following chapters. The end result is a simple design with an easy-to-use structure. Clearly the focus here is on investor relations, rather than the company's actual business of selling chemicals. Sites that have been planned using techniques similar to the ones we describe in this book are easy to discern—they are organized, easy to navigate, and because the site designer has a

→ Determining the Site's Objective

Determining the Site's Audience

→ Surveying the Content

handle on where each document is in the structure, the Web site works. Moreover, just as when you undertake any creative process, it's helpful to develop a clear notion as to the goal of the site: How you want it to function, what tools you'll use in creating the pages, and so on.

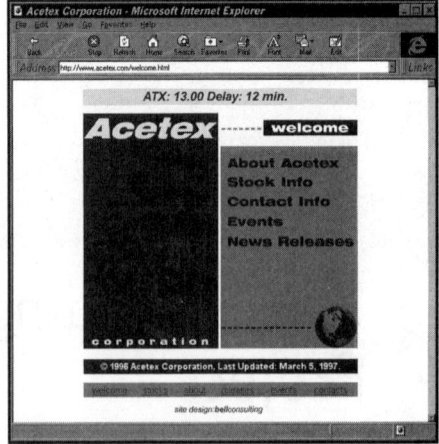

Figure 1.1
Acetex Corporation's Web site: Stock Quotes and Investor Information.

Determining the Site's Objective

What is the Web site you're designing trying to achieve at its most basic level? Is it a site catering to customers who need product support, or is it a project where you're collecting information from your users and allowing them to pull dynamic data or order product? Most small to medium scale business-related Web sites serve one of two main functions (or combinations of the two): inform or interact.

Informative

These sites are deceptively simple. Although you don't have to worry about having dozens of forms or doing any advanced programming, you probably have the problem of effectively organizing a large body of documents. You're likely to be serving up scores of nice, visually appealing, static Web pages, but you probably won't require functions such as CGI server-side interfaces or advanced Java applets. Again, your prime focus as a designer is to ease navigation to the documents people are searching for.

Chapter 1 Understanding the Project

The value of such a site then lies in its capability to present the desired information to its audience in an organized fashion. Many companies who contract someone to develop a site aren't fully cognizant of the reasons for its existence, and they're relying on the designer to guide them through this process.

Figure 1.2 is an example of a site that does an excellent job of navigating customers to support, software updates, and product information. It does this with a minimum of fuss and doesn't overdo the graphics. Each graphic is useful and consistent with the others.

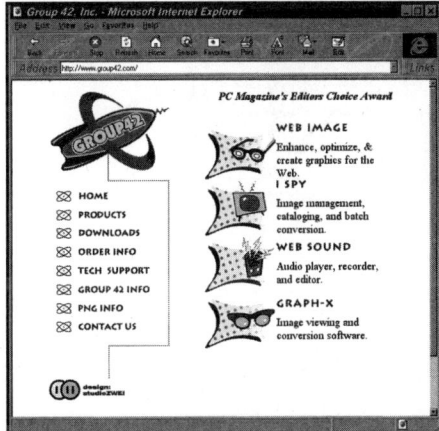

Figure 1.2

Group 42: A small software company with an informative site.

Fortunately for NASDAQ, our new client Rocco has yet to undergo his first round of Investment Capitalization, and so the informative aspects of the Rocco's Radios Web site are primarily contact information and availability. The real crux to his site is his online catalog, which brings us to the second category, interaction.

Interactive

Simply put, interactive sites are sites whose success rides on a useful feature or an application. Although interactive Web sites don't necessarily have a higher use value than informative sites, they definitely represent a greater challenge to build. Interactive sites rely heavily on processing, and anything that relies on processing requires some advanced programming.

In our running example, Rocco wants us to build an online catalog for some of his "hot" products. He wants his Web customers to generate orders for stereo equipment that he has on sale and for those orders to be sent to him. He sees this as the crux of the site, and for him it's a big "selling point" for putting his site on the Web.

Figure 1.3 is a good example of a site built around an interactive core. When the project was undertaken, the Web designer observed people walking into the store and "building" boxes by picking individual chocolates from a display case. This was replicated on the site and has created the same interactivity as exists in the store.

Figure 1.3

Over The Moon's "Build Your Own Box" Interface at `http://www.over-the-moon.com/moo`.

In HTML, your use of forms is the primary instrument in creating interactivity. As we'll learn in Chapter 7, forms can pass data entered by the user to server-side programs called CGIs. Often times, forms can operate without the user's knowledge, using hidden fields and images. Other technologies we'll discuss in Chapter 11, such as Java, also enable you to use interactivity—often in concert with forms.

After you ascertain the direction of your site, you can begin to plan where different features appear. Your key task as a designer is to make sure that users don't get lost in the dazzling array of text boxes and pop-up menus that you're about to present to them. It's important to develop a sense of who will be using which features and in what ways.

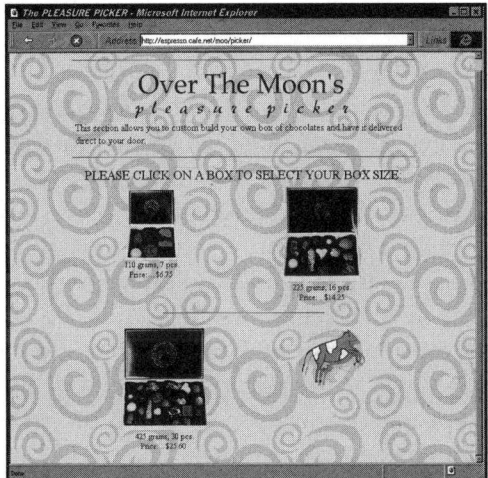

Figure 1.4

Where's the form? Each chocolate box actually represents a form submit button, though you can't see it.

Determining the Site's Audience

Now that you have determined what your site will be like, it's a little simpler to conclude who will visit the site. This information is critical in determining which of the more advanced Web elements (if any) you use in the creation of your site. Several factors influence how you're going to design and tailor your site to your users' needs and limitations.

Bandwidth: How Fast Is Their Connection?

Are your users Net heads or are they bandwidth-starved? Bandwidth determines the speed of someone's Internet connection, which could range anywhere between a lowly 14.4K modem or a high-speed fiber-optic connection.

This is a major consideration. Imagine you went to the shopping mall only to discover that none of the escalators or elevators worked. How long would your patience run before you headed for the exit because you were tired of climbing and descending hundreds of stairs, just so that you could do a little browsing? People won't wait around for big bandwidth sites without a good reason, but by the same token they like to see pretty ones. What to do? The best idea is to go for the best possible interface and make a compromise based on their available bandwidth.

If, for example, you're designing a Web site for use on a university campus where everyone is using high speed Ethernet connectivity, then you can probably afford to be less judicious in your use of bandwidth. On the opposite end of the scale, when designing a Web site for less-privileged users, you might want to constrain your use of fancy graphics files to situations where they are absolutely necessary because these users are not likely to be patient while a 200K GIF animation downloads on their 14.4K modem. Your other options are offering a text-only version of your site or making graphics a less essential element of your design so that people can surf your site with the browser's image loading function turned off.

Because every situation is different, there are no hard and fast rules to follow. Rest assured that you'd eventually be beleaguered by complaints if you ventured too far in either direction. You could learn the hard way that people are not interested in sifting through a mishmash of graphics and applets just to get to your information, or you may have to answer some very difficult questions as to why the impact of the site is lower than expected.

Platform

What computer software are your users viewing your site with? If you're exceptionally lucky, they are using freshly downloaded browsers on the same operating system with the same plug-ins (for advanced techniques such as video or audio) installed. This is possible in corporate environments, where intranet projects (projects geared towards servicing internal, rather than external, needs) rely upon baseline standards as maintained by local MIS personnel, but otherwise it is not likely.

More commonly, sites are developed specifically for Mac or PC users. When creating your site, you need to determine:

Chapter 1 Understanding the Project

▶ What operating system your users are running

▶ What browser software they are using

▶ What plug-ins they have

The content of a site defines the audience, which can define the tools they work with. Not many users on a Mac Web developer's site, for example, are going to be surfing your way with Windows 95. In addition, operating system platforms can cause variations in page layout in several ways:

▶ Colors don't always look the same

▶ Window width is rarely identical

▶ Some fonts available on Windows aren't available on Macs

As we'll learn in Chapter 11, implementations of technologies such as ActiveX and Java are at differing stages of evolution and could really cause problems when implemented on a page.

Although it's not likely that you can prevent one platform or the other from visiting your site strictly through the use of obscure HTML, you *can* add beneficial features, such as an ActiveX component, that are specific to a particular platform. This is an excellent time saver, and most Web designers will look to you with envy if you're able to pull it off without alienating any users.

That said, there's great merit in making your site work with all of the other kids in the playground. You would do well to consider future growth in any situation involving platforms.

The irony, though, is that although a site may function correctly, they can sometimes look completely different on another Web browser (as seen in Figures 1.5 and 1.6).

Obviously, this company isn't too interested in servicing Netscape users, which is too bad because they still account for more than 50 percent of the Web users out there.

Figure 1.5

Aiko, a Web site Design company, as viewed by Internet Explorer v3.1.

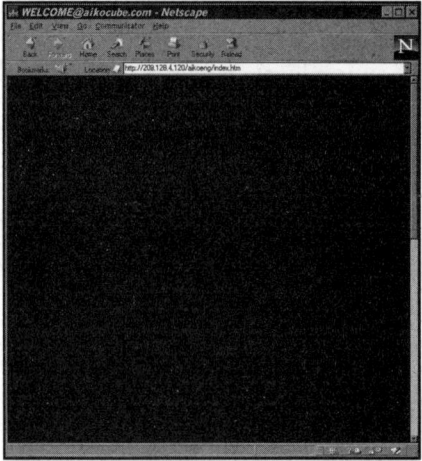

Figure 1.6

Aiko as viewed by Netscape 4.0. Can you see the difference?

For our purposes, Rocco is pretty adamant that the Rocco's Radios site be viewable without any added fuss or plug-ins, but at the same time he wants the site to be visually innovative. Therefore, we've chosen to go with simple, standard tools such as JavaScript (covered in Chapter 11). Our only indulgence is to incorporate some Microsoft-specific HTML tags because we enjoy the precision with which the documents lay out in Internet Explorer. In effect, our site will look better with Explorer, but will still lay out fine on Netscape.

Chapter 1 Understanding the Project

This won't be particularly detrimental for Netscape users, as browsers tend to ignore HTML tags they don't understand.

Demographics

A final consideration is the profile of your users. Are these people the info-rich or the info-poor? Are they coming to you for information on returning their broken toaster or for reconfiguring their TCP/IP router? If you're able, you can look at the customer profile and take into account both their experience within your client's industry and with the Web in general. From that point you can determine whether you ought to get fancy with your interface or keep it simple.

You also have to judge whether your users are can or will bother to install any plug-ins required to view your site. As we have experienced, people are always reticent to engage in a time-consuming download when they're not even sure why they need it. Make sure that the light at the end of the tunnel is bright enough to inspire your audience to travel through it.

User demographics also determine the look and feel of your site. Younger, more net-savvy audiences respond better to the hip, postmodern approach, whereas older audiences who've grown up bombarded by other media might prefer simpler, to-the-point appeals. Culture, language, and any number of other considerations are also significant factors, as they would be in any other medium.

Figure 1.7 shows us one of the Web pages developed by Apple for its 20th anniversary special-release Macintosh. The site represents solid innovation in Web design, but is this page really worth the lengthy download of a large QuickTime file and potentially the added complication of installing plug-ins? Only the most die-hard fans are likely to go through the bother, but then again, they're only making 10,000 copies of the computer this site is advertising.

Again, even a cursory analysis of the project reveals whether information about your users is a significant determining factor. You might simply have to assume the worst, push for a wider more general audience, and challenge yourself by working within the structure as defined by the lowest common denominator (that is, users who don't know anything about the Net, use old browsers, and so on).

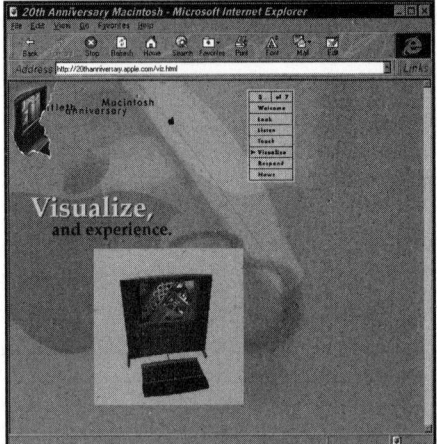

Figure 1.7

Preaching to the Already Converted: Apple's 20th Anniversary Mac.

Surveying the Content

Before beginning development, any responsible site designer spends some time going over the material proposed for the site. When you're embarking on a new project you want to learn everything you can about the content, which helps you gain a better understanding of what its needs are.

Examine Current Communication Practices

It's a good idea to take a peek at any already-existing publications you can get your hands on, get a feel for their existing communications channels, observe their operations, and see where the Web can add value. Look at each company individually, observe their current communications practices, then duplicate and extend on the site what they already provide in terms of information services.

For larger companies you can examine current marketing campaigns and devise a way to create a site that leverages on the presence they already have in print, radio, TV, or anything else.

Typically, smaller companies may require you to be more creative. What types of phone calls do their receptionists or help desks receive on a daily basis? Are they a public company? If so, is investor relations a significant concern? It never hurts to ask a lot of questions.

Size Up Web Competition

Check out the competition. If you're doing a site that sells CDs or books, you should stop at `http://www.cdnow.com` or `http://www.amazon.com`. These two sites are the leaders in their markets online. Why develop something inferior? Take note of where your approaches can improve upon the competition's model, and pay particular attention to how the competitors deal with the technical limitations of their users.

This is a great way to accelerate a better understanding of an industry to which you have no previous exposure. Much like other media, the Web is a morass of ideas, and we're all contributors. Your goal should always be to take what is done, and build upon it—enhancing its reach both technically and socially. This is called "Embrace and Extend," a term coined by our friends at Microsoft. Your observations here will help you in further development.

Conclusion

The importance of completely understanding where your project is going before you start designing cannot be overstated. It's important to make your interpretations and to communicate them to the client or your supervisor and see if they agree. You never want to waste time going too far afield only to discover that a complete re-work is the only thing that will save you.

Many times in this young industry projects are started and completed before anyone on the development team truly comprehends what the needs of the client and the audience are. In these cases a lot of companies and organizations have been gravely disappointed by Web projects that failed to attract people and keep them coming back for more. They underachieved not because no one was really trying, but because the site didn't cater to the audience properly.

In the world of marketing, most people are suspicious of using the Internet as an effective tool as disappointment after disappointment has lined the pockets of Web designers while disaffecting their customers.

Now that you know what you're up against, you should be ready to start planning the layout of the site. We're busily preparing ourselves for our first meeting with Mr. Rocco.

chapter 2

Site Mapping and Blocking

Some of your most important tools in Web site design have little to do with a computer, but they are essential in site design visualization—the process whereby we conceive the structure of a project before we embark upon it. If you haven't guessed already, these tools are pens, pencils, or markers. The drawing surface you pick is up to you, though the authors of this book prefer white boards, Post-It notes, or napkins from Mexican restaurants. Surprisingly, you can identify problems with even the smallest of sites using techniques such as site mapping and blocking.

Site Mapping

You can impress your clients or employers by drawing a site map when they first raise the specter of a new project; this helps them to add focus to their ideas. A site map is best described as a flow chart for your Web design

→ Site Mapping

→ Page Blocking

project. Figure 2.1 shows the site map we designed for Rocco's Radios, as we discussed his site for the first time. As we mention later on in this chapter, the site map gives you an added tool in developing your Web site in an organized manner.

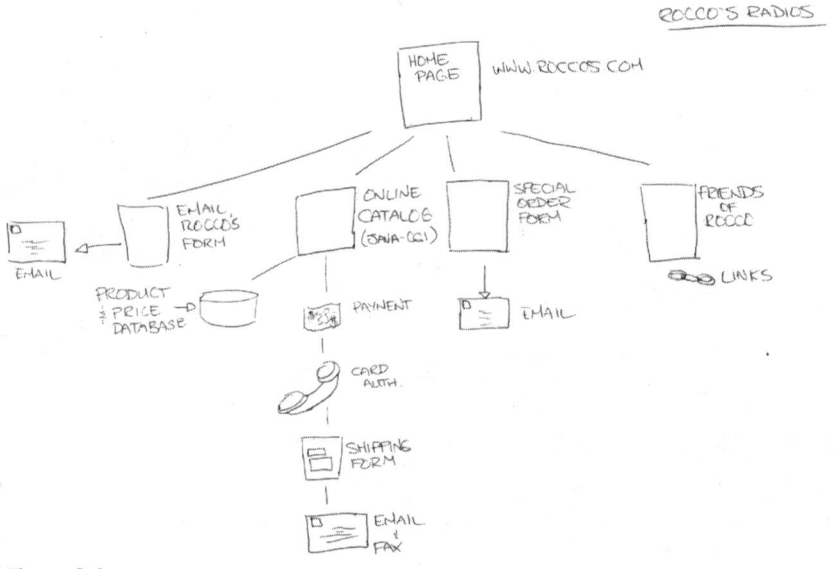

Figure 2.1

Rocco's site map.

Put this way, Rocco's is a pretty insignificant site. At this stage, though, we have yet to flesh out our online catalog (on the near left), which will surely be a multi-page series of complex documents. Other than that relative unknown, we have a good idea of what we have to deal with on this project. By being more detailed at the outset, we will have a better idea of the length of time we'll need. Rocco also has a few napkins to take home to peruse while he dreams of making his fortune on the Internet.

Chapter 2 Site Mapping and Blocking

More complicated site maps help you to plan out how to stage the development process and how to delegate tasks among teams. As you move forward as a designer and approach sites that make use of highly advanced technologies such as database servers, CGIs, and integration with other Internet services, the site map will become a prerequisite for all project plans. Figure 2.2 is a basic site map for a fictitious realty company. It illustrates the complexity of such a major site and how that can be articulated easily to help people understand how it works.

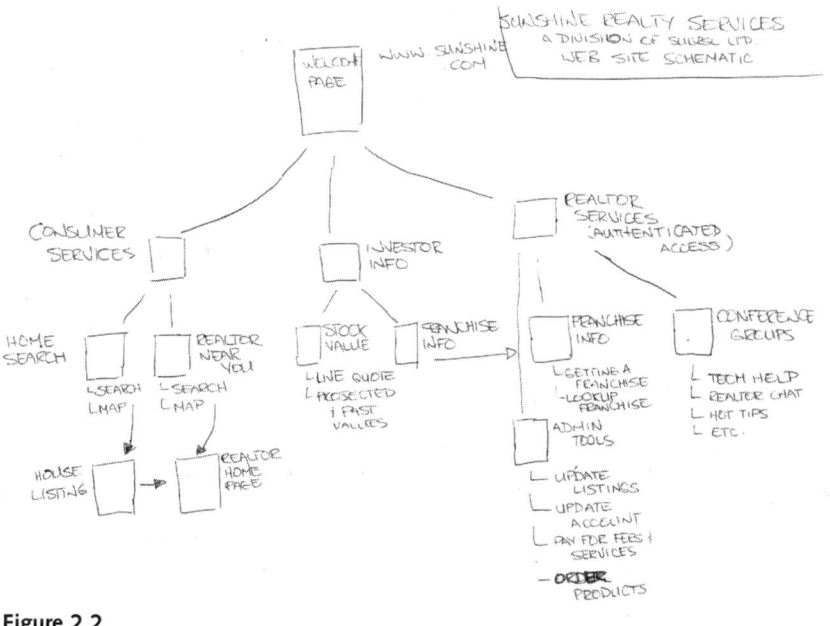

Figure 2.2

Basic design for an advanced Web site for a realty company.

Figure 2.3 shows a screen capture from Microsoft's FrontPage Web site editor and management tool, which features the capability to map and manage the structure of a site. It's no coincidence that this looks a lot like our hand-drawn site map for Rocco's.

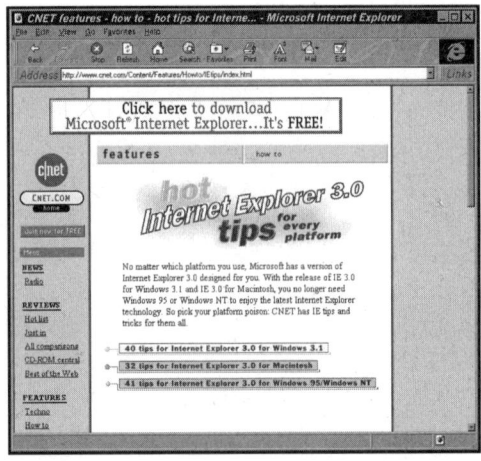

Figure 2.3

Acetex Corporation's Web site map in FrontPage (http://www.acetex.com).

As we've learned, site mapping enables you to see your entire site on a few sheets of paper, but what does it really show you? The features it should articulate are the flow of interactivity, points of entry and exit, and resource points.

Flow of Interactivity

Also called the "Click-Through Process Model," this function is intended to communicate how users navigate their way through your site. It's vital to be able to see this from the get-go, because all of your navigational aids in the site (menu bars or pull-down menus, icons, and other functions) will be dependent upon your understanding of how people will get from the home page to a particular file.

On small to medium-scale sites, your site map should be wider than it is deep, for the solitary reason that you want to reduce the number of layers your users have to go through to get to the section they want to use.

> **Note**
>
> The "width" of a site is a term that refers to how many subsections there are on a Web site, whereas the "depth" of a site refers to the functions or information contained within each of those sections.

Chapter 2 Site Mapping and Blocking

The Click-Through Process Model enables you to figure out where your Web site is difficult to use (by shaking out bugs), where people might become lost, and how to design your menu systems and navigational tools. Is, for example, a frequently used resource such as an FAQ for a particular department too low in the site map? Why not link to it somewhere in the home page?

Points of Entry and Exit

The concept of entry and exit points refers to how people get to your site's information. Although many users don't even realize when they've left one site and hopped over to another, you have the problem of keeping them oriented no matter where they come from.

Not everyone enters your site by typing www.mycompany.com into their browser window. If your company is engaging in an extensive Web-based marketing campaign for a particular product, people will likely be following a link from outside of your site and clicking their way to the page for that particular product, rather than surfing their way through your entire site.

If you have a secure area on your site for particular types of users, they might be likely to start at that point rather than from the main home page. The implications of knowing your points of entry again influence the design of your navigational tools, and based on this information, you might have to rework your site's structure to make sure people aren't disoriented when they pay you a visit through a side door.

By the same token, you might be forced to rely on resources outside of your Web site to inform your users. These various links to the outside world might be points of no return. It's probable that some users (especially now that we have WebTV users to contend with) won't be able to figure out how to get back to your site once they're gone. It's up to you to determine whether you want to let them go or if keeping them in a "frames" (discussed in Chapter 9, "Advanced Graphics") interface is a worthwhile compromise to the worse option.

Steering clear of both of these potential pitfalls will allow you to accommodate those lost surfers and keep people happily making their way to the vital information that your site delivers.

Identifying Resource Points

Your resource points are basically items that make up your site that aren't HTML files or images. This would include Java, database technologies, forms, CGIs, scripts, and so on.

It's difficult to build a Web site without the use of these tools. These should pop up in your site map as early in the development stages as possible for two primary reasons. First, you learn what you're up against; and second, you'll find that you can create an amazing number of areas in which you can re-use existing applets or server-side programs for a number of different pages.

If you're forced to do some programming instead of re-using someone else's code, then this is the point at which you'll be able to ascertain the possibility of writing CGIs that are applicable for several different uses. Why, for example, use a different CGI to handle the data from five different input forms when you can use a more generic CGI engine that is able to service all five?

In the last few pages we've outlined some steps to help you conceptualize and plan the structure of your site. What you've learned about your project in this process directly influences your future planning and design.

Page Blocking

It should go without saying that it is vitally important to have a consistent look and feel to your Web site. Templated sites, as we call them, are a lot more efficient in terms of their use of bandwidth, not to mention ease of navigation. Linking together a bunch of disjointed documents with a few URLs is a bad way to go about building a site, and it's rare to see sites like this these days (unless they're old or very large). On the other hand, sites that seem to "switch channels," for lack of a better term, are common. These sites break down into different interfaces for subheadings and departments, but why?

Some of the best sites on the Internet manage to keep you working within a consistent, comfortable interface. This is a vital tool, especially when dealing with sites with complex organizational structures, but c|net's site (as seen in Figure 2.4) in particular demonstrates why this is

Chapter 2 Site Mapping and Blocking

important. The expression "wherever you go, there you are" never meant so much as when you've been surfing their site for everything from free software to video game reviews. In a nutshell, you're never really lost.

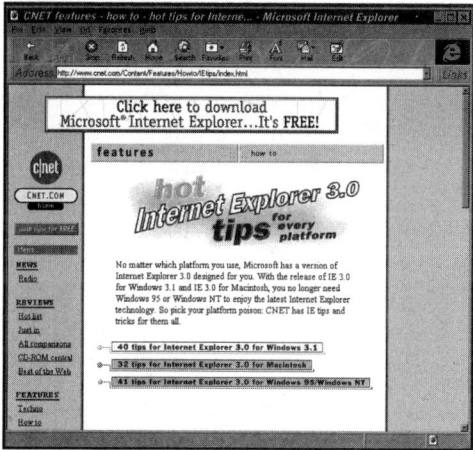

Figure 2.4

c|net's site keeps you from getting lost (http://www.cnet.com).

The design originally used frames after they were first implemented by Netscape. Although frames are a great way to maintain a consistent "shell" around a site's content, they can interfere with page layout options, and if they use borders and scrolling, waste a large number of pixels. Now that frames are better implemented, this is less of a problem.

c|net's Web site elected to use table tags (discussed in Chapter 6, "The Fine Art of Tables") to maintain the layout, and a vertically tiling background to delineate screen real estate. This has proven to be an effective method, although it is sure to be a maintenance nightmare down the road because rather than maintaining a single menu bar document that appears beside every page, they must now maintain the same menu bar in each document and keep it consistent.

The look of your site will depend on many things, but the c|net site serves as a reminder that whatever look you choose, you may be stuck with it for a long time. This is where you'll put on your "interface designer hat" and begin experimenting with different looks for your main template. The process can take as many as three stages.

Laying It Out on Paper

Flip over the writing surface on which you've drawn your wonderful site map, and start to doodle. Play with a few different options until you find something you like. This process is subjective and we don't want to snub your creativity by giving you hard and fast rules.

In our example in Figure 2.5, we doodled a site that eventually used a frames interface to keep the reseller's menu and navigation information onscreen even when the site linked out to vendor-specific information. In this way we see how earlier planning influenced our visual design process.

Figure 2.5

Quick layout idea for a computer reseller's Web site.

Doing It in Style

Next, load your favorite graphics application, such as Photoshop or Illustrator. It's important to flesh out your ideas without taking into consideration the actual limitations or even your perceived limitations of the HTML language. Formulate the look of your site with as much creativity as you can muster, and worry about how you're going to lay it out later. It's been our experience that there are few things that can be done in a graphics application that can't be mimicked in HTML. This is a great way to come up with some of the graphics that you'll later use throughout your site, so take an example of your favorite page from the site map and just "roll with it."

If you're familiar with Photoshop, make sure to use the layers feature by adding each element on a different new layer with a transparent background (see Figure 2.6). This will make future changes easy and enable you to quickly separate the graphics you want to keep for later use. For more information about using layers in Photoshop, you can reference the examples and instructions contained in Chapter 9.

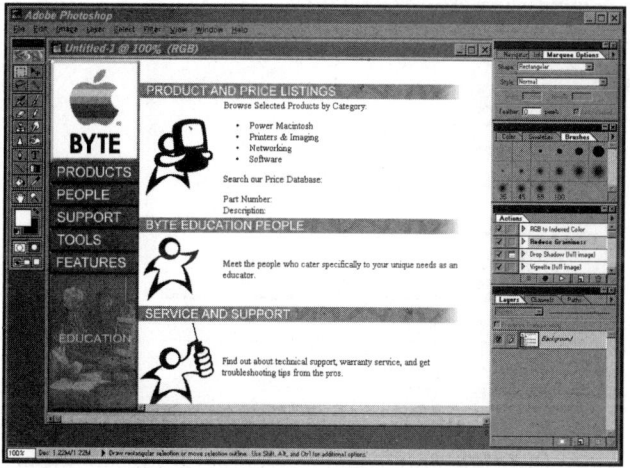

Figure 2.6

Photoshop file of the layout concept, as presented to the client for approval.

Designing the HTML Template

Now you'll call upon your extensive skills at HTML wizardry to make the vision of your Photoshop dreams come to life. Use the tools we give you in later chapters to bring your HTML layout as closely into line with your Photoshop fantasy as you can—and you should be able to get pretty close. You might as well cut, paste, and crop your original design and incorporate the results as your GIFs throughout the site.

The resulting HTML file (as seen in Figure 2.7) will serve as the template for the rest of your site's design. If you've done it right you should be able to slip the text and any changing graphics in while keeping the headers, footers, backgrounds, and any body attributes unscathed. Make sure you keep the design nice and clean so that it's not a pain to incorporate into the rest of your pages.

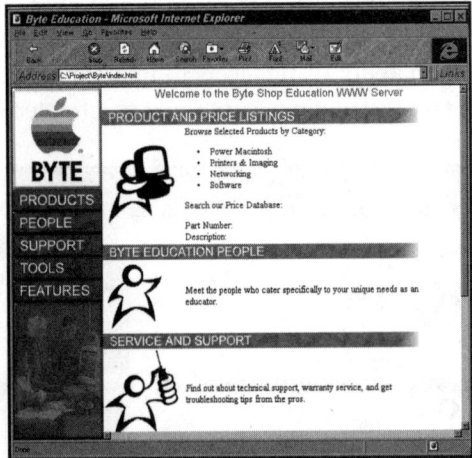

Figure 2.7

The final result: A mocked up treatment of the site's template.

Now that the template is done, refer back to your site map. How well does this style apply? Is it scaleable as the site grows? How will you take into account really long files (if you have any)? Can you keep the look consistent, even with someone else's CGIs? How fast does the page load over a modem?

One of the great advantages to making use of HTML-based templates created in this way is the efficiency with which you can use many rich graphics. Within reason you can frame your pages with images and load yet more graphics within the body of each document. Because you load the graphics that will appear throughout your site at the outset and augment them with specific graphics for specific information pieces, you're able to get a good level of visual appeal within limited bandwidth.

Although in some cases the first page of a site might take a bit longer to load, users tend to be a little more patient when subsequent pages are loaded quickly.

Conclusion

You should now have a clear notion as to what your Web site will look like and how it will function. Aided by your maps and templates, you can now take a site from a concept scribbled on a beer-stained napkin to a fully functional Web site servicing thousands of users per month.

The essential step here is making the best use of the abilities you have and the tools you will opt to work with. As we've said from the start, this book will chip away at the intimidation factor of working with advanced technologies and let you explore your own creativity. Although setting realistic goals is important, don't let any limitations get in your way during the conceptual design phase at all—ask the questions, and search for the answers. If you're not a programmer and can't find a ready-made CGI to process your forms somewhere down the line, then so be it.

What makes HTML and the Web as a whole so challenging and interesting is the infinite range of possibilities within finite boundaries. The dynamic element here is your brain. When you encounter problems or limitations the proof of our success as teachers and yours as a learner will lie in how you work around them. As you're reading this book you hopefully have a project in mind, and in the production chapters, you'll see exactly how the tools we teach you to use will solve problems you might be dealing with.

Onward!

chapter

The \<HEAD\> and \<BODY\> Elements

HTML is the language you use to create a Web page. Commands inside the HTML language are called tags or elements. When you create an HTML document, you are creating source code, just as programmers do, and as with all programmers it's important to understand the language. The HTML language has gone through many changes from 1.0 to 2.0 to the current 3.2 and will probably change again.

Information on the Web page is contained within these tags, and each tag can contain many options or attributes. In this chapter, we will deal with the \<HTML\>, \<HEAD\>, and \<BODY\> tags, and they're associated attributes. Let's begin with the core tag, \<HTML\>.

Every HTML document starts with the \<HTML\> tag and ends with the \</HTML\> tag. Some HTML tags need to be closed by using the same tag

 The Head Section

 The Body Section

name and adding the '/' character before the tag name. This is what we mean when we refer to closing the tag.

Between the <HTML> tags is the actual Web page, which is broken into the following two sections:

▶ The head, which uses the <HEAD> tag and must be closed

▶ The body, which uses the <BODY> tag, and also must be closed

The most basic HTML document you can make is this:

```
<HTML>
     <HEAD>
     </HEAD>
     <BODY>
     </BODY>
</HTML>
```

It does nothing, but it contains the fundamental components of an HTML file.

The head contains information related to the workings of the document, whereas the body *is* the document. The head contains items such as the title of the document, information for search engines, and document refresh information, whereas the body contains the images, text, as well as the background music and other content and cosmetic pieces.

This chapter provides a breakdown of all the tags and attributes that belong to the <HEAD> and <BODY> tags.

The Head Section

The <HEAD> or header tag contains all the information needed for the browser or server to process the HTML document for things such as title, search information, author info, anchor info, and whatever else needs to be read by the browser before the HTML document is shown onscreen.

Let's look at some of the tags and attributes that make up the head section.

Chapter 3 The <HEAD> and <BODY> Elements

> **Note**
> Try and keep your title name as short as possible. You don't want your title cut off because the user has a low resolution and the words are running off the edge of the screen. It's also good to remember that the browsers sometimes add the browser name before the title. That is: Netscape: Document Title.

<TITLE>

Syntax: `<TITLE>This is the document's Title</TITLE>`

The title does not contain attributes, superfluous tags, or characters —just the document's title. It also should only appear once within the head, and it should be closed with the `</TITLE>` tag.

The `<TITLE>` tag originally was added so that Telnet clients could tell what an HTML document's content was without actually looking at the document. Now we see the title in our browser in the top window title bar (see Figure 3.1). The `<TITLE>` tag should contain only text—no other tags or attributes apply to it. Also, when dealing with frames, use the `<TITLE>` tag only in the document that creates the frames. All subsequent documents don't need the `<TITLE>` tag because it is only read once.

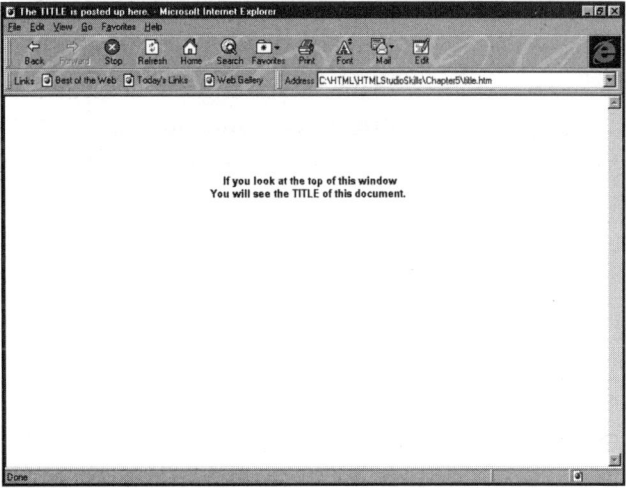

Figure 3.1

The document title.

<META>

<META>, or MetaInformation (information about information) is used primarily by the server to parse (or convert/translate) certain types of information about things such as the following:

- Document keywords
- Searchable index words
- Author
- Expiration date
- Design date

<META> also has the capability to refresh itself within a specified time or even chain itself to another HTML document within a time limit. The <META> tag's main use is to prepare a site for search engines by determining keywords used on the site. Also with the timed refresh function, it can be used as a sort of slide show of Web pages.

Search Engines

Many search engines, such as Yahoo!, Magellan, HotBot, and Lycos, provide an option for you to list your site there. But just how do these sites know what to add to the description and keyword fields from your site? Besides requiring the user to submit basic information, most search engines send out bots or spiders—small programs that search your site and all your HTML files to see the contents.

Some search engines only search your main or index.htm (index.html) file for text occurrences and see which words come up the most. This becomes the basis for how important your site is on that search engine. But this is hardly fair because many pages can contain graphics for text instead of actual text, or even have title pages with no text that link to the more informative pages. This mean the bots or spiders would miss the information.

HTTP-EQUIV

Syntax: <META HTTP-EQUIV="##">

is the name or option of the protocol response you want to use. (Whatever name or option is used here generates a response from the

Chapter 3 The <HEAD> and <BODY> Elements

server and server software). The server parses or translates the name (provided the server was designed to respond to that particular name) and then it responds to it, either sending back some information or running a task. CONTENT, another attribute that can be used with the <META> tag, enables the server to respond to more information than just the HTTP-EQUIV name.

You can use the <META> tag to add important keywords to your site within the head of your document. This is done using <META> tags and the HTTP-EQUIV and CONTENT attributes.

The name or command that is put between the brackets of the HTTP-EQUIV attribute is the activating factor to what the server, browser, or these bots do. Without this attribute, the <META> tag is powerless.

Although most commands depend on server or browser capabilities, let's deal with the search engines for now.

The name or option for the HTTP-EQUIV attribute that tells the search engine what keywords are important to the document is HTTP-EQUIV="Keywords". This enables you then to use the CONTENT attribute, which contains all of the keywords you use.

CONTENT
Syntax: <META CONTENT="##">

is the information you are to send to either the server, browser, or other program to be processed. The type of content you are using is determined by the HTTP-EQUIV attribute—it tells the server or browser what is coming.

The CONTENT attribute enables you to place whatever information you are processing to the server, browser, or bot. Whereas the HTTP-EQUIV and NAME attributes tell the server or browser what you are

> **Note**
> When using the CONTENT attribute, use no more than 255 characters for your keywords. (If you need to type more words, create another keywords line; you can have more than one.) Your contents are what become your description after the search engine has checked your site.

about to do, the CONTENT attribute deals with the information that needs to be passed. In this case, we're dealing with keywords, so this is where each keyword would go.

The tag would now look like this:

`<META HTTP-EQUIV="Keywords" CONTENT="Stereos, Radios, Electronics, TV, VCR">`

This tells the search engine bot that the main focus of the site is stereos, radios, electronics, TVs, and VCRs.

Refresh/Slide Show

Another great trick that can be done with the `<META>` tag is REFRESH, the HTTP-EQUIV command that refreshes the current HTML after a set amount of time. You give it a specific time with the CONTENT="##" attribute (where ## is the number in seconds), and then the current document reloads after waiting that amount of time. You also can have it load another document by adding the URL="##" attribute (where ## is the URL of the file you want to load). This creates a chain or slide-show type effect.

This can be useful if you want to show a short basic title page that chains to another more intricate one. (Although this technique is used often, it isn't liked by many good Web designers.) If you want to create a site that chains a user after a certain amount of time for no reason, this is perfect. If, however, you want to chain a user to another page that is specific to his browser or monitor resolution, you may want to learn more about CGI and Java programming. Both of these languages facilitate some effective uses of timing and chaining.

Here's an example:

`<META HTTP-EQUIV="Refresh" CONTENT="6; URL=http://www.example-site.com/slide2.html">`

> **Note**
>
> All search engines deal with the HTTP-EQUIV attribute and Web sites differently. Whereas some search engines want to see text in your document, others might rate your site based on how many times a keyword is repeated. Still others might penalize a site for repeating keywords too many times. It can be next to impossible to please all of the search engines.

Chapter 3 The <HEAD> and <BODY> Elements

This chains to the slide2.html file after six seconds and is great for creating a slide-show effect.

Remember to leave enough time for the page to load before sending the user to the next page.

The Body Section

The body is the main portion of all HTML documents, and nothing would exist on a Web page without it. The body is where you place text, forms, tables, images—everything. It also is where you set up the page background, the links and text colors, and even the music.

To understand the <BODY> tag better, first look at its attributes.

BACKGROUND

Syntax: <BODY BACKGROUND="##">

is the URL or location of the image file you are using as the background.

BACKGROUND is another important addition to the HTML family. It enables a tileable background to be shown behind the text and images on the page. This spurred the graphical revolution that we see on the Web today—the end of text-heavy sites, and the birth of more visual theme parks. Graphic artists now can create watermarks, tiles, and border backgrounds to use in their HTML files, which adds to the tools or creativity that a designer has, moving the medium a lot closer to desktop publishing.

But one common negative we find when surfing—and this one is classic—is the 300K Photo GIF format background image of a supermodel, game box logo, sports star, or other interest. Not only does this background take a few days to load, but text in the document can sometimes disappear against the

> **Note**
> It's important to remember that backgrounds tile; they do not remain static, therefore you cannot justify or center them.

many colors of the photo image background. Another great background blunder is the bright text on the bright background. Not only does this give you a headache after a few seconds of viewing, but it has been known to cause seizures in lab rats.

Backgrounds should be GIFs or JPEGs (or BMPs if you use Explorer). Use GIFs for large colored backgrounds that use simple shapes, and use JPEGs if you need to use a photograph or photographic quality image as the background. (I tend to use GIFs for almost all my backgrounds. I even dither the photo quality images down so that I can use them as GIFs.)

If you're careful to avoid the pitfalls described here, there are many different effects that can be created with backgrounds using these techniques.

Horizontal Tiling

Otherwise known as using horizontal tiles, this technique creates a vertical effect (or a top to bottom look, where the background starts at the top and seamlessly repeats down). It is probably used on about 50% of the good sites out there and can achieve many effects. Use this horizontal tiling whenever you want to split your information vertically or when you need to create a line or space between the left side and the right side of the Web page.

This technique creates a wide, short, tileable image that seamlessly repeats from top to bottom. If, for instance, you create two rectangles, one longer than the other, both different colors, you would create a border type effect from top to bottom (see Figure 3.2).

> **TIP**
>
> Although many Web designers believe there is a perfect combination of background and text color, there isn't. If you look around at some of the greatest Web pages, you often see colors and backgrounds that on paper should not go well together, yet create a harmony and a balance that many users like.
>
> The best thing to do is to experiment with your use of colors and backgrounds. Don't be afraid to use bright reds and blues, provided the page is still readable and isn't annoying to look at over time. How do you know if the page looks good? Show your mate, your friends, the dog, anyone who will look and listen. Then when you are comfortable with designing your color schemes, be your own judge.

> **Note**
>
> GIFs and JPEGs are graphical file formats. They represent the way a certain image is stored on the hard drive, just as a word processor document might be saved as a .DOC file, images can be saved as .GIF or .JPG (or even .JPEG) files.
>
> The difference between image file formats and normal file formats is that images can be saved as a loss format, or in a

Chapter 3 The <HEAD> and <BODY> Elements

format that loses some of the original look; file formats never lose anything from the original.

Both JPEG and GIF are loss formats, but in different ways. GIFs are stored as indexed color images, meaning that a GIF can drop the range of colors in an image to create a smaller file size. (The range of colors a GIF can have is between 1 and 256.) The lower number of colors an image has, the less it looks like its original. JPEGs, on the other hand, are not indexed. They can be 24-bit color and they save the image by compressing parts of the image that are similar, blurring the parts of the image that have the same color or texture. The higher the compression, the worse and more blurred the image looks.

Note

To actually create these effects, refer to the section, "Creating Backgrounds," in Chapter 9.

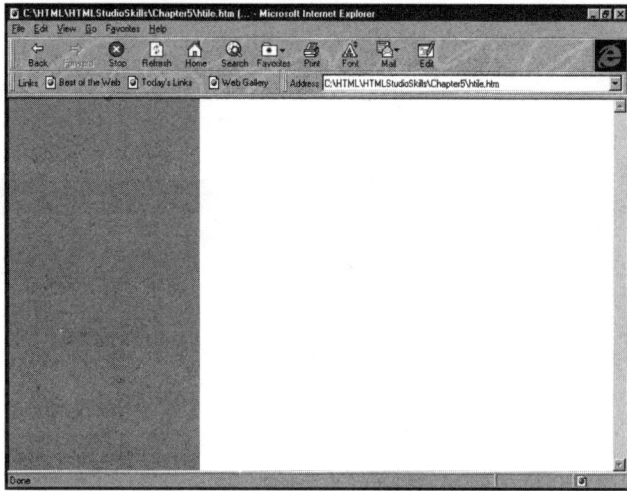

Figure 3.2

Horizontal tiling.

All we did to create this image is make one line of orange and one line of white. Then it just repeats from top to bottom. (This section shows you the effect, and how it affects your document.)

The secret to this horizontal tiling is to understand how long and high to make the image. If you are at 800×600 resolution, making the image 800 pixels wide would tile fine at your resolution. But what about the user who uses a resolution of 1,024×768 or 1,280×1,024? Then the tiled background would look more like a checkerboard than a border. Most Web designers create a horizontal image that is 1,280 pixels wide and then try to keep it as short as possible so that the image size stays small.

We created a smaller file size by using a GIF instead of a JPEG. Why? JPEGs are based on size and complexity of colors in the image, whereas GIFs are based on how many colors are used and any repeating patterns. Our two-color background is just that: two colors taking up almost no space when we save it as a GIF. The JPEG was 1.62K, and the GIF was 0.2K—a major size difference.

Another more complex background is the Full Scap paper effect. A completely cosmetic effect, it serves no other purpose than to show that you can create a paper-like background using a horizontal tile. This effect is often overused and often created incorrectly (see Figure 3.3).

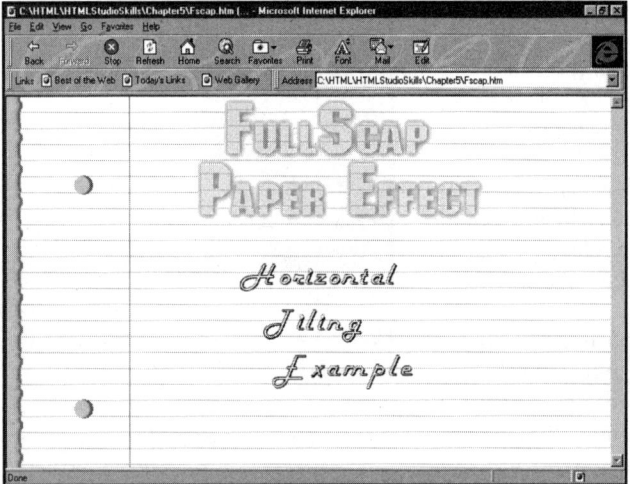

Figure 3.3

Full Scap paper effect.

Let's take a look at how to create the paper effect.

1. First, create a blank white image 1,280 pixels wide by 40 pixels high.

2. Add three lines (two green and one red). Shade the left side to give the illusion of ripped paper.

3. For cosmetic effect, create a 28×28 pixel image, and make a little shaded paper hole. That's it! We create a wide image that lays out to look like a tall image. Because we made both images GIFs, they amount to less than 1K. Now that's bandwidth control.

There are many other ways to utilize horizontal tiling, so experiment and have fun.

Vertical Tiling

The effects created with vertical tiling aren't as common as horizontal because most Web pages scroll down, making it harder to decide on the proper height for the background. That being said, we'll show you a simple effect—the fence background (see Figure 3.4).

Figure 3.4

The fence (vertical tiling).

To create the fence background, we needed to create a wood-like texture. Instead of drawing the wood for the fence, you can substitute a photographic image or texture as we did here. This causes the size of the background to increase, however, because converting a photographic image to GIF or JPEG creates more loss. It's a complex image, thus creating a larger file size.

This wood image was long, so we resized the image to 1,060 pixels high by 100 pixels wide (see Figure 3.4). We then used one of Photoshop's plug-ins, Alien Skin's bevel effect, to give the wood a 3-D effect. We drew some stars at the top, added some mountains, and voilà, it was finished. (We go over many of these techniques step-by-step in the advanced section of this book.)

> **Note**
>
> Pictures of wood and other such images can be found on the Web quite readily. Make sure to use public-domain or royalty-free images.

The problem with this effect, besides the size of the images, is that if text were added to this page, it wouldn't be very readable because there are so many color variations in the image. In addition, if the page got too long, the tile would wrap, and the top of the tile would be visible again.

Vertical tiling can be used effectively, but it is based on the dimensions of your Web page and how detailed an effect you want. The less detailed, the smaller the image size.

Small Image Tiling

Using small tiled images can create some wonderful and effective backgrounds. These bandwidth-friendly effects can do wonders for your page (see Figures 3.5 and 3.6).

The effect shown in Figure 3.7 creates a pattern throughout the entire background.

Create an image 40×40 pixels, draw a horizontal and vertical line, and draw a small globe in the middle. Examine it inside the document, and something doesn't look right (see Figure 3.7).

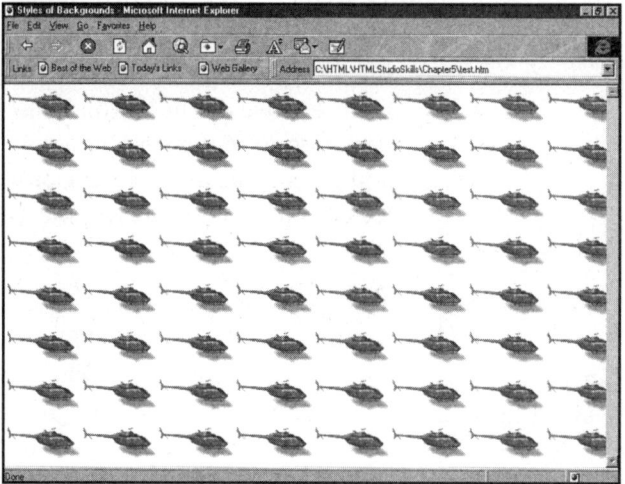

Figure 3.5

An icon tiled.

Chapter 3 The <HEAD> and <BODY> Elements

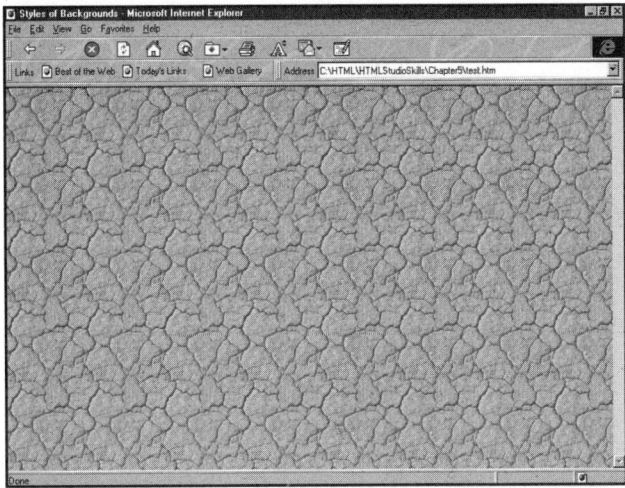

Figure 3.6

A perfect mathematical tile (the tile is seamless).

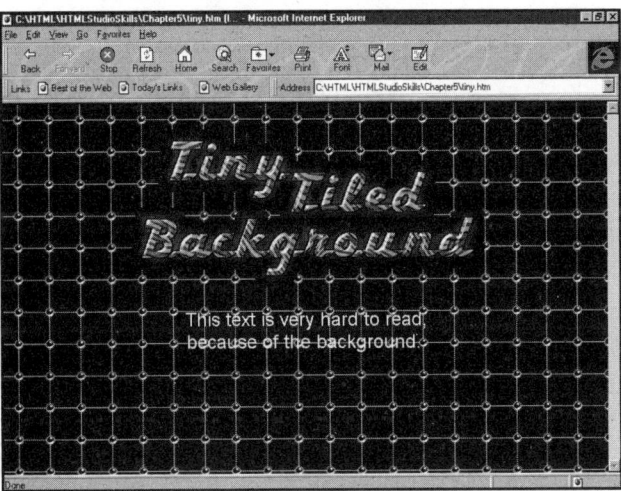

Figure 3.7

Tiny tiles (un-muted).

The white text that we added was hard to read because even though the tile was mostly black, the white in the image was so bright that it overpowered the text in some places. This is the most common background problem—when the background image overpowers the content of the document.

One of the best options is to make your background faint or faded. To do this, add a certain percentage of whatever background color you are using. In this case, the tile is mostly black and the text is white, so going with a dark color would be the best choice.

We added a little black to our image and then saved it. Next, we loaded it in our browser so that we could tell if we achieved the effect we needed. We did this until we added about 70% black to the image. Although this made the image look faded, it still kept its pattern and the text was clear and easy to read (see Figure 3.8).

When you are muting your images, remember, there is no definite percentage for the amount of color to add; it's all trial and error, so experiment.

Figure 3.8

A clear and easy-to-read image.

Texture Tiling

Texture tiling creates a texture-type look over the entire background, as though you created your Web page on canvas, concrete, or recycled paper. The types of textures you can come up with are endless.

Chapter 3 The <HEAD> and <BODY> Elements

> **Note**
>
> You always should mute your backgrounds, even textures. If the concrete looks perfect, add some white or gray to it so that the text won't be overpowered by the background.
>
> A wonderful Photoshop 4.0 feature is the capability to create textures automatically, which we did in Figure 3.9.

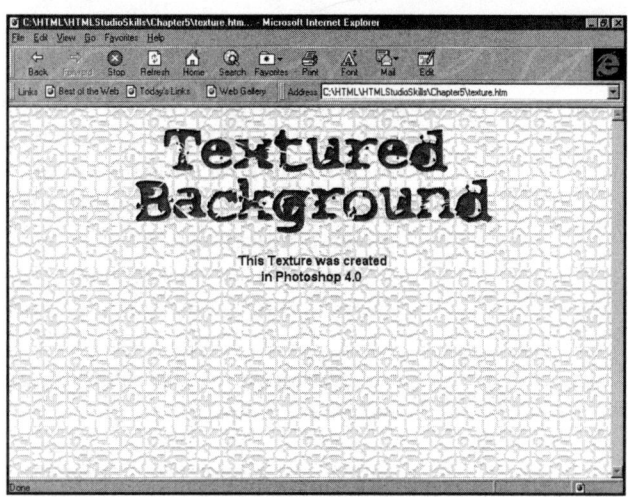

Figure 3.9

A sample texture.

All we did in Figure 3.9 was create a 100×100 pixel image and fill it with a pinkish white background color. We then used the Texture, Craquelure filter in Photoshop 4.0 to create the actual texture, and added some of the background color (60%) to mute the texture. The effect is quite subtle.

Now let's see some other attributes in action.

> **Note**
>
> Whenever you're creating textured tiles, you may want to check the end result at different color depths or resolutions. Sometimes a tile looks great at 24-bit, but looks like mush at 256 colors.

BGCOLOR

Syntax: `<BODY BGCOLOR="##">`

is either the color name, or the number (in hex) of the color you want as the document background.

If you aren't creating a background for your page, then using the BGCOLOR attribute is very effective. It paints the entire background of the document the color you select.

RGB Values

Coloring on the Web is based on the RGB palette, which is red, green, and blue respectively. Almost all paint or drawing programs use the RGB color scheme, so the Web coloring scheme was based on it. The limits of colors also are based on numbering each color from 0 (none of that color) to 255 (all of that color). So if you wanted to see red and only red, the color number would be 255, 0, 0, which means all red, no green, and no blue. Green would be 0, 255, 0, and blue would be 0, 0, 255. The great thing about using a universal coloring scheme such as RGB is that when you're in a paint program, you can make your own colors and know exactly what the red, green, and blue amounts are. And many paint programs enable you to select a color in a picture, which then tells you what the RGB numbers are. (Windows 95 also enables you to select colors based on red, green, and blue amounts.)

Choosing a background color by name is simple. Just type the name, and the browser figures out what color it should show. To choose white as the color of the background, for instance, type <BODY BACKGROUND= "white"> in the <BODY> tag (see Figure 3.10). The browser automatically parses this information and turns it into the RGB value of 255, 255, 255, which is all red, all green, all blue—creating white.

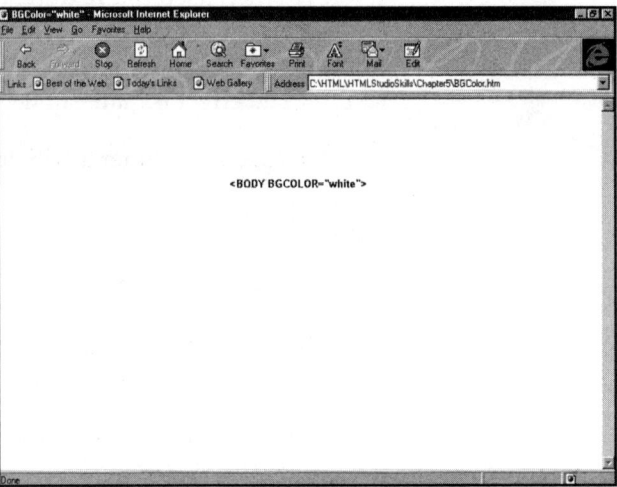

Figure 3.10

Background="white".

Most browsers have a list of color names that you can use to create background colors. Some of the basic ones are white, black, red, green, blue, and gray. Although there are many more, each browser converts these color names differently.

Chapter 3 The <HEAD> and <BODY> Elements

Hex Numbering

Although many novice Web designers use the name method of choosing a color, the hex number method is much more accurate. Just as the RGB model uses the standard base 10 numbering system, the hex numbering system uses base 15, or when a digit goes past the 15th number it adds a number to the left, except that it uses both letters and numbers.

Hex is based on the principle that when you get to the 10th number, you use the alphabet to replace the numbers.

Therefore, the numbers 0 to 16 would look like this: 00, 01, 02, 03, 04, 05, 06, 07, 08, 09, 0A, 0B, 0C, 0D, 0E, 0F, 10. Hex also uses two digits to express numbers, so 1 would be represented by 01, and 0 would be 00.

Notice how we only need to use the letters A–F. These represent the numbers 10 to 15.

If this were the base 10 counting system, 09 would change to 10, because that is the point where it rolls over to the next digit. With hex we rollover at 0F to 10. So the range of numbers of 0 to 255 in hex is 00 to FF.

Using this method of numbering in our BGCOLOR attribute, we must append an # to the beginning of the number to tell the browser that we are going to use the hex method of choosing a color. Then we add our hex values for each RGB color, or #rrggbb.

Here are some examples:

White would now become: <BODY BGCOLOR="#FFFFFF"> which is all red, all green, all blue.

Blue becomes: <BODY BGCOLOR="#0000FF"> or no red, no green, all blue.

Black becomes: <BODY BGCOLOR="#000000"> or no red, no green, no blue.

> **Note**
> Cyan may look great in one browser and completely different in another, which makes designing graphics and text for a specific color background almost impossible. This is why it's best to use numbers rather than color names.

> **Note**
> Don't use commas or spaces with our numbering, just one hex value after another.

Green becomes: `<BODY BGCOLOR="#00FF00">` or no red, all green, no blue.

Red becomes: `<BODY BGCOLOR="#FF0000">` or all red, no green, no blue.

To use any of the colors you see in Figure 3.11, copy the hex value. Each color has a corresponding name, hex number value, and RGB number value. There are many more color charts at Mark Koenen's site as well as some color utilities. Check it out at http://www.sci.kun.nl/thalia/guide/color/

> **Note**
> Even though you may be using a background tile, you should always set the background color because many viewers use the option of not showing images in their browsers.

BGPROPERTIES (Explorer Only)

Syntax: `<BODY BACKGROUND="URL" BGPROPERTIES="FIXED">`

This attribute has only one option—FIXED—which locks the background in place while the document scrolls over it. You must use a background for this attribute to work.

This attribute freezes the background from scrolling. Then as the user scrolls down the page, the text and content scroll, but the background doesn't move. Some Web designers use this technique to create a sized or frozen background (they think because the background doesn't move that they can create a static or sized background), but if the user is at a higher or lower resolution than what the background was created at, it looks weird, or if they use Netscape the background will not freeze, definitely not what the designer wanted.

LEFTMARGIN and TOPMARGIN (Explorer Only)

Syntax: `<BODY LEFTMARGIN="##" TOPMARGIN="##">`

is the number in pixels of the where the left margin or the top margin start. `LEFTMARGIN="10"` and `TOPMARGIN="16"` are the defaults.

Chapter 3 The <HEAD> and <BODY> Elements

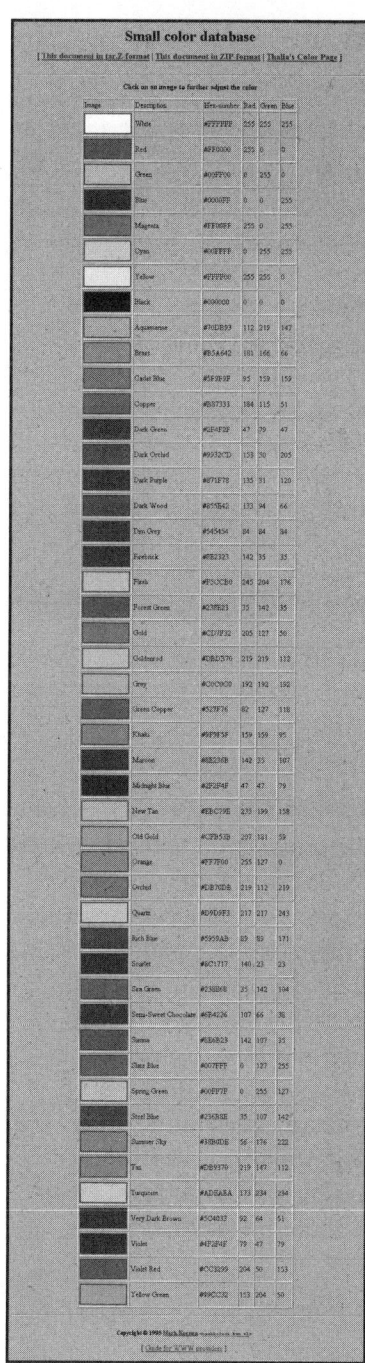

Figure 3.11

Hex and RGB color chart.

This is a great attribute that enables absolute positioning and layout on your Web page. If you set the LEFTMARGIN to 0, it places the contents of the document against the left side of the browser, with no spaces between the browser and the content. The same rule applies to the TOPMARGIN, enabling exact borders and alignments (see Figure 3.12).

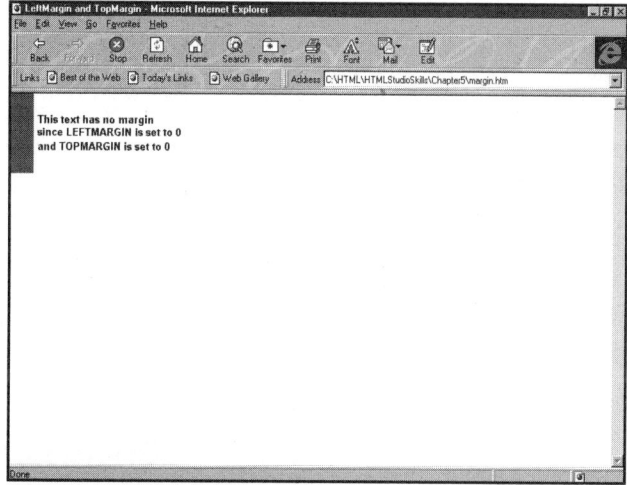

Figure 3.12

LEFTMARGIN and TOPMARGIN=0.

LINK, VLINK, ALINK, and TEXT

Syntax: `<BODY LINK="##" VLINK="##" ALINK="##" TEXT="##">`

is the color name, or the hex color number.

These attributes affect the links you add to your page. LINK affects the color of all links on your page that haven't yet been accessed, VLINK affects the color of links that have been seen or accessed, and ALINK affects the currently ACTIVE links. TEXT affects what default color the text is in your document (see Figure 3.13).

> **Note**
> Refer to the section on BGCOLOR and hex numbering if you don't know how to use the hex color numbering system.

The color is chosen much the same way BGCOLOR colors are chosen.

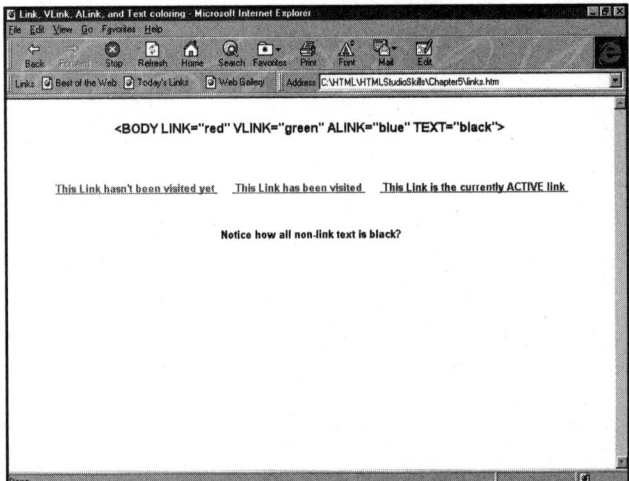

Figure 3.13

LINK, VLINK, ALINK, and TEXT.

Conclusion

This chapter provided a breakdown of tags and attributes that need to be understood before you start adding content to your Web page. From the <HEAD> tag, which holds information for the server and the browser to translate, to the <BODY> tag, which contains all the information related to the actual Web page, you learned how certain background techniques affect the look of the page and how to choose the proper background, link, and text colors. This chapter also discussed the art of hex numbering. The following chapters explain the tags and attributes contained within the body, how to use them, what they do, and when they should and shouldn't be used.

chapter 4

Text Elements

Now that you've learned about the head and body elements, it's time to start using tags and elements that affect visual portions of your Web site: the text elements of HTML design. Because most desktop publishers have had a slew of great software programs from which to choose to make their designs more colorful and effective, it was only natural that the Web design community would receive some of those features as well—through HTML and the evolution and use of tags such as <FONT>, <IMG>, <EMBED>, and <BGSOUND>. This chapter deals with everything text-related.

Fun with <FONT>

The <FONT> tag sets things such as size, color, and face. If you want to set the font style for the *entire* document, you should use the <BASEFONT> tag after the <BODY> tag. Just as with the <FONT> tag, <BASEFONT> enables you to set up default parameters for each <FONT> attribute, such as SIZE, COLOR (remember you can set the default

- → Fun with <FONT>
- Pagination
- Lists
- → Links and Anchors

font color in the <BODY> tag, using the TEXT= attribute), and FACE. <FONT> must be closed with </FONT>.

The <FONT> tag has quite a few options and it can achieve some pretty cool effects. The <FONT> tag can be placed at the beginning of a document to denote a default setting for the document's font, or you can use it on any piece of text that you want to change font settings on. The only syntax you need to remember with this tag is after you have opened it, you must close it after the last character you want to change. For example: this text is normal, <FONT SIZE="5"> This text is bigger, </FONT> This text is normal again.

There are three attributes that can be changed with <FONT>: SIZE, COLOR and FACE.

SIZE

<FONT SIZE="##">

With the SIZE attribute, ## is either the number in size from 1–7, or you can increment the default font size (or <BASEFONT> size) a specific amount by adding either a + or a - in front of the number. For instance, <FONT SIZE="+2">. If the <BASEFONT> size was 2, then the font size would now be 4. The default font size is 3 (see Figure 4.1).

> **Note**
> Explorer enables FACE to be set within the <BASEFONT> tag, but Netscape does not.

> **Note**
> When using the + numbering in your sizing remember to use quotes, such as "+2"; some browsers do not recognize the + and – without them.

Chapter 4 Text Elements

Figure 4.1

Font size adjusted using the <BASEFONT> tag.

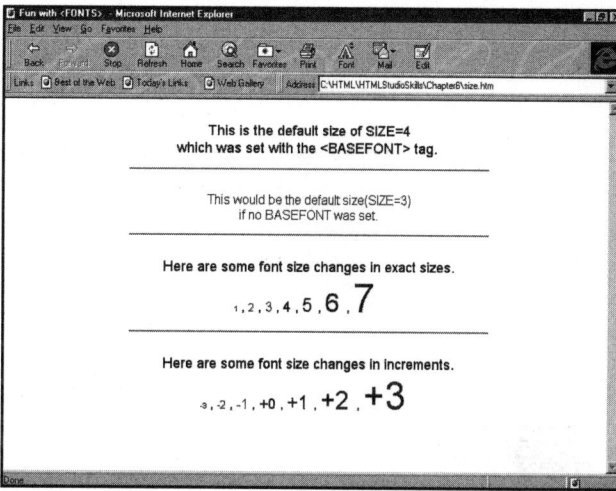

In the first text example in the figure, we set the <BASEFONT> size to 4. We can also see, in the second example, what size the text would be if we hadn't set a <BASEFONT> size.

And in the third example, we can see how large the text is by setting the SIZE from 1–7, showing the smallest to the largest font size (see Figure 4.1).

The fourth example uses the increment method of sizing to show smallest to largest. The smallest, SIZE="-3" (because the default is 4), makes the font size 1. And the largest, SIZE="+3", makes the font size 7. To see more examples of sizing "in action" check out the next section, "COLOR."

COLOR

`<FONT COLOR="##">`

With the COLOR attribute, ## is either the name, or hex number, of the color you want as the text color.

The colors for fonts are numerous and can literally be anything within the RGB spectrum.

> **TIP**
>
> If you don't understand the hex numbering system for colors, or if you don't know what the RGB spectrum is, then please read the section on BGCOLOR under the <BODY> tag in Chapter 5.

With so many colors available within the RGB spectrum, the looks you can achieve are infinite. Let's check out some text that mixes colors and font sizes (see Figure 4.2).

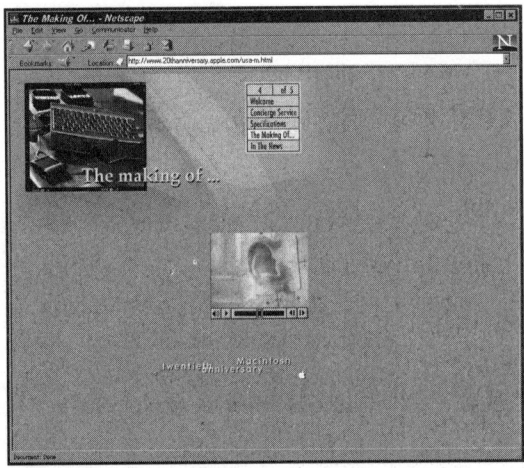

Figure 4.2

Font color; example 1.

In the first example, we can see that the default color is white, nothing fancy.

In the next example, we made our text go from large to small, back to large, light blue to dark blue, and then back to light blue again (see Figure 4.3).

All we did was change each text character's font size and color, and although it creates a nice effect, let's see what the HTML code looks like.

```
<FONT COLOR="#0000FF" SIZE="6">U</FONT>
<FONT COLOR="#0000DF" SIZE="5">S</FONT>
<FONT COLOR="#0000BF" SIZE="4">I</FONT>
<FONT COLOR="#00009F" SIZE="4">N</FONT>
<FONT COLOR="#00007F" SIZE="3">G</FONT>
```

Chapter 4 Text Elements

```
<FONT COLOR="#00005F" SIZE="3">M</FONT>
<FONT COLOR="#00004F" SIZE="2">A</FONT>
<FONT COLOR="#00004F" SIZE="2">N</FONT>
<FONT COLOR="#00005F" SIZE="3">Y</FONT>

<FONT COLOR="#00007F" SIZE="3">B</FONT>
<FONT COLOR="#00009F" SIZE="4">L</FONT>
<FONT COLOR="#0000BF" SIZE="4">U</FONT>
<FONT COLOR="#0000DF" SIZE="5">E</FONT>
<FONT COLOR="#0000FF" SIZE="6">S</FONT>
```

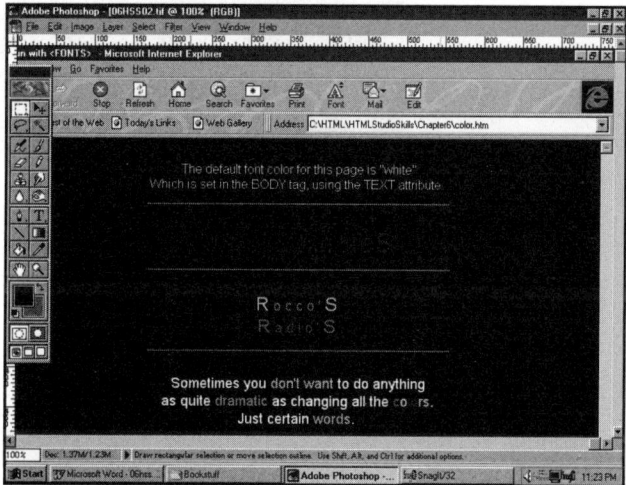

Figure 4.3

Font color; example 2.

Each character of text was dealt with separately. We changed each character's color from light blue (COLOR="#0000FF") to dark blue (COLOR="#00004F") and then from large (SIZE="6") to small (SIZE="2").

In the next example, we've taken a more basic approach: only two size changes and two color changes (see Figure 4.4).

Figure 4.4

Font color; example 3.

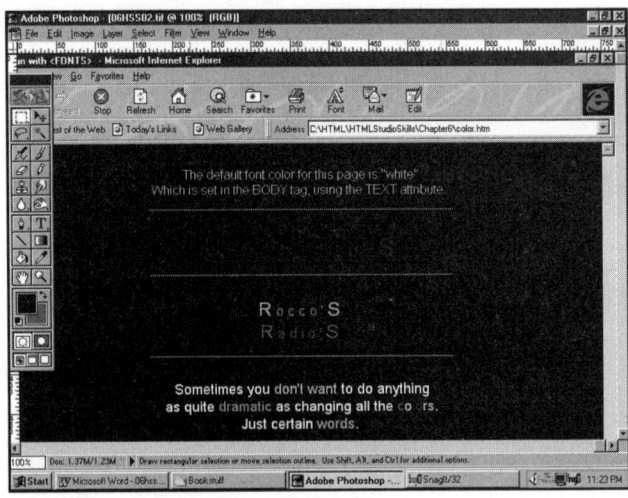

Here's the code:

```
<FONT COLOR="#00FFFF" SIZE="5">R</FONT>
<FONT COLOR="#109F9F" SIZE="4">o c c o '</FONT>
<FONT COLOR="#00FFFF" SIZE="5">S</FONT>
<BR>
<FONT COLOR="#FF00FF" SIZE="5">R</FONT>
<FONT COLOR="#9F109F" SIZE="4">a d i o '</FONT>
<FONT COLOR="#FF00FF" SIZE="5">S</FONT>
```

This example is much simpler than the last one. We only needed to change the first and last letters and the text in the middle.

In the third example, we've used the COLOR attribute to change only the words we needed to. But this draws attention only to those colored sections. This has been used very effectively with some sites, where only certain words have slight color changes that draw your attention to key words in the text. Otherwise, this attribute can get old and tired pretty fast.

> **TIP**
>
> We can see that it took a lot of code to produce somewhat minor effects, which is why most text effects should be done in a graphical program, such as Photoshop. This enables you to create better effects in less time, using small palettes for fast load times and less bandwidth. See Chapter 9, "Advanced Graphics," for details.

FACE

`<FONT FACE="##, ##, ##, ##">`

With the FACE attribute, ## is the actual font name, not the filename, that is to be seen by the user. If the user doesn't have the font specified or loaded, the browser then looks for the next available font in the computer (the next font name after each comma) until it either finds the font on the user's system, or it runs out of font names and uses the default browser font.

The default browser font can be very boring and basic, but now Web designers can use the HTML font attribute FACE to select another font to use as the text. The only problem is that the font must be loaded onto the user's computer. Otherwise it just shows the default font.

If one font you name isn't found, then the browser goes to the next font (just separate the font names with a comma). If you know what the basic default fonts of Macintosh and Windows systems are, then you can use fonts similar on both machines to create a list of font names that both machines will accept at least one from.

Let's take a look at an example (see Figure 4.5).

In Figure 4.5 we've set the font for four drop-down faces. If the user doesn't have the Comic Sans MS font loaded (the first text example), the browser uses the next one, which is Arial if it's loaded. If neither Arial nor Comic are loaded, but Americana is loaded, the user sees the third example, and so on. If he has none of the fonts you've suggested (essentially that's what the FACE attribute is doing, suggesting which fonts should be used), the browser now uses the default font associated with the browser.

> **TIP**
>
> IBM systems loaded with Windows 95 or Windows contain at least these fonts—Courier, Arial, Times New Roman, and Comic Sans MS. Most Macs come preloaded with Helvetica, Times, New York, and Palatino. This information should help you in choosing your list of font faces.

Figure 4.5

Font Face.

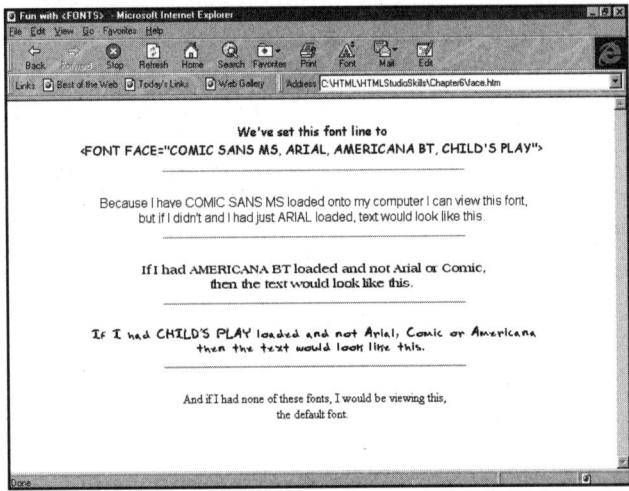

Pagination

Pagination is essentially all the features and strategies of text layout that you need to know. There are a variety of tags, such as `<P>` for paragraph, `<HR>` for horizontal rule, `<BR>` for line break, `<I>` for italics, `<B>` for bold, and `<U>` for underline. If anything, this chapter will hammer home proper syntax and usage, so if you know the tag, just check it for any attributes you may not recognize and then move on.

`<P>` or Paragraph Tag

`<P ALIGN="##">`

With `<P>`, ## is the alignment of the text: left, center, or right. If no alignment is given, the default is left aligned.

> **Note**
> Although closing this tag is not mandatory, it is recommended so that your code looks clearer.

Although this tag is somewhat out of use, it does have its place, specifically if you are showing a lot of text and it isn't in the confines of a table. (This is rare. Because you are learning to place most of your text and content within a tabled structure, this doesn't mean you won't use it. It's just better practice to master text layout with tables.) Essentially all this is used for is to align the text. The <P> tag has the same function as does the ALIGN attribute within the <TD>, or table data tag.

Let's take a look at the tag in action (see Figure 4.6).

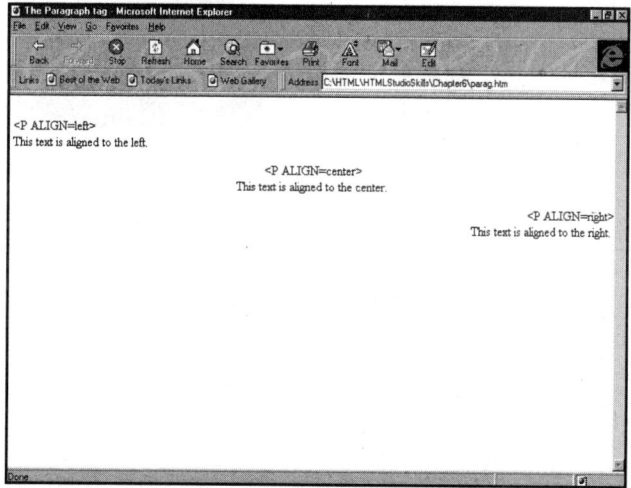

Figure 4.6

The <P> tag.

As you can see, we have three pieces of text and we have aligned them to three different positions in the browser using the <P ALIGN> tag. The text has been aligned to the left, center, and right, respectively.

 or Line Break Tag

When HTML was first used, browsers weren't very good at parsing text, and because so many platforms can make HTML documents for the Web, there was no universal way to tell the text in an HTML document when to go to the next line. That's why the <BR>, or line break tag, was added.

Every time you want a line break, add the <BR> tag. Remember with the <P> and the <TD> tags that text just keeps wrapping. It only drops to the next line when space runs out. To force a line break, you *must* use the <BR> tag.

When using images with text, we often wrap the text around the image by using the <IMG> tag's ALIGN attribute (see Figure 4.7).

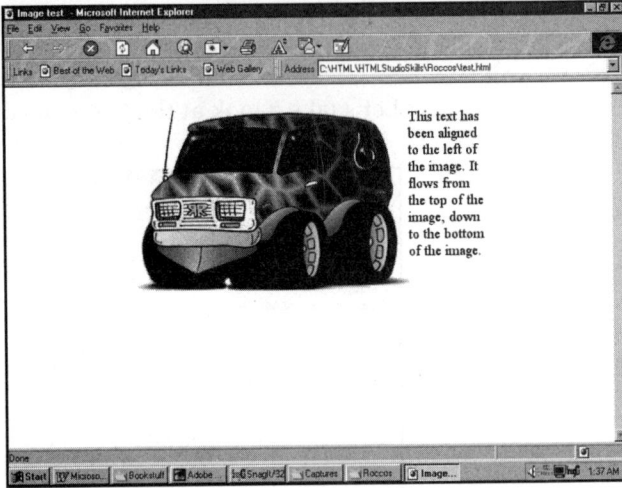

Figure 4.7

Wrapping text around images.

TIP

Read the section on images to see how alignment works with all of its options.

As you can see in our example, the text has been aligned to the right of the image because the image's alignment is set to the left.

But what if we wanted to align just part of the text on the right, a few words on the right, and then the rest of the text below the image? The CLEAR attribute used with the <BR> tag was designed to solve those problems.

CLEAR

<BR CLEAR="##">

With the CLEAR attribute, ## is the alignment of the image to clear: left, right, all, or none. (None is the default.)

The CLEAR attribute will clear the aligned image and then show the text following the break.

If, for example, an image is aligned (or embedded) on the left (<IMG ALIGN=left>) and you want the text to show up below the image, add a <BR> after the image to solve this problem. The text would then follow the image.

But if the image is aligned to the right (`<IMG ALIGN="RIGHT">`) and you add the `<BR>` tag after the image tag, the text does not appear below the image, rather it appears to the left of the image, but a line down.

So how do you make sure that the text appears below the image? By using the `CLEAR` attribute. You use it right after the image, and you align the `CLEAR` to the same side as the image. If the image is aligned to the right, for instance, setting `CLEAR="RIGHT"` will not show the text until the right aligned image is cleared. Then the text will show up below the image.

Let's have a look at the line break in action (see Figure 4.8).

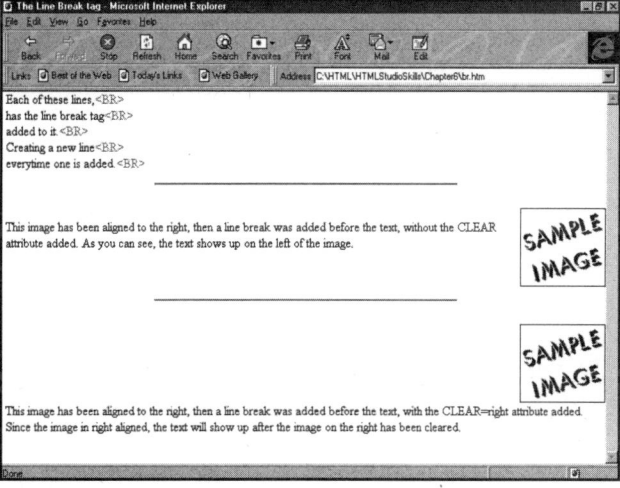

Figure 4.8

The line break.

In the first example, a new line occurs whenever you add the `<BR>` tag.

In the second example, you can see what happens when you place text after a right-aligned image without the `CLEAR` attribute added.

The third shows you that adding the `CLEAR="RIGHT"` attribute (matching the `IMG ALIGN="RIGHT"` attribute) clears the right-aligned image. It shows the text below the image and not beside it, which is the desired effect.

The great thing about this attribute is that you can use it when you want. You can have some text align beside the image, then add a line break with the `CLEAR` attribute added and make the rest of text appear below the image. This is a very useful tool.

`<HR>` or Horizontal Rule Tag

`<HR>`

The tag isn't closed, which creates a break between paragraphs or sections by creating a horizontal line.

Creating a rule or line between paragraphs of text can be quite pleasing to the eye, and it makes reading large pieces of text easier. The `<HR>` tag creates a 100% wide, 3D, shaded horizontal line. Using a darker background color for the top and right parts of the line and a lighter background color for the bottom and right sections of the line gives it a beveled or 3D look.

This tag acts like the `<BR>` tag, but it has more options.

ALIGN, WIDTH, and SIZE

`<HR ALIGN="##" WIDTH="??" SIZE="++">`

When dealing with these attributes, ## is the alignment for the rule, either to the left, center, or right; ?? is the width of the rule, either in pixels or percentages; and ++ is the size in pixels of the height of the line.

These two attributes almost always go together. You can't set the alignment without making the width less than the default of 100%. You can set the width without using the alignment, but the alignment will be defaulted to the center.

> **Note**
> SIZE is basically the height of the line. It can only be set in pixels, not percentages.

COLOR (Explorer Only) and NOSHADE

`<HR COLOR="##" NOSHADE>`

COLOR is an Explorer-only feature.

With these attributes, ## is either the color name or the hex color number. NOSHADE is an on/off type attribute, which means it has no options, and it doesn't work if it isn't added.

The default of the <HR> color is based on the background so that the 3D effect can be achieved.

NOSHADE creates a flat color line, with no bevel or 3D effect. The color of the line is then based on the darker part of the line.

Let's look at some examples (see Figure 4.9).

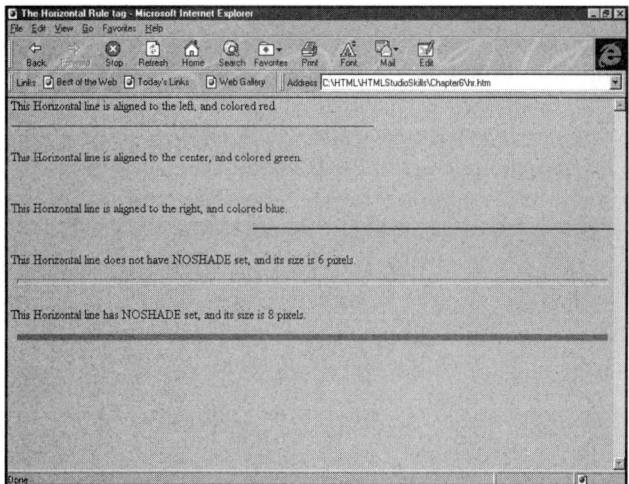

Figure 4.9

The horizontal rule.

In the first three examples, we've set the alignment and the colors (only in Explorer will you see the colors). The first is aligned left and colored red, the second is centered and colored green, and the third is right aligned and colored blue. Also, we've set each of their widths to 60%.

The next line is 6 pixels high (SIZE="6") and it has no attributes added to it. Now you can see the 3D effect we were talking about earlier, where the top-right portion of the line is darker and the bottom-right portion is lighter.

The last line has NOSHADE added to it, and it's 8 pixels high (SIZE="8"). As you can see, the darker color is now the line's entire color.

In the advanced section you will learn how to create horizontal lines using images for a much more effective and appealing look.

<I> Italic, <U> Underlined, and <B> Bold Tags

<I>, <U>, and <B> must all be closed with the appropriate </I>, </U>, and </B> tags, respectively.

Font altering with the use of *italicizing*, <u>underlining</u>, or making text **bold** has always been a useful way of bringing attention to certain pieces of text, and HTML has not ignored this.

You can add any of these features to text by using the <I> tag for italicizing, the <U> tag for underlining, and the <B> tag for bolding.

Just as when we added the <FONT> tag to change text size, face, or color, we do exactly the same with these tags (see Figure 4.10).

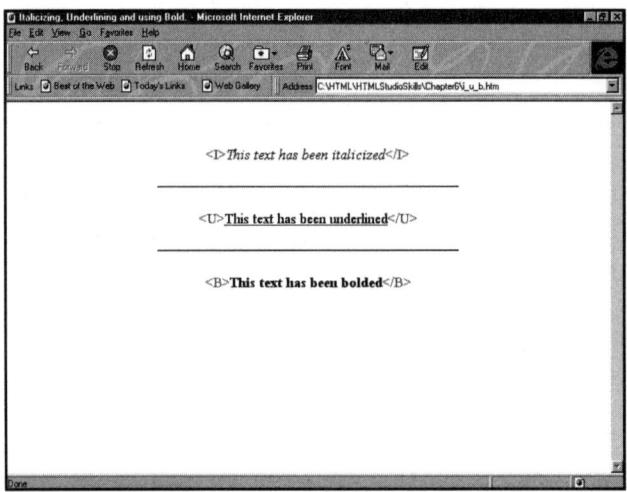

Figure 4.10

Italicizing, underlining, and bolding.

You will find that you use these tags quite often, but don't over do it. Italicizing a line or two is fine, but an entire page of italicized text can be very annoying, unless of course this was the desired effect.

Lists

Lists are a wonderful series of tags that let you present items, definitions, or lists of information. Bulleted, numbered, lettered, or even definition lists can all be achieved with these tags:

- <UL> for unordered lists
- <OL> for ordered lists
- <DL> for definition list

Lists are best used whenever subject, definition, or list information is given, such as in shopping lists, résumé information, definitions, and so on.

<UL> Unordered Lists and <OL> Ordered Lists

<UL> (Unordered list)

    <LI> ## (This is for each List Item)

    <LI> ## (They are usually multiple and are NOT closed)

</UL> (List must be closed)

<OL> (ordered list)

    <LI> ## (List Item)

    <LI> ## (Doesn't need to be closed)

</OL> (List must be closed)

Whereas <UL> or <OL> determine what type of list you are using, the actual information is placed after the <LI> or list item. ## is the content for each list item.

All lists need information tags. That's where <LI> comes in to create each individual list item. Both ordered and unordered lists use <LI> for each list item.

Let's take a look at a basic unordered and ordered list (see Figure 4.11).

Figure 4.11

Unordered and ordered lists.

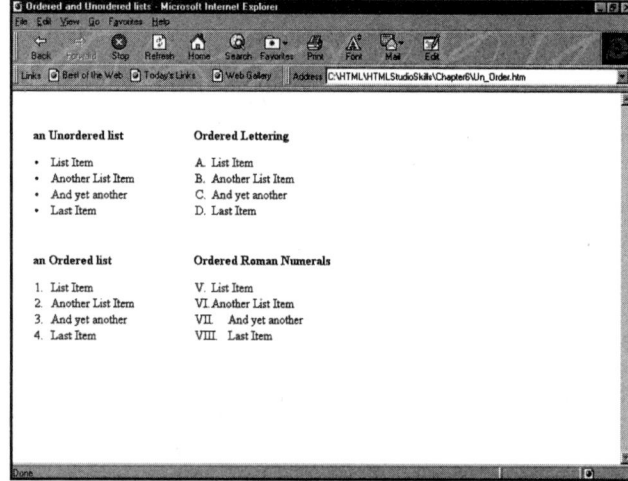

The first list is bulleted and is an unordered list. The code is identical for both except for the type of list.

```
<UL>
<LI> List Item
<LI> Another List Item
<LI> And yet another
<LI> Last Item
</UL>


<OL>
<LI> List Item
<LI> Another List Item
<LI> And yet another
<LI> Last Item
</OL>
```

In the second list, the items are numbered. This is an ordered list.

You can change the type of item numbering to lettering or even Roman numerals by placing the TYPE attribute within the <OL> tag. The options for TYPE are:

> **Note**
>
> In Netscape, you can change the type of bullets by adding the TYPE attribute to the <UL> tag. The options for the TYPE attribute are TYPE="CIRCLE" (default), TYPE="DISC", TYPE="SQUARE".

▶ TYPE="1"—Numbering. This is the default.

▶ TYPE="A"—Capital lettering.

▶ TYPE="a"—Lowercase lettering.

▶ TYPE="I"—Capital Roman numerals: I, II, III, IV, V, and so on.

▶ TYPE="i"—Lowercase Roman numerals.

You can also tell the list where to start the lettering or numbering by adding the START attribute to the <OL> tag:

<OL START="##">

Here, ## is the number of the starting point for the list. Although ## needs to be a number, it affects all type, Roman numerals, lettering, and numbering. For example, <OL START="3" TYPE="A"> would mean that the first list item would start with the letter C because we've set START to 3, which means that the lettering will start from the third letter on.

If we look at the example of the two lists on the right in Figure 4.12, the top list uses lettered ordering (TYPE="A"), whereas the bottom list uses Roman numerals (TYPE="I") as its ordering, with the START attribute added and set to 5.

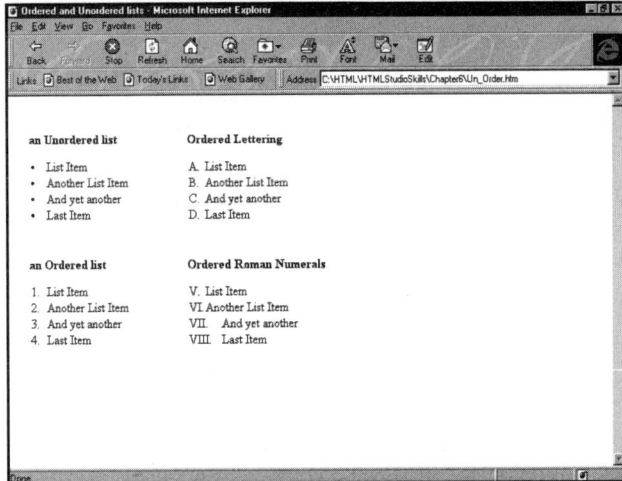

Figure 4.12

Lettered and Roman numeral lists.

> **Note**
>
> The START attribute can be very effective if you need to start off ordered lists and then finish them in other places, such as a list that states five items, has a small paragraph explaining each item, then a new list showing the next five items, and so on.

<DL> Definition Lists

<DL> (Starts the definition list)
    <DT> Definition term or term to be defined
        <DD> Definition Defined
    <DT> Term to be defined
        <DD> Definition Defined
    <DT> Term to be defined
        <DD> Definition Defined
</DL> (Closes the definition list)

Definition lists enable you to create dictionary-type lists for your information. The term is left justified and the definition is slightly tabbed over so that you know which is the term and which is the definition.

Whereas ordered and unordered lists use the <LI> for each piece of content, here the <DT> and <DD> tags are used for "term to be defined" and "actual term definition," respectively.

Let's take a look at a definition list (see Figure 4.13).

Figure 4.13

Definition lists.

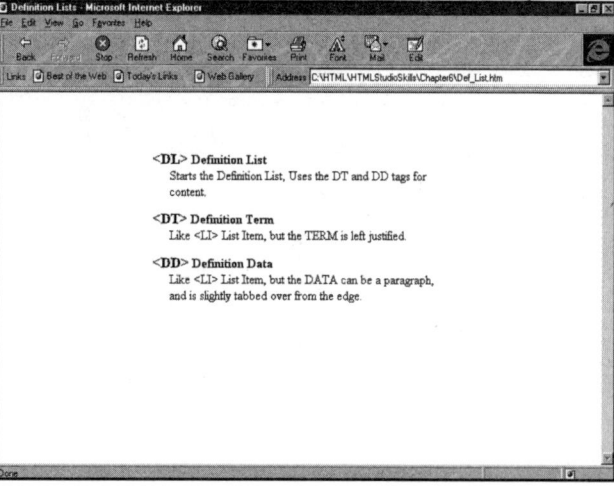

Chapter 4 Text Elements

Here each tag is a term and then the explanation becomes the definition. So the tag, and the tag name, is the <DT> information, and the explanation goes into the <DD> tag. Here's what the code looks like:

```
<DL>
<DT><FONT SIZE="+1"><B>&ltDL&gt</FONT> Definition List
</B>
<DD>Starts the Definition List, Uses the DT and DD tags
for content.

<DT><FONT SIZE="+1"><B>&ltDT&gt</FONT> Definition Term
</B>
<DD>Like &ltLI&gt List Item, but the TERM is left
justified.

<DT><FONT SIZE="+1"><B>&ltDD&gt</FONT> Definition Data
</B>
<DD>Like &ltLI&gt List Item, but the DATA can be a
paragraph, and is slightly tabbed over from the edge.
</DL>
```

We've made the term a little fancier by increasing the size of the tag and bolding the text so that it stands out. This is a good example of functional definition lists.

Lists can be effective presentational tools, enabling you to lay your information out in a much more readable format. Remember to use lists whenever list, definition, or subject information is used. Start experimenting and come up with some cool variations.

> **Note**
>
> Lists seem to format better in Netscape than in Explorer, which means your lists will look a little clearer and more precise when viewed in Netscape.

Links and Anchors

A link is a reference point to another place; it could be a document, a file, an email recipient, or an Internet newsgroup. An anchor is a reference point in a document that enables a link in another place to access it. Both links and anchors use the <A> tag, but they use different attributes to activate the different functions.

The link uses the HREF attribute, and with certain parameters it can access FTP files, HTML files, Gopher information, email addresses, newsgroups, and even open up a Telnet client.

The anchor uses the NAME attribute, followed by the name of the anchor so that a link could send the user to the anchor automatically.

<A HREF> Links

`<A HREF="##">`

This tag must be closed with the `</A>` tag, and ## is either the URL (www.place.com), the anchor (#orderinfo), or another option.

The most common HREF (Hyperlink Reference) link is a link to another HTML file.

Here are a few examples:

- `<A HREF="http://www.example.com/people/home.html">` is a link that tells the browser to load the file home.html in the people directory of the domain www.example.com.

- `<A HREF="home.html">` works exactly the same. It tells the browser to look for the home.html file in the same directory and path as the current file.

- `<A HREF="home.html#orderinfo">` is a link that searches the same directory for the home.html file. When it loads, it then searches for the orderinfo anchor, which has been set using the NAME attribute.

- `<A HREF="www.example.com/places/">` is a very interesting link because it tells the browser to search for the root HTML file in the places directory of the www.example.com domain. But this link will only work if the server software on www.example.com has been setup for a specific file. Most servers are setup so that if a filename isn't included in a link, it then searches for the index.html or index.htm file, but this is not guaranteed. It's important to remember this when creating your links; otherwise, you could create a link that goes nowhere. It's good practice to use the full path in the link; then check your links to make sure they work.

You can also access files with links. These automatically download to the user, and they follow the same rules as an HTML file.

`<A HREF="http://www.example.com/demo.exe">` would access and download the file demo.exe from the root directory at the `www.example.com` domain.

There are many other options to the `<A HREF>` tag and attribute:

- `HREF="http://##"`

    Here, `##` is the URL of the document you want to access, such as `www.domain.com/home.html`. If no URL is given, and no http:// is used, the tag looks for the HTML document in the same directory as the current document. This is the default option type, and it doesn't need to preface the URL.

- `HREF="mailto:##?subject=$$"`

    `##` is the email address, such as `marcus@fluidu.com`, and `$$` is the subject of the email message.

- `HREF="ftp://##"`

    `##` is the FTP server you want to connect to, followed by the path, and filename, such as `HREF="ftp://ftp.example.com/bin/public/test.hqx"`

- `HREF="gopher://##"`

    `##` is the gopher server you want to connect to.

- `HREF="news:##"`

    `##` is the Usenet newsgroup server and newsgroup.

- `HREF="Telnet://##"`

    `##` is the Telnet server you want to connect to. This activates a telnet session, but the user must have an external telnet client installed.

Let's take a look at one of these: the `mailto: ?subject=` option. It enables us to create a link that when pressed, opens up the browser's mail message window. It is then ready to send an email message to the `mailto:` person, and it has the subject filled in (see Figure 4.14).

> **Note**
>
> The person's actual email address must be used with `mailto:`, such as `mailto:bob@hangout.com`.

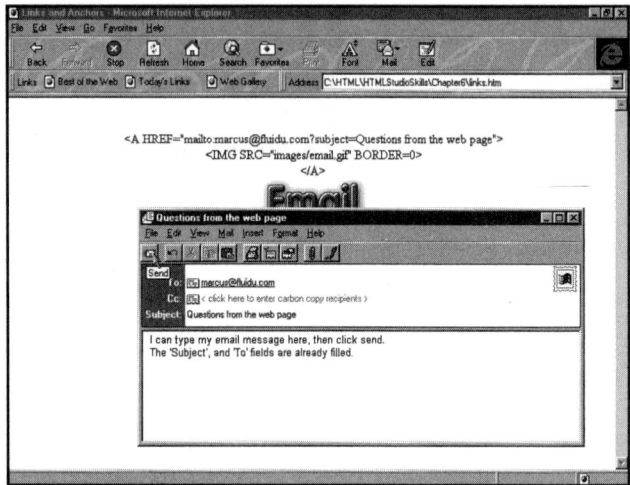

Figure 4.14

The `mailto:` option.

We've created a link around an image so that when the user clicks the image, whatever the link is set for is accessed.

The code for this `mailto:` looks like this:

```
<A HREF="mailto:marcus@fluidu.com?subject=Questions from the web page">
<IMG SRC="images/email.gif" BORDER="0"></A>
```

We've set the `mailto:` option to send mail to `marcus@fluidu.com`, and we've set the `?subject=` option to Questions from the Web page. When we clicked the email image, an email message box popped up with the TO field and the SUBJECT field already filled in. All we need to do now is type in a message and press send.

> **Note**
>
> It's important to remember that when creating a link around an image, the image border should be set to `BORDER="0"` or there will be a colored border around the image (which is fine if that's the look you want).

`<A NAME>` Anchors

`<A NAME="??">`

Anchors aren't closed, and they are referred to by the `<A HREF="#??">` tag.

Chapter 4 Text Elements

?? is the name of the anchor, which is usually placed before a certain section or subheading and then named accordingly. `<A HREF="orderinfo">`, would be a good anchor name if the following text related to ordering information.

Creating an anchor is a lot like naming sections or subjects on your Web site. Say, for instance, you've got a Web page on fixing fuel pumps, and it's broken down into categories such as parts involved, electrical, tools needed, and so on. You could then add anchors to the beginning of each section, such as `<A NAME="electrical">`, `<A NAME="tools">`, and so on. Then to access these from the same Web page, or even another, you could create a series of links at the top of the page that enable the user to click the subject they want to read about, and they're sent to the subject.

Let's have a look at some anchors in action (see Figure 4.15).

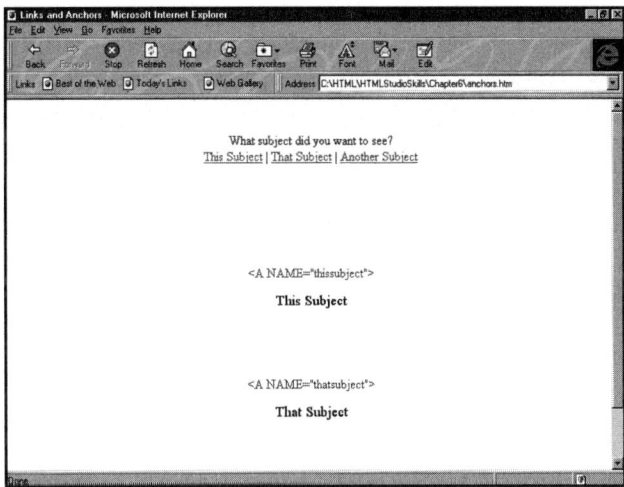

Figure 4.15
Anchors.

We have a subject menu, created with links.

```
<A HREF="#thissubject">This Subject</A>
<A HREF="anchors.htm#thatsubject">That Subject</A>
<A HREF="#anothersubject">Another Subject</A><BR>
```

And if any one of these subjects is pressed, it will drop down to the corresponding anchor.

Every subject has its own anchor. Just above "This Subject," for example, we've added the anchor:

`<A NAME="thissubject">`

The interesting thing about anchors is that they can be accessed at the end of HTML links. In the second subject link example, you can see that we have created the link `<A HREF="anchors.htm#thatsubject">`. This tells the browser to look in the same directory for the anchors.htm file and then find the `thatsubject` anchor. The same path rules used by links apply to anchors.

Conclusion

In this chapter, you learned the basics of HTML, from text attributes, such as `FONT` with all of its colorful options, to italicizing and underlining text, to using line breaks with images to get the text layout you want. We also discussed how to create lists using Roman numerals as bullets, and definition lists that present dictionary style terms and definitions. You also learned all about links and anchors, how to create subject lists in your documents, and easy ways for your users to access them. You even saw ways to set up a quick `mailto:` option with the address and subject pre-filled so your users can contact you from your Web page.

Now it's time to move on to the visual and aural aspects of design by integrating sound and multimedia into your Web site.

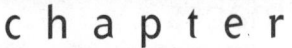

Images and Multimedia

The Web would not be where it is today had Tim Berners-Lee not had the foresight to include specifications for inline images in the original HTML draft. Simply put, you download HTML files and GIF or multimedia files from the server separately, and then the browser draws them all together in the browser window. Although the HTML file describes the look and the layout of the document, the actual images, sounds, and movies are contained in separate files.

Inline images are images and therefore contained within, rather than referenced by, a document structure; and adding them to a page is the best way to make your site distinctive, useful, and attractive. There are a growing number of features you can use to enhance the functionality of your images. As the Web grows, you have the benefit of additional tools in the form of multimedia. This chapter helps you to get a handle on both.

 Placing Inline Images

    <IMAGE> Tag Attributes

    Adding Imagemaps to Pages

 Adding Audio and Video to Web Pages

Placing Inline Images

The two formats most commonly used for inline images on the Web are GIF and JPEG. The GIF specification is a highly evolved, extensible, and relatively efficient format that enables animation, transparency, and interlacing, whereas JPEG is a simple format that uses more optimized compression to preserve color content in photorealistic graphics. Other file formats, such as PNG, are permissible but have not yet been embraced with quite the same fervor as GIF and JPEG and may not work with all browser software. In essence, you'll probably find yourself using GIFs for most of your graphics, especially those needing transparency and animation, whereas JPEG will be reserved for instances where you're frustrated by GIF's poor quality and compression on a photorealistic image.

Adding an image to a Web page is simple:

```
<IMG SRC="http://espresso.cafe.net/ian/ianelvis.gif">
```

The SRC= attribute is the only essential attribute of the <IMG> tag. This specifies where a client's Web browser will find the image file you're referring to. Placing this tag somewhere in a Web page will lay out the image on the left-hand side of the page. Notice that this tag uses a full path URL, specifying the name of the server and the full directory path to locate the image file. You can also use relative path URLs similarly to when you build links. This is handy if you want to build your files on a local machine and then upload them to the server. Rather than using full path URLs, which require you to upload the GIFs and HTML to a server before you can view the page properly, you can test your work locally using relative path URLs and see the document's layout exactly as it will look when the site is up and running.

> **Note**
>
> Relative Path URLs look for a file's location in relation to the location of the file that refers to it. If, for example, within a document located at `http://ian.cafe.net/doc/bob.html` I use the command `<IMG SRC="bob/bobanim.gif">`, the Web browser assumes that what I really mean is `<IMG SRC="http://ian.cafe.net/doc/bob/bobanim.gif">`. If `bob.html` gets moved to my hard drive at the path `C:\www\`, then my Web browser will look for the image in `C:\www\bob\bobanim.gif` when I attempt to view the page.

`<IMAGE>` Tag Attributes

Now that you have some images on a Web page, let's look at attributes you can use to make them look, load, and lay out better. The tools we discuss here cover image alignment, alignment of text around the images, borders, alternate display options, clickable menu graphics called imagemaps, and several more advanced tricks to help you make your images appear on the page exactly as you'd like.

ALIGN

Values: TOP, MIDDLE, CENTER, BOTTOM, LEFT, RIGHT

This attribute enables you to set the alignment of the image or the text that surrounds it. The default value is TOP. Table 5.1 suggests how each of these values of the ALIGN attribute will affect surrounding text.

Table 5.1
ALIGN Values and Descriptions

Value	Description
TOP/TEXTTOP	Text is aligned with top of the image.
MIDDLE/ABSMIDDLE	Text is aligned with middle of the image (vertical).
CENTER	Text is aligned with center of the image (horizontal).
BOTTOM/BASELINE/ABSBOTTOM	Text is aligned with bottom of the image.
LEFT	The image is aligned to leftmost point possible, and text flows around it.
RIGHT	The image is drawn to rightmost point possible and text flows around it.

> **Note**
> Although the TOP, MIDDLE, and BOTTOM attributes start the text flowing at the desired point, the rest of the text drops curiously below the image once a single line is filled. Using LEFT or RIGHT values in conjunction with your desired text or table formatting options (Chapters 4 and 5, respectively) will help you achieve a block of text running contiguously alongside an image.

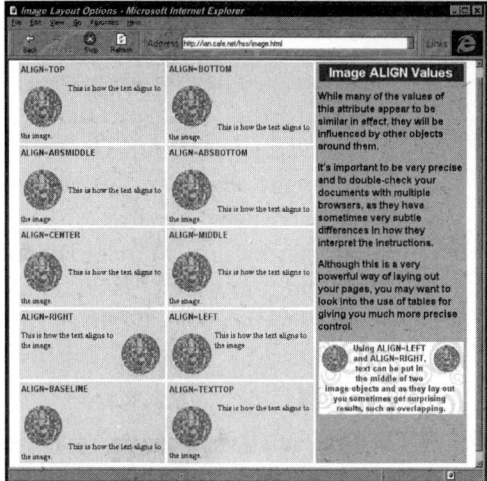

Figure 5.1

Checking out how your ALIGN attributes work.

BORDER, HSPACE, and VSPACE

Values: η (integer)

Every image, when placed on a page, has a 2-pixel border drawn around it. Unless that image becomes a link, the border is invisible. Usually when you make an image into a link, you won't be happy with how that border affects the look and feel of your page—specifically if you're using a transparent image file as the link. In such cases, the BORDER attribute is most commonly set to 0 (zero) to turn off the image's border altogether.

As we see in Figure 5.2, an undesirable result of turning off the border is the text butting up against the edge of the image, making it difficult to read. Using the HSPACE and VSPACE attributes, you can define a transparent "no-fly zone" or a margin where text won't dare to venture. This gives you plenty of options for making text readable and giving images added dimension.

Curiously, Internet Explorer chooses to draw the borders of images (unless they are links) as transparent, which renders the HSPACE and VSPACE attributes essentially redundant. Netscape draws these borders using the color attribute of the surrounding font.

Chapter 5 Images and Multimedia

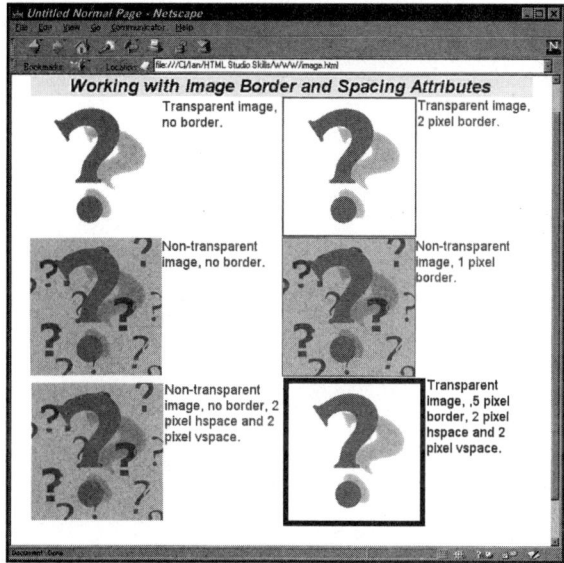

Figure 5.2

HSPACE, VSPACE, and BORDER in action.

HEIGHT and WIDTH

Values: η (integer)

The HEIGHT and WIDTH attributes enable you to specify the size of the image, which can create two possible effects.

First, when the browser knows how big the image is going to be, it can lay out the rest of the page *while* the image is downloading, instead of waiting until after all of the images download. This enables users to read the page while they wait for the images to download, which is a real plus.

Second, you can use the HEIGHT and WIDTH attributes to resize and reuse the same image file at different sizes (within reason). This doesn't add pixels to the graphics—it makes them bigger, which means that they suffer in quality. At most, an image can be scaled about 50% up or down before looking completely hideous; this is an imprecise science, however, and you'll need to judge what's tolerable. Of course, this doesn't make your files any larger or smaller, but it does enable you to re-use images at different sizes. This saves download time because the files only need to be loaded once to work many times on a page or series of pages. Figure 5.3 shows the same image loaded at three different sizes.

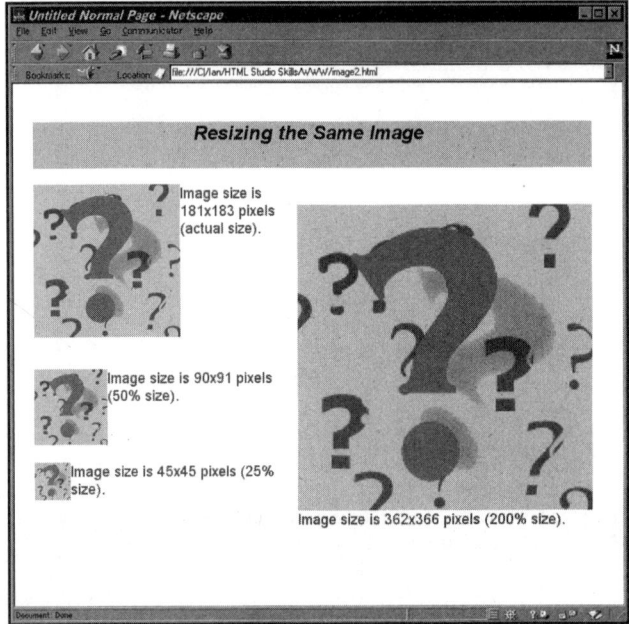

Figure 5.3

Reusing and resizing a single image.

Proper usage is as follows:

```
<IMG SRC="http://ian.cafe.net/HSS/BitBall.GIF" WIDTH="75"
     HEIGHT="75" HSPACE="2" VSPACE="1" BORDER="0">
```

LOWSRC and ALT

Value: URL (LOWSRC), Text (ALT)

The LOWSRC attribute, which works only in Netscape, supports the downloading of the specified LOWSRC image prior to the downloading of the SRC image. The impact of this is that you can now load a low-resolution or grayscale version of a large GIF so that the layout phase is completed quickly. The high-resolution version will replace it in the event that the user chooses to wait.

The ALT attribute serves several purposes. By placing text in the quotes you can describe the image being loaded to the user. This information is drawn in the image frame and is replaced when the image is loaded. This is not only handy for people with slow connections but also for people who turn off Auto Image Loading in their browser so that they can surf faster, or who are using text-based Web browsers such as the venerable Lynx. The text values placed in the ALT attribute also get indexed by some search engines.

This is also handy if you are using GIFs to express text or headings and still want that text to be indexed by a search engine.

```
<IMG SRC="http://ian.cafe.net/HSS/bitball.GIF" LOWSRC="http://ian.cafe.net/HSS/smallball.GIF" ALT="A big yellow ball">
```

Adding Imagemaps to Pages

Imagemaps enable you to link to several different files or Web locations from a single graphic. Let's say you want to create an image that serves as a menu for your site. Based on where a user clicks, you want the user to be directed to the appropriate file resource. How do you do this? Simple. It's called imagemapping. In a few short steps you can make your site faster and more interactive by adding this tool to your page in the form of a navigation menu or button bar.

You can also turn objects in a picture into hot spots that point the user toward varying resources depending on the object they click. Imagemap hot spots can be circular, rectangular, or made of polygons.

How Imagemaps Work

When creating an imagemap, you lay out a grid, which based on the points you define, references a specified file. The interpreter then handles the click point and redirects the user's browser to that file (see Figure 5.4). There are essentially two different ways of doing this, either on the client side or on the server side.

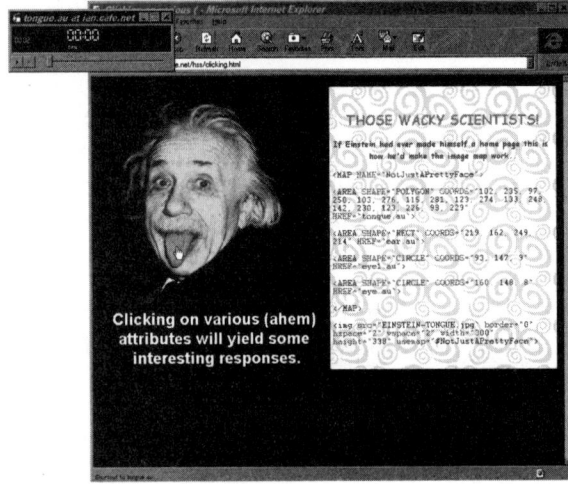

Figure 5.4

Our example imagemap shows how to use client-side mapping to link to audio files.

Comparing Map Formats

Client-side mapping has so many advantages over its predecessor that it is hard to resist. Specifically, it

- Enables users to see which areas are links as the mouse rolls over them.

- Enables users to see where each link will carry them as they roll over the hot spot by displaying the URL in the lower left-hand corner of the browser window.

- Is substantially faster.

- Saves you time, because it's directly supported in most of the visual HTML page layout tools.

- Is easier to integrate with technologies such as Java, JavaScript, and ActiveX.

- As with server-side imagemapping, client-side imagemapping enables you to maintain one .map file that is referenced by multiple documents.

Note

The map format you use depends on whether you choose to use a server-side or a client-side implementation of the interpreter. Although server-side processing was the original implementation and still deserves some respect, the advantages to using client-side image-mapping are hard to resist. Be forewarned, though, because client-side image-mapping is available only to Web browsers that conform to HTML 2.0 and greater. Netscape 1.1 users and others who have not updated to recent browsers cannot make use of this feature.

Chapter 5 Images and Multimedia

The two attributes of the <IMAGE> tag that activate imagemaps on a Web page are ISMAP and USEMAP.

ISMAP

Value: Empty

ISMAP is the original specified method for using imagemaps, and it is the most widely supported. This implies that you will be using server-side coordinate translation, and that the map coordinate information is loaded from a separate .map file. ISMAP could function in one of two possible ways.

Most likely, your server supports imagemap translation as a built-in function. You need only to determine whether it prefers CERN or NCSA-compatible imagemap styles and call upon the .map file either from a specific directory or from anywhere on the server. You can then call it with a reference such as:

```
<A HREF="menu.map"><IMG SRC="menu.gif" ISMAP></A>
```

In the event that your server does not support imagemap translation as a built-in function, you can use a third-party CGI to do it for you. The syntax of the URL is specific to the CGI and where it locates its image files, but it could function as follows:

```
<A HREF="/cgi-bin/imagemap/ian/menu.map"><IMG SRC="menu.gif" ISMAP></A>
```

Of course, in both cases the HREF specifies where to find the map file it will use to return the coordinates.

USEMAP

Value: URL

USEMAP makes use of client-side imagemapping; therefore, implementation is simpler. USEMAP gives you the option to embed the map coordinates information within the same file as the reference or to call a standard file from the server. The beauty of either function is that your imagemaps can work independently of the Web server, meaning it's one less thing to worry about in the event that you move your files or if your site suffers from frequent server "upgrades." The syntax is as follows:

```
<IMG BORDER="0" SRC="menu.gif" USEMAP="#menu">
```

or

```
<IMG BORDER=0 SRC="menu.gif" USEMAP="http://ian.cafe.net/menu.map">
```

Obviously, the latter refers to a different file containing the map information, whereas the former refers to an anchor that exists in the current document. After you've added this tag to your document you must add the `<MAP>` element to define the hot spots on your document. This sample shows an imagemap of four equal squares on a 200×50-pixel rectangle.

```
<MAP NAME="Simple">
    <AREA SHAPE="RECT" COORDS="0,0, 50,50" HREF="file1.html">
    <AREA SHAPE="RECT" COORDS="51,0, 100, 50" HREF="file2.html">
    <AREA SHAPE="RECT" COORDS="101,0, 150,50" HREF="file3.html">
    <AREA SHAPE="RECT" COORDS="151,0, 200,50" HREF="file4.html">
</MAP>
<IMG SRC="simle.jpg" BORDER="0" WIDTH="200" HEIGHT="50" USEMAP="#Simple">
```

The `<MAP>` Tag

Attributes: `NAME`

Syntax: `<MAP NAME="Simple">`

As with all other element tags, the `<MAP>` tag must open and close, acting as a container for the attributes within it. The value of the `NAME` attribute is arbitrarily assigned by the Web designer, and it enables the browser to locate the map when it's referenced in the `<IMG>` tag as a value of `USEMAP`.

The `<AREA>` Tag

Primary Attributes: `SHAPE, COORDS, HREF, NOHREF, TARGET, ALT`

Extended Attributes: `CLASS, ID, NOTAB, TABINDEX, TITLE`

Syntax: `<AREA SHAPE="RECT" COORDS="0,0, 50,50" HREF="file1.html">`

The tag defines hot spots: where they go and what they do. The values can be separated according to the ones you'll use most often (the primary attributes) and those which are used in advanced documents (extended attributes).

Chapter 5 Images and Multimedia

SHAPE
Values: RECT (rectangle), CIRC (Circle), POLY (Polygon)

SHAPE tells the browser how your hot spots will be defined. Rectangles are the simplest, using two basic X,Y coordinates to place the hot spot. Circles require you to plot the center and then define the radius, and polygons plot individual points on the map and connect them together to define the space in between as a hot spot.

COORDS
Values: x1, y1, x2, y2, (RECT)

x1, y1, Rad, (CIRC)

x1, y1, x2, y2, x3, y3, and so on, (POLY)

These values plot the dimensions of the hot spot area along the X and Y axes. If two areas overlap, then the first area in the listing gets priority.

HREF and NOHREF
Values: URL

Where does this link go? HREF, as you should already be recalling, specifies where this link leads. Using NOHREF in the same way, you can cut holes in hot spots—a very useful trick!

TARGET
Values: Window

As we will learn in greater detail in Chapter 8, this value specifies into which window space the link will be loaded. These windows use names and are always alphanumeric, except for the following four values, which start with an underscore character so you don't call them accidentally:

- _BLANK—Loads the link into a blank window
- _PARENT—Loads the link into this window's parent
- _SELF—Loads the link into this window
- _TOP—Loads the link into the browser's complete window

ALT
Values: Text

The ALT attribute is used to provide text labels that are displayed in the browser's status line as the mouse or other pointing device is moved over the hot spots. The tag also enables the construction of a textual menu for non-graphical Web browsers. It's a good idea to use this tag as it helps search engines to index your site, in addition to making your site more accessible to users.

TITLE
Values: Text

This is a rarely used means of identifying the hot spot. It has no effect on how the map displays or loads in the browser.

CLASS and ID
Values: URL, (Class); Text, (ID)

This is a back door that enables Java to act on the clicking of the hot spot. The ID attribute represents the name of this map area, and the CLASS attribute represents the Java applet that will be used to handle this information. Java and applets are introduced in Chapter 11, but you probably won't soon be using this attribute.

TAB and NOTAB
Many viewers use the Tab key to highlight and cycle through the links on a page. NOTAB can exclude an area from this process, whereas using TAB with an integer can define the order in which they are highlighted.

Creating Map Coordinates

Now that you know how to put an imagemap on the page, how will you generate the complex coordinates that will enable the hot spots? All of the imagemap configuration tools work in much the same way. In many visual HTML editors such as Microsoft FrontPage, Claris HomePage, and HotDog Pro, you can click an image after you add it to the page to bring up the Image toolbar.

As Figure 5.5 shows, selecting the object type (RECT, CIRC, or POLY) immediately enables you to draw an area. Click your first point and drag the box, circle, or line to the next. In the instance of using the polygon, click at each point and return to somewhere near the starting point.

Chapter 5 Images and Multimedia

> **Note**
> Check out the external image-map creators included on the CD-ROM!

After you draw your hot spot, a window appears enabling you to make this a link and add other attributes, as in Figure 5.6. After you press OK, you can move on to the next one until you're finished—with no added heartache.

Figure 5.5

Drawing hot spots in FrontPage.

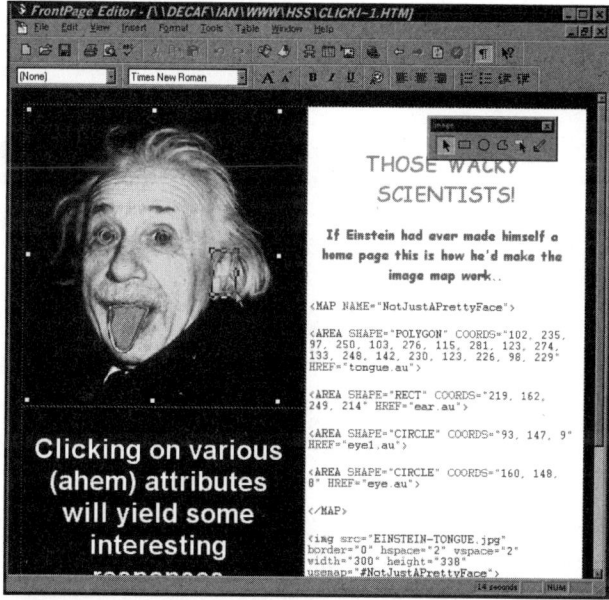

Figure 5.6

The Insert Hyperlink dialog box in FrontPage.

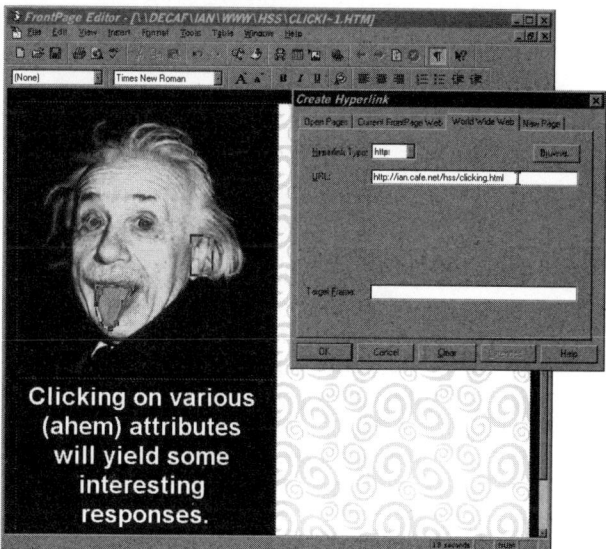

The MapEdit software from Boutell, Inc. can edit existing files or create new ones (see Figure 5.7). This includes HTML, which means that you can create and work with client-side imagemapping as well as server-side maps. Because FrontPage does not have this option, third-party applications such as MapEdit are necessary if you plan to use server-side maps. MapEdit for Windows/Unix is available from http://www.boutell.com/mapedit/, whereas a similar program for the MacOS, simply called Mapper is available from http://www.calles.pp.se/nisseb/mapper.html.

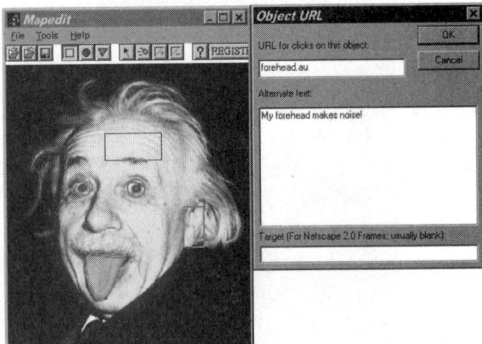

Figure 5.7
The Insert Hot spots Link dialog box in MapEdit for Windows 95.

As shown in Figure 5.8, saving as a stand-alone .map file enables you to use your CGI to interpret the click coordinates when the client selects a hot spot. Be careful to remember which format (CERN or NCSA) your CGI requires!

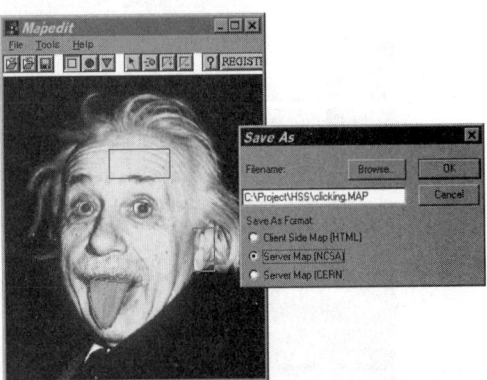

Figure 5.8
Saving as a CERN imagemap file from MapEdit.

Chapter 5 Images and Multimedia

> **Note**
> After you've put the file on the server it can be referenced by multiple HTML files, if needed.

Adding Audio and Video to Web Pages

More active pages are definitely becoming the norm on the Web. Adding audio and video in place of static images may well be a good start for your Web site.

<BGSOUND> and <EMBED>

Adding sound is possible through two different means, of course, one for each browser type. Although Explorer uses and implements the very effective <BGSOUND> tag, Netscape has embraced the <EMBED> tag, which had originally been implemented to support the PlugINS framework. To make matters worse, Explorer also supports the <EMBED> tag, but in a slightly different way.

The <EMBED> tag will likely be your best bet until <BGSOUND> becomes approved and standardized, and Netscape must implement it. Until then, they're unlikely to support any tag that extends the reach of Microsoft-Centric initiatives. That said, we'll start with the Explorer tag.

The <BGSOUND> Tag

Attributes: LOOP, SRC

Syntax: `<BGSOUND SRC="bite.au" LOOP="INFINITE">`

You can use this tag to add sounds in the form of .WAVs, .AUs, .MIDs, AIFFs, .RAMs, or anything else that's readily usable by your viewers. The two attributes associated with <BGSOUND> are easy to work with.

Although .AU files (Sun's ULAW format) files are universally acceptable, Webmasters are turning to .WAVs (a Windows-specific sound format) and .AIFFs (common audio standard with varying acceptance) to achieve better sound quality. MID files (which use MIDI instructions standard to Netscape 2.0-compatible browsers) are a byte-size economical way of adding sound to your page, albeit with varying degrees of cheesiness. RAM files are RealAudio format files that "stream" the audio data, which means they play as they download, but you need access to a RealAudio server to use them.

The LOOP Attribute
Value: η, or "INFINITE"

This value specifies how many times the sound file will loop. Using INFINITE makes it loop until the page is exited. The sound starts playing automatically as soon as it is downloaded.

The SRC Attribute
Value: URL

This value designates the sound file's location.

The <EMBED> Tag

Attributes: AUTOSTART, LOOP, SRC, HEIGHT, and WIDTH

Syntax: <EMBED SRC="bubbles.au" AUTOSTART="TRUE" LOOP="TRUE">

<EMBED> tags activate plug-ins within Netscape and Internet Explorer that are built-in to the browsers. The significance of this is that the attributes we pass to the different plug-ins lack consistency between media types. The SRC attribute works as you would expect; there are some differences, however, in the implementation of <EMBED> across browsers.

The LOOP Attribute
Value: TRUE, FALSE

This value specifies whether the sound file loops. But unlike its cousin, Microsoft's <BGSOUND> tag, LOOP cannot specify how often.

The AUTOSTART Attribute
Value: TRUE, FALSE

This value specifies whether the sound begins playing automatically or waits for a user action on the sound control panel that pops up in the Netscape browser window when a sound is downloaded.

Chapter 5 Images and Multimedia

HEIGHT and WIDTH

Unfortunately, the <EMBED> tag causes the sound control panel to appear as a part of your document. This can really mess up your page layout if you're not careful, but only in Netscape. Internet Explorer does not display the sound control panel at all. The actual size specifications of the control panel are WIDTH="146" and HEIGHT="58".

This ensures that the control panel displays properly on your page. But what if you don't want to see it? The best idea would be to give the <EMBED> tag a size of 0,0, but for reasons unknown this causes it to break in Netscape. Therefore, the best possible compromise is to use WIDTH="146" HEIGHT="0". Your own experimentation may reveal a better combination that works for you (see Figure 5.9).

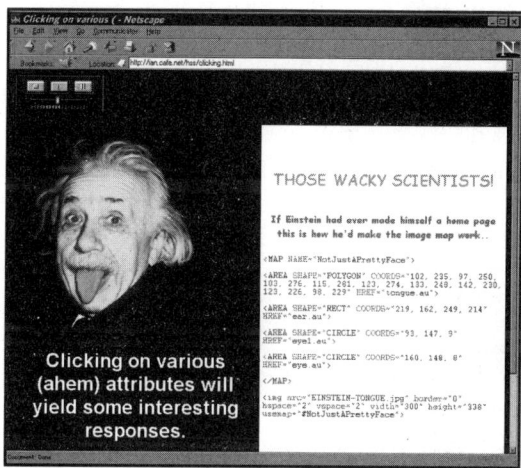

Figure 5.9

Using <EMBED> causes your page layout to change dramatically.

Adding Inline Video/VRML

You can also add video and VRML to your Web pages using one of two different methods. VRML stands for Virtual Reality Markup (or Modeling) Language and it's been called the 3D equivalent to HTML. One of the best books on VRML is Mark Pesce's book, *VRML: Browsing and Building Cyberspace,* from New Riders Publishing.

Internet Explorer enables you to activate video within image tags and gives you some control, although again the standard is the <EMBED> tag as implemented by Netscape. Of course, as with the use of <EMBED> for sounds, this technique can be messier and doesn't have the kind of control that you get with Internet Explorer.

Using the <IMG> Tag

Attributes: DYNSRC, LOOP, START, CONTROLS

Syntax: <IMG DYNSRC="happy.avi" LOOP="3" START="MOUSEOVER">

The addition of video and VRML as inline elements of pages is accomplished courtesy of an extended set of attributes for the <IMG> tag. You can add motion in the form of QuickTime movies, AVIs, or MPEGs using these attributes, assuming you can count on the end user having the appropriate decoder. The nice thing about using the <IMG> tag is that it is easy to integrate seamlessly into your Web documents. Some designers find the controls and borders of most inline movies annoying. The benefit here is that you get to use all of the image attributes, including those previously listed, to customize the look of your video window (see Figures 5.10 and 5.11).

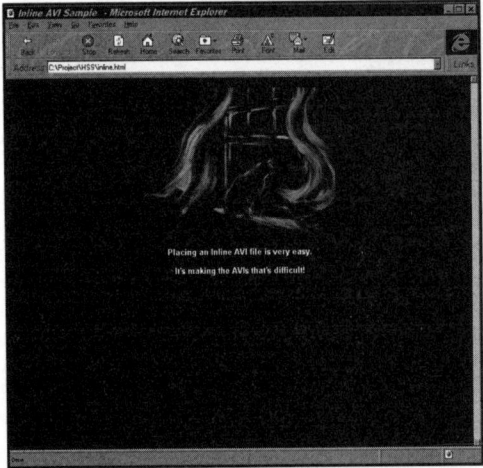

Figure 5.10

A seamlessly integrated movie demonstrates the visual power of using the <IMG> tag for inline movies.

Chapter 5   Images and Multimedia

> **Note**
> None of the video formats will work for every user on every platform. QuickTime (pioneered by Apple) is currently the most popular for MacOS and Windows browsers, with .AVI (a Windows format) running a close second. MPEG usually requires external decoder software on most platforms.

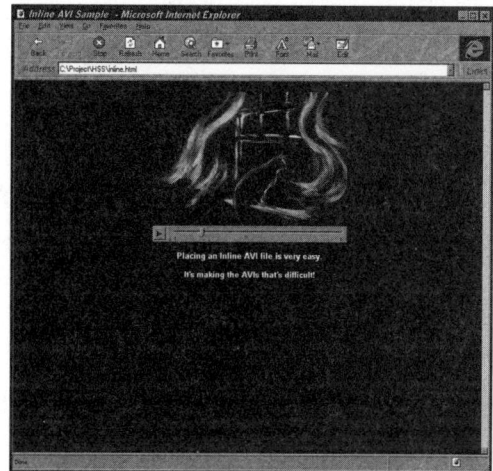

Figure 5.11

The same movie displayed inline with the controller activated.

The DYNSRC Attribute
Values: URL

This value specifies where the file is located. It is possible to use the SRC= in conjunction with this to provide a placeholder until the file's download is complete.

The LOOP Attribute
Value: η, or "INFINITE"

This value specifies how many times the video file loops. Using INFINITE will make it loop until the page is exited. The video starts playing automatically as soon as it is downloaded.

The START Attribute
Value: FILEOPEN, MOUSEOVER

This value specifies when the movie starts playing. FILEOPEN is the default setting, although both settings can be present, separated by a comma.

▶ FILEOPEN—Start playing as soon as the file is downloaded.

▶ MOUSEOVER—Start playing when the user moves the mouse pointer over it.

The CONTROLS Attribute

If CONTROLS is present, browser controls appear onscreen to operate the video clip. If not, the movie simply floats over the page. This attribute has no value.

Using the <EMBED> Tag

Attributes: SRC, LOOP, AUTOPLAY, CONTROLLER, HEIGHT, and WIDTH

Syntax: <EMBED SRC="FOO.MOV" LOOP="TRUE" AUTOPLAY="TRUE">

Most of the attributes used in this tag are slightly different from those for using audio in pages. At the very least, SRC works as promised, and this is supported in both browser types provided your users have the correct browser-enabled movie decoder.

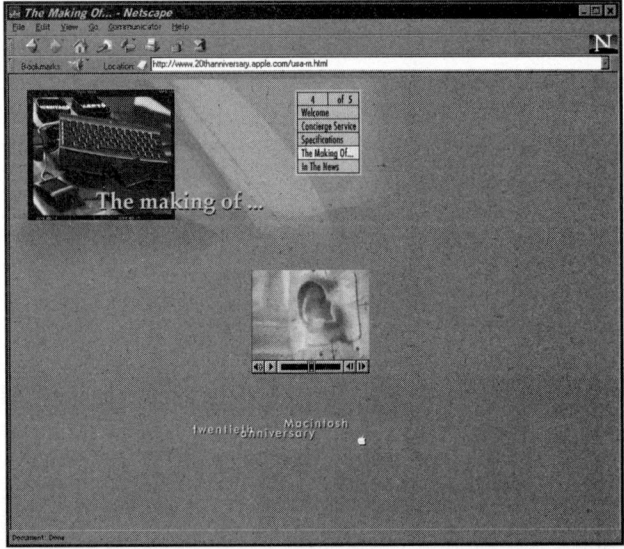

Figure 5.12

Apple uses an inline QuickTime movie to great effect for its 20th anniversary site.

The LOOP Attribute
Value: TRUE, FALSE

This value specifies whether the video file loops, but it cannot specify how often.

The AUTOPLAY Attribute
Value: TRUE, FALSE

This value specifies whether the video begins playing automatically or waits for a user action on the video control panel. It works like the AUTOSTART attribute in using video files.

The CONTROLLER Attribute
Value: TRUE, FALSE

If CONTROLLER="TRUE", browser controls appear to operate the video clip. If not, the movie simply floats over the page.

Conclusion

In this chapter, you've absorbed a lot of information about using the <IMG> tag to really control the look and feel of your Web pages. You should also be developing a sense that the real value of the related tags and attributes is letting you tweak your documents to create the perfect look: The attributes of the <IMG> tag combine to give you some expert-looking layouts. As the use of images, animated GIFs, and multimedia snippets such as movies and sound files propagate, however, it's important to recognize the impact of these larger files on your site.

chapter 6

The Fine Art of Tables

When tables were first introduced to the HTML standard, programmers were elated: "Finally, a way to display list and database information in a hypertext format!" It wasn't until the Web and graphic designers got ahold of it, though, that the power of tables truly became apparent: "Finally a way to use page layout and graphic design in a hypertext format!"

Tables essentially took the basic "content" structure of the Internet and added a new element: Excitement! (see Figures 6.1 and 6.2). Old, drab, text-based pages were now being replaced by graphical amusement parks—places for users to explore, and enjoy.

- → <TABLE> Tag
- <TR> Tag
- <TD> Tag
- <THEAD>, <TBODY>, and <TFOOT> Tags
- → <COLGROUP> and <COL> Tags

92 HTML Studio Skills

> **Note**
> Most hard-core Web enthusiasts believe that HTML would never be, and should never be, a page layout medium/language. Well, they're wrong! After reading this book, you should be able to design or emulate any magazine, Web, or graphic layout you see.

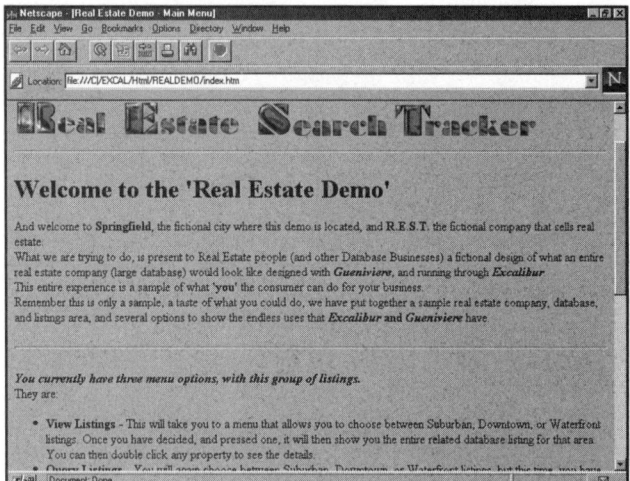

Figure 6.1
Before tables.

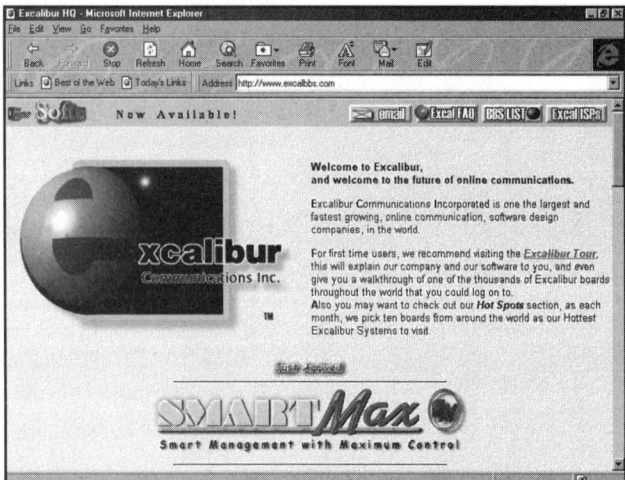

Figure 6.2
After tables.

<TABLE> Tag

The tag that creates a table within your HTML document, <TABLE>, must be closed with the </TABLE> tag.

Chapter 6 The Fine Art of Tables

> **Note**
>
> Many tags have repetitive attributes that affect each tag differently. These "common attributes" have an order of importance.
>
> <TD> is the most important tag, and if you set an attribute inside that tag, it overrules all other tags, including <TR>, <THEAD>, <TBODY>, <TFOOT>, <COLGROUP>, and <TABLE>.
>
> <TR> is the second most powerful tag, overruling settings in <THEAD>, <TBODY>, <TFOOT>, <COLGROUP>, and <TABLE>.
>
> Without these options, or commands, a table can be a very boring thing (as seen with our basic table earlier).

The <TABLE> tag is very diverse in that it has a lot of attributes or commands that can be used within it: 20 attributes within the <TABLE> tag and eight tags that can be used within the active table.

The most basic table you can create needs only one other tag: the <TD> or table data tag. The <TD> tag creates a cell, or a place where you can put text or images. When you open a cell, you must close it with the </TD> tag. Here's an example:

```
<TABLE>
<TD>Cell Number 1</TD>
<TD>Cell Number 2</TD>
</TABLE>
```

The concept behind a table is basically a box containing several smaller boxes that contain data, text, or images. These boxes are then placed in rows. Each box can have its own options, including colors, background graphics, borders, alignments, and sizes.

Let's spend some time learning all of the attributes and tags that make tables interesting.

ALIGN Attribute

`<TABLE Align=##>`

With the ALIGN attribute, ## is the alignment of the table; left, right, or centered. It aligns all of the cells accordingly, with the default being aligned to the left.

Although this attribute is used to align your elements on your Web page, it is seldom used within the <TABLE> tag. Instead it is used within the table data (<TD>) and table row (<TR>) tags to achieve concentrated aligning (each cell or row can be aligned) that doesn't affect information surrounding the table.

> **Note**
>
> Aligning your table within the `<TABLE>` tag causes the same affect as aligning text around an image. If you haven't planned for this, information can wrap around your table when you don't want it to.

Although this attribute is used to align your elements on your Web page, it is seldom used within the `<TABLE>` tag. More often the `ALIGN` attribute is used within the `<TD>` and `<TR>` tags to align your table on your Web page.

VALIGN Attribute

`<TABLE VALIGN=##>`

`##` is the vertical alignment of the table itself, either top, middle, bottom, or baseline.

Much like the `ALIGN` attribute, you will find that using the `VALIGN` attribute within the `<TD>` and `<TR>` tags is a more common and effective practice.

BGCOLOR Attribute

`<TABLE BGCOLOR=##>`

`##` is the number (in hex), or name, of the color you want as the table background.

This changes the background color of the "entire" table to whatever you choose.

While you can change each individual cell background color by using this attribute within the `<TD>` tag, using it within the `<TABLE>` tag affects the entire table and all of its cells.

Let's take a look at three colored tables (see Figure 6.3).

In the first table, the color is green, or `BGCOLOR="#00FF00"`; in the second, the color is red, or `BGCOLOR="#FF0000"`; and the third table is blue, or `BGCOLOR="#0000FF"`.

> **Note**
>
> When learning some of the advanced layout techniques later on, you will find certain instances when using the `ALIGN` and `VALIGN` attributes within the `<TABLE>` tag is a useful and necessary tool, but they are rare. Most of the time, you will use these attributes within the data cells themselves.

Chapter 6 The Fine Art of Tables

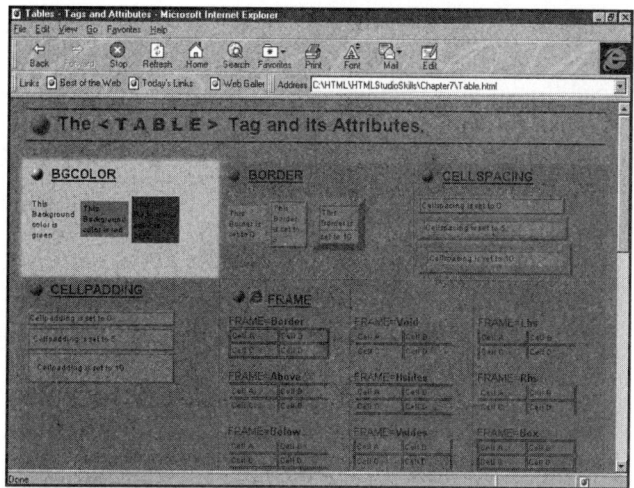

Figure 6.3

BGCOLOR.

BORDER Attribute

`<TABLE BORDER=##>`

Here, ## is the number (in pixels) of how large the outside border will be.

The BORDER attribute creates a border around the table and between each data cell within the table.

The size of the border only relates to the outside border, or the outer edge of the table; the inner border (the border between the cells) remains at 1 pixel in size.

Take a look at the three examples of different border sizes (see Figure 6.4).

In the first table, the border is set to 0, or BORDER="0", making the border invisible. This is the default.

In the second table, the border is set to 3, or BORDER="3", and because there is only one data cell, the border is only visible on the outside of the table.

In the third table, the border is set to 10, or BORDER=10, but there are two data cells. Therefore, you can see the inner border, which remains at 1 pixel thick, while the outside border is 10 pixels thick.

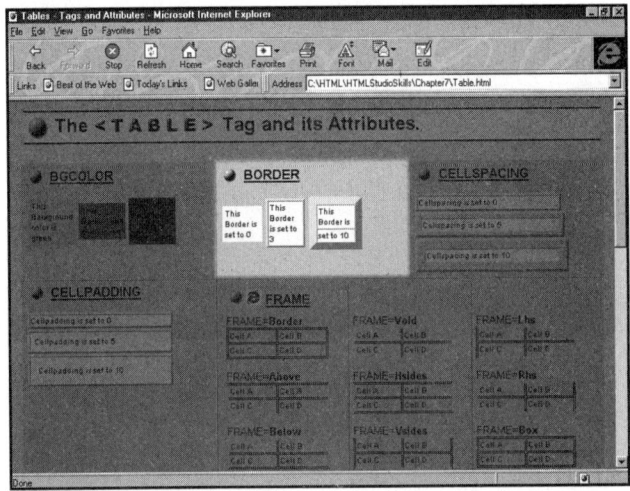

Figure 6.4

Border.

CELLPADDING Attribute

<TABLE CELLPADDING="##">

Here, ## is the number (in pixels) of the distance between the outside of the data cell and the data inside. Cellpadding is just that, the padding space in each data cell between the outside of the cell and the data.

Let's take a look at the attribute (see Figure 6.5).

In the first table, CELLPADDING="0", making the text, or data in the cell, align against the outside of the cell. In the second table, CELLPADDING="5", moving the text 5 pixels away from the outside of the cell. In the third table, CELLPADDING="10", creating a larger gap between the outside of the cell and the data.

Although CELLPADDING's sister attribute, CELLSPACING, acts in the same way, the main difference between the two attributes is that CELLPADDING deals with the inside of the cell, and CELLSPACING deals with the outside.

Chapter 6 The Fine Art of Tables   97

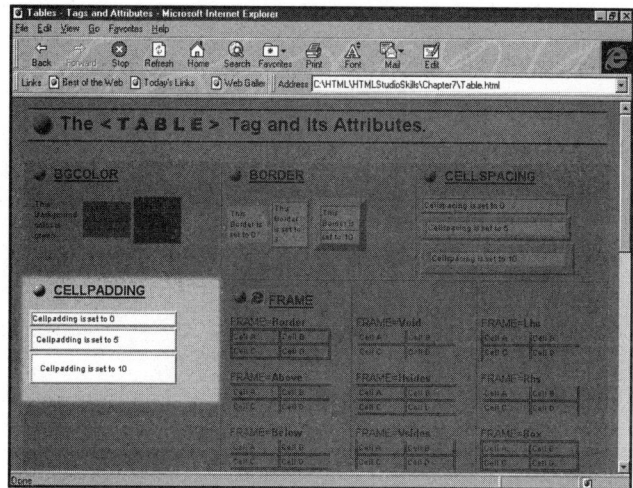

Figure 6.5

The CELLPADDING attribute.

CELLSPACING Attribute

<TABLE CELLSPACING="##">

With the CELLSPACING attribute, ## is the number (in pixels) of the distance between each data cell and the outside of the table. Cellspacing is just that, the spacing between the data cells and the outside of the table.

Let's take a look at the attribute (see Figure 6.6).

In the first table CELLSPACING="0", which aligns the cell against the outside of the table. In the second table, CELLSPACING="5", which adds 5 pixels of space between the data cell and the outside of the table. In the third table, CELLSPACING="10", creating an even larger space.

FRAME Attribute (Explorer Only)

<TABLE FRAME="##" BORDER="1">

Here, ## is the option of the frame type you want; BORDER, ABOVE, BELOW, VOID, HSIDES, VSIDES, LHS, RHS, or BOX.

Figure 6.6

The CELLSPACING attribute.

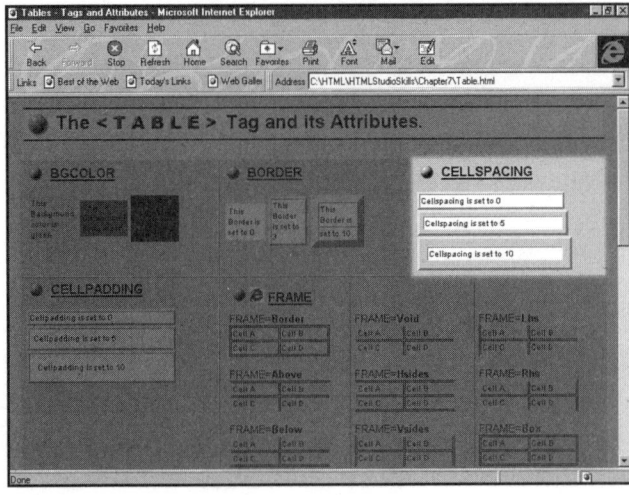

> **Note**
>
> Border attributes must be set larger than 0 for this attribute to work.

After you have the BORDER attribute turned on by setting it to something larger than zero, you can control exactly how you want the border to look by using the FRAME attribute. The frame is the border around the table—not the individual cell borders.

There are nine options with the FRAME attribute.

Table 6.1

FRAME Attribute Options	
Option	Result
FRAME="BORDER", FRAME="BOX"	Creates a border all around the table. It is the same as using a border without the FRAME attribute, and it is the default.
FRAME="ABOVE"	Creates a border along the top of the table.
FRAME="BELOW"	Creates a border along the bottom of the table.
FRAME="VOID"	Removes all outside borders from the table, but leaves all the inside cell borders in tact.
FRAME="HSIDES"	Creates a top and bottom border.
FRAME="VSIDES"	Creates a left and right border.

Chapter 6 The Fine Art of Tables | 99

FRAME="LHS"	Creates a left-hand side border.
FRAME="RHS"	Creates a right-hand side border.

Let's take a look at how they affect the border (see Figure 6.7).

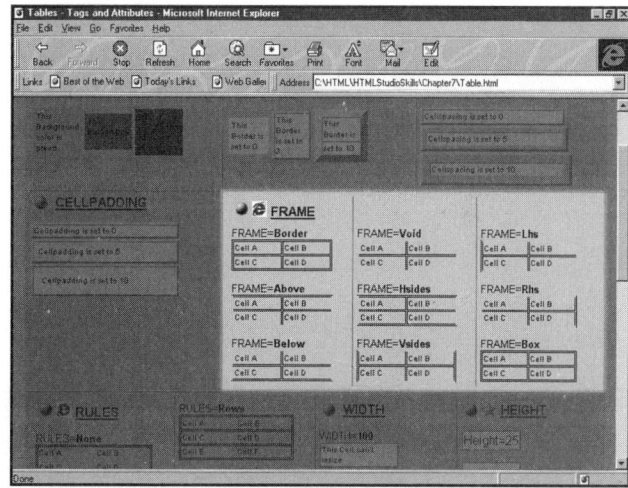

Figure 6.7
The FRAME attribute.

> **Note**
> The BORDER attribute must be set larger than 0 for this attribute to work.

RULES Attribute (Explorer Only)

`<TABLE RULES="##" BORDER="1">`

Here, ## is the option of the rule type you want between the cells; NONE, GROUPS, ROWS, COLS, or ALL.

Whereas FRAME deals with the look of the border surrounding the table, RULES deals with the lines or borders between each cell. Once again, in order for this attribute to work, you must have the border turned on and set to larger than 0. Also, if the CELLSPACING attribute is set higher than 0, the space between the cells will show, even though the border may not. Table 6.2 lists the values for RULES and what the result is.

Table 6.2
RULES Attribute Options

Option	Result
RULES="NONE"	Takes away all borders between the cells.
RULES="GROUPS"	Creates borders between groups of data cells, created with the THEAD, TBODY, TFOOT, or COLGROUPS tags.
RULES="ROWS"	Creates borders between all cell rows (created with the <TR> tag).
RULES="COLS"	Creates borders between all data cell columns (created with the <TD> tag).
RULES="ALL"	Creates borders between all data cells. This is the same as not using RULES and is the default.

Let's take a look at the RULES attribute in action (see Figure 6.8).

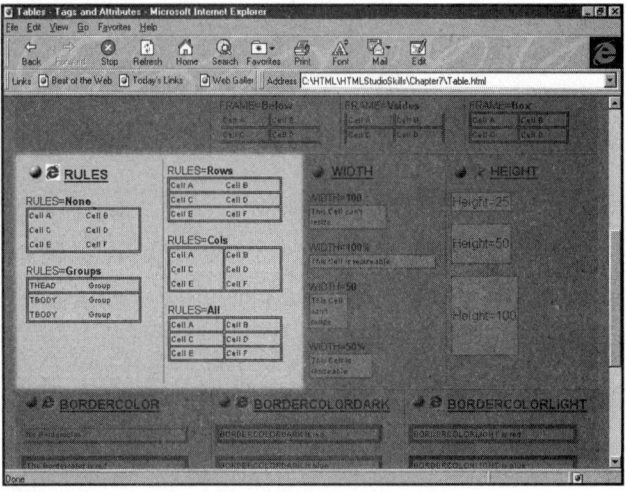

Figure 6.8

RULES.

Chapter 6 The Fine Art of Tables

WIDTH and HEIGHT Attributes

`<TABLE WIDTH="##" HEIGHT="##">`

Here, ## is the size in either pixels or percentages.

Tables can be very versatile. If you removed the height and width from the `<TABLE>` tag, your table size would be based on what was put into each data cell. Or you could size just the width, or just the height inside the `<TABLE>` tag and control which way the Web page scrolled, either vertically or horizontally because you would be constricting either the width (which would make it scroll vertically) or the height (which would make it scroll horizontally). You can use pixel sizes to make your tables definite or a fixed size, but then the table size may be too large for a low resolution or too small for a large resolution. If so, you could make your table based on percentages so that no matter what resolution the user is, the basic layout would be viewable. You can even mix and match between pixel sizes and percentages to keep certain effects and sizes perfect, while allowing the page to be completely resizeable.

The `HEIGHT` and `WIDTH` attributes used within the `<TABLE>` and `<TD>` tags make tables a powerful page layout medium (see Table 6.3).

Table 6.3

WIDTH and HEIGHT Attribute Options	
Option	Result
`WIDTH="100"`	Makes the table width exactly 100 pixels; and therefore, the table cannot resize.
`WIDTH="100%"`	Makes the table 100% the width of the browser window, or in this case, because we embedded this table, 100% of the space we put it into. The table will then resize; if the user resizes the browser window to be smaller, the table width will get smaller.
`WIDTH="50"`	Makes the table width 50 pixels, and non-resizeable.
`WIDTH="50%"`	Makes the table 50% of the browser window or 50% of the space it has left.
`HEIGHT="25"`, `HEIGHT="50"`, `HEIGHT="100"`	Means the table will be those pixel sizes high. Notice how we don't have any percentage examples for `HEIGHT`; read on to see some of the rules associated with `HEIGHT` and `WIDTH` in the `<TABLE>` tag.

Let's take a look at some different width size examples (see Figure 6.9).

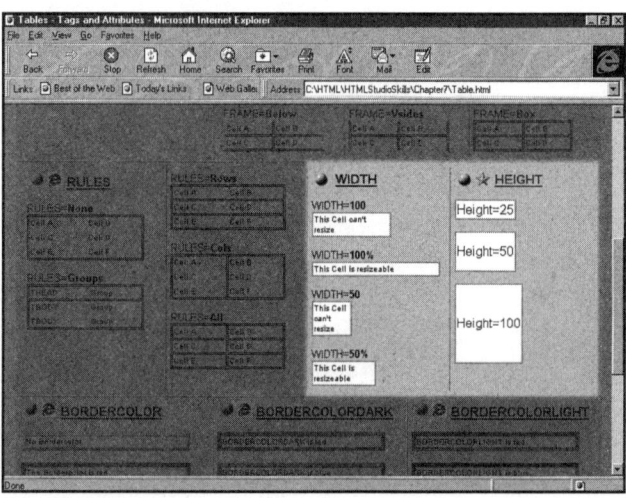

Figure 6.9
The WIDTH and HEIGHT attributes.

Mixing and matching sizes within a table can't be done within the <TABLE> tag itself. You need to change each individual data cell height and width in the <TD> tag.

Also, there are a few rules involved with HEIGHT and WIDTH in the <TABLE> tag.

Tables are only as small, or as large, as what data is inside each data cell. If you have an image that's 350 pixels wide inside one of your data cells, then making your table width=300 would not work; your table will then become 350 pixels wide. Many Web pages are easily viewed at 800×600 resolution or 1024×768, but they may look like garbage at 640×480 because their layouts were designed for that resolution only (see Figures 6.10a and 6.10b).

> **Note**
>
> One of the more confusing rules with height and percentages is that you can only use it on the outside or master table; you won't be able to size with percentages when embedding tables. This is best accomplished within the <TD> tag (see Figure 6.10).

Chapter 6 The Fine Art of Tables

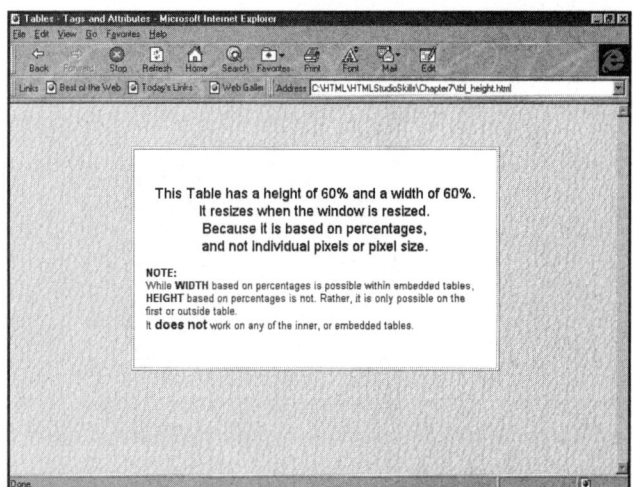

Figure 6.10

HEIGHT rule.

Figure 6.10a

Notice that the images and the Web page look fine at 800×600 resolution.

Figure 6.10b

The same Web page at 640×480 video resolution. Notice that the images seem cut off, and now both the horizontal and vertical scrolls bar are now active because the Web page doesn't fit in the window.

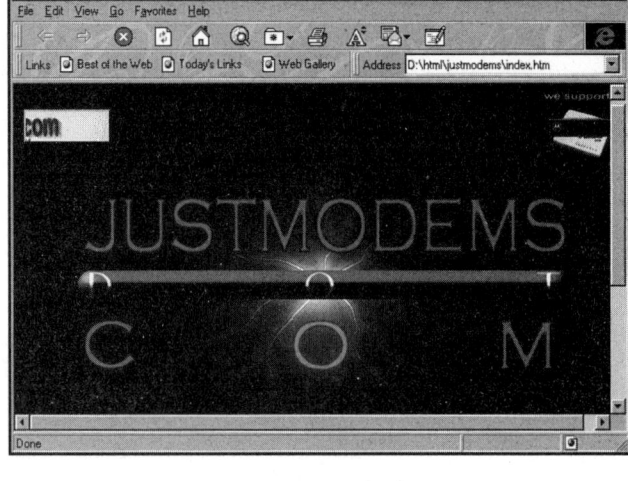

At the end of this book, you should be able to create platform- and resolution-independent Web sites, meaning anyone, anywhere, can view your Web pages.

BORDERCOLOR Attributes (Explorer Only)

```
<TABLE BORDERCOLOR="##" BORDERCOLORDARK="##"
BORDERCOLORLIGHT="##" BORDER="1">
```

With this attribute, ## is the number (in hex) or name of the color you want.

There are two parts to the border. BORDERCOLORLIGHT is the top and left of the outer border and the bottom and right of each cell border. BORDERCOLORDARK is the bottom and right of the outer border and the top and left of the smaller inner cell border. BORDERCOLOR changes both of the border sections to the same color.

Let's look at the example (see Figure 6.11).

> **Note**
>
> The BORDER attribute must be set larger than 0 for this attribute to work.

Chapter 6 The Fine Art of Tables

Notice that when you change the border color to either red or blue, the entire border becomes that color. Changing BORDERCOLORDARK to another color affects the bottom-right parts of the outer table border and the top-left parts of the inner cell border.

BORDERCOLORLIGHT affects the top and left parts of the outer border, and the bottom-right of the inner cell border.

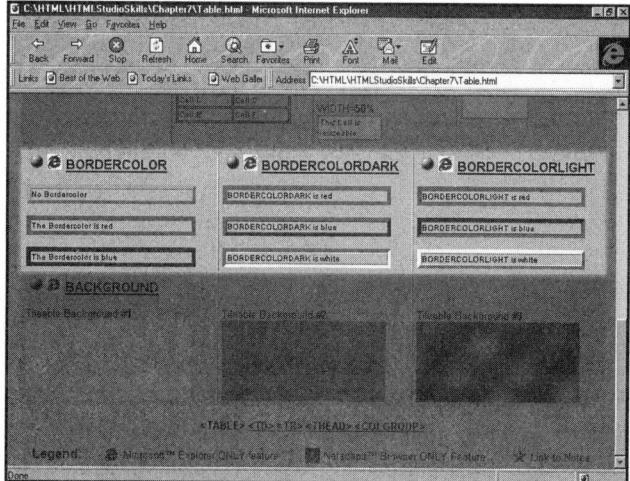

Figure 6.11

The BORDERCOLOR attributes.

BACKGROUND Attribute (Explorer Only)

`<TABLE BACKGROUND="##">`

Here, ## is the URL or location of the image that you would like tiled as the background of the table.

The BACKGROUND attribute, much like the BACKGROUND attribute used in the <BODY> tag, enables you to load a background (<TABLE BACKGROUND="images/gfx1.gif">, for example) that will then tile inside the table.

Three different tileable backgrounds were loaded into each of the three tables; the backgrounds are named tile1.gif, tile2.gif, tile3.jpg respectively. The big thing to remember is that they tile; they aren't loaded as a single image inside the table, so you couldn't load images that don't tile properly into a table without it looking strange. If that's the look your going for, though, that's fine.

Let's take a look at the BACKGROUND example (see Figure 6.12).

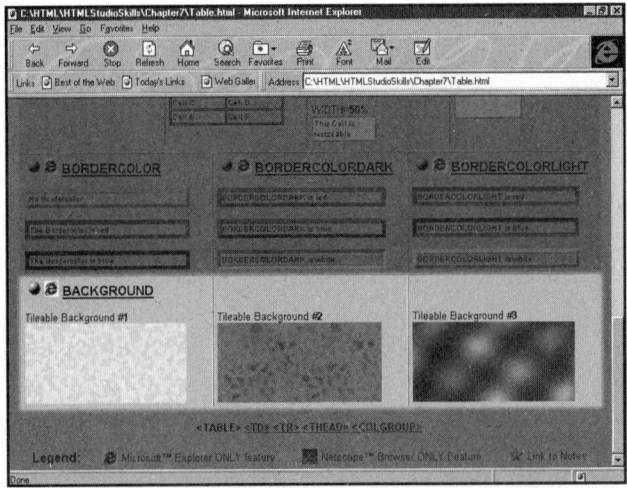

Figure 6.12

The BACKGROUND attribute.

This is definitely an effect that can get overused because not only can you tile a background in a table, but you can also tile a background within each and every data cell, so please use it sparingly.

<TR> Tag

The <TR> or table row tag is closed with the </TR> tag, but it doesn't need to be closed. Closing it, however, enables you to understand your code better and makes your HTML code more readable.

The <TABLE> tag is just the housing structure for the data cells, or <TD> tags. As shown in this simple table example:

Chapter 6 The Fine Art of Tables

```
<TABLE>
<TD>Cell Number 1</TD>
<TD>Cell Number 2</TD>

</TABLE>
```

The <TD> tag creates a data cell. Creating a second cell places it to the right of the first; not below or above, but beside that cell. In order for you to create a new line, or a new row in a cell, you must use the <TR> tag.

Let's take a look at an example (see Figure 6.13).

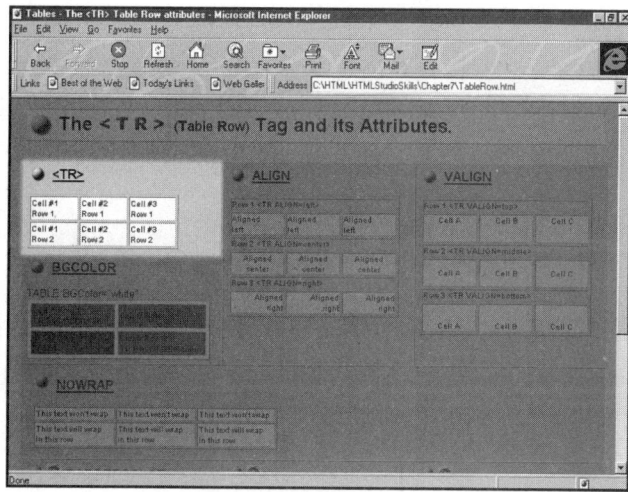

Figure 6.13

The <TR> tag.

We have created six <TD> data cells, but after three of them we have added the <TR> tag. This created the second row, while each of the three cells now makes up its own column as well. Cell #1 becomes a column, so does cell #2 and so on.

With the addition of a single tag, a table that would have had 1 row and 6 columns now has 2 rows and 3 columns.

ALIGN Attribute

`<TR ALIGN="##">`

With this tag, ## is the horizontal alignment of the text within the following row: left (default), center, or right.

Using ALIGN within the `<TR>` tag aligns all of the text and data in that row horizontally.

Let's take a look at the attribute in action (see Figure 6.14).

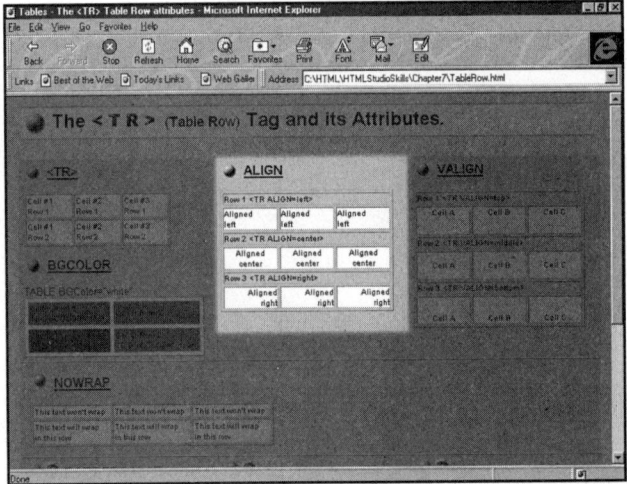

Figure 6.14

`<TR ALIGN>`.

Aligning the first row with `<TR ALIGN="LEFT">` aligns all of the row text to the left; the second row is centered with `<TR ALIGN="CENTER">`; and the third is aligned to the right.

The ALIGN attribute can be used either to align the whole row, or, when used in the `<TD>` tag, can align each cell individually. Using ALIGN within the table row can be a time saver for large portions of a table that need the text aligned.

VALIGN Attribute

`<TR VALIGN="##">`

Here, ## is the vertical alignment of the text within the following row, either middle (default), top, or bottom.

Using VALIGN within the <TR> tag aligns all of the text and data in that row vertically.

Let's take a look at it (see Figure 6.15).

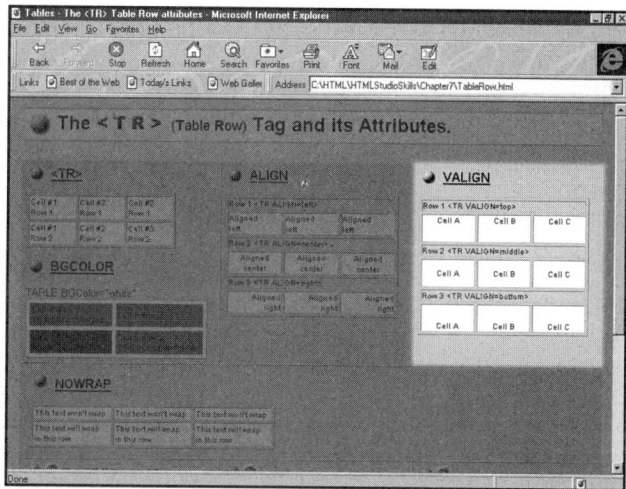

Figure 6.15

<TR VALIGN>.

Aligning the first row with <TR VALIGN="TOP"> aligns all of the row text to the top of the cell; the second row is centered with <TR VALIGN="MIDDLE">; and the third row is aligned to the bottom.

Like the ALIGN attribute, VALIGN can be used to align the whole row, or it can be used in the <TD> tag to align each cell individually. Using ALIGN within the table row can be a time saver for large portions of a table that need the text aligned.

BGCOLOR Attribute

`<TR BGCOLOR="##">`

With this attribute, `##` is the number (in hex) or name of the color to be used as the background for the following row of cells. The BGCOLOR attribute changes the background color of the *entire* following row of data cells.

If used within the `<TABLE>` tag, BGCOLOR colors the entire table; and if used within the `<TD>` tag, it colors only the individual cell. You can use this as a powerful presentation feature to make your tables colorful, easier to read, and easier to understand.

Let's take a look at this attribute in action (see Figure 6.16).

> **Note**
>
> You can see the outer TABLE BGCOLOR (white) in Explorer. It is not visible in the Netscape browser because Netscape doesn't color the space between the table and the cells. This is known as CellSpacing space; it is only colored in the Explorer browser.

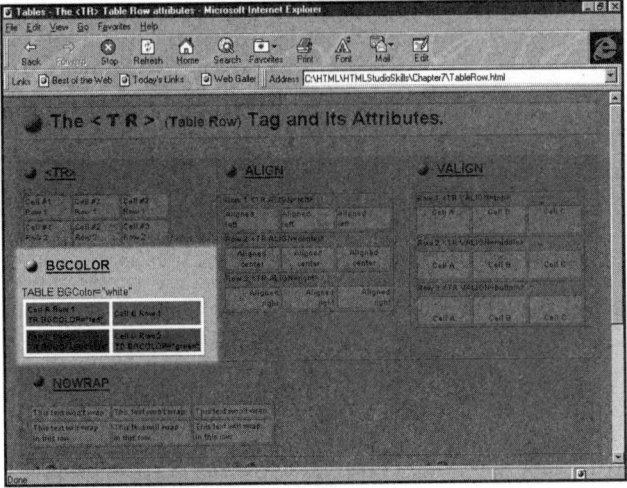

Figure 6.16

BGCOLOR.

There are two rows of two cells; the `<TABLE>` tag has been set to white or `BGCOLOR="#FFFFFF"`.

The first row has been set to red, or `BGCOLOR="#FF0000"`, which overrules the TABLE BGCOLOR. The second row has been set to blue, or `BGCOLOR="#0000FF"`, which overrules the TABLE BGCOLOR. The second cell of the

Chapter 6 The Fine Art of Tables

second row has been set to green, or BGCOLOR="#00FF00", which overrules the TABLE and TR BGCOLOR.

NOWRAP Attribute

<TR NOWRAP>

This attribute has no options or commands, and it controls whether the text will wrap in the following row, or not (default).

NOWRAP enables the cells in the following row to show the text in the cells without wrapping to the next line when space runs out. It creates more space for the text by expanding the table size (see Figure 6.17).

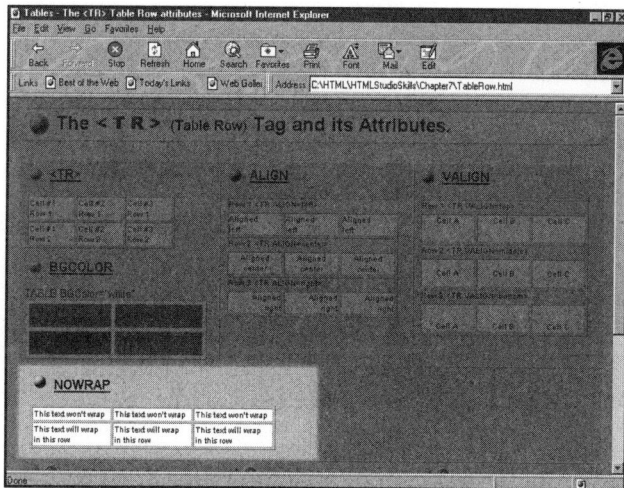

Figure 6.17

NOWRAP.

You'll notice three cells in each row with text that have no breaks or new lines.

The top row is set to <TR NOWRAP>, which enables all the text to display without wrapping to the next line. The second row is set <TR> (the default), which enables text to wrap to the next line when it's too large to fit on one line.

Note

The BORDER attribute must be set larger than 0 for this attribute to work.

BORDERCOLOR Attributes (Explorer Only)

`<TR BORDERCOLOR="##" BORDERCOLORDARK="##" BORDERCOLORLIGHT="##" BORDER="1">`

Here, ## is the number (in hex) or name of the color you want.

There are two parts to the border. BORDERCOLORLIGHT is the bottom and right of each cell border. BORDERCOLORDARK is the top and left of the cell border. BORDERCOLOR changes the entire border to the same color.

Let's take a look at an example (see Figure 6.18).

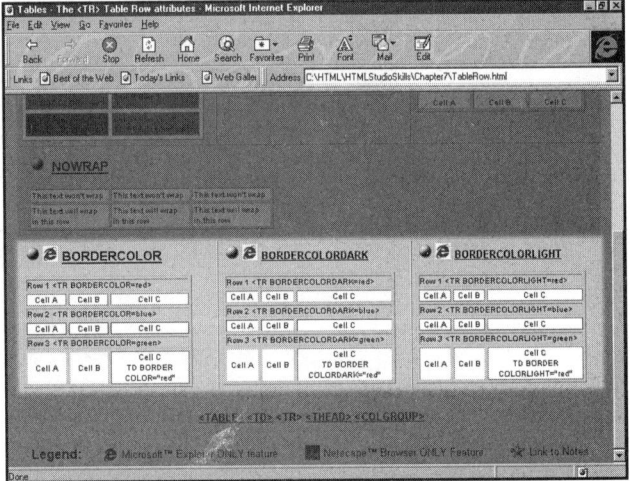

Figure 6.18

The BORDERCOLOR attributes.

Under the BORDERCOLOR attribute, the first two rows have been set to red, `<TR BORDERCOLOR="#FF0000">` and blue `<TR BORDERCOLOR="#0000FF">`, respectively.

The third row is set to green, `<TR BORDERCOLOR="#00FF00">`, but the last cell in the row has been set to red, `<TR BORDERCOLOR="#FF0000">`. This shows order of importance: the `<TD>` settings overrule the `<TR>` settings, which in turn overrule the `<TABLE>` settings.

Note

If the BORDERCOLOR attributes are used within the `<TABLE>` tag, they affect the outer border as well as each cell border. If used within the `<TR>` or `<TD>` tags, they only affect each cell border.

Chapter 6 The Fine Art of Tables   113

> **Note**
> <TD>, or table data tag, should be closed with the </TD> tag. This tag creates the individual data cells.

Under the BORDERCOLORDARK attribute, only the top-left portion of the cell border is affected; under the BORDERCOLORLIGHT only the bottom-right of border is affected.

<TD> Tag

This is the most important tag in the table because it actually creates the data cells that images and text are placed into. It is also the leader in order of importance. If you set a common attribute in the <TD> tag, whatever similar attribute you have set in the <TR> or <TABLE> tag is ignored.

There are three <TD> data cells here, placed one after the other. Because we haven't created a second row, by adding the <TR> tag all the data cells are horizontal and on a single row.

Figure 6.19

The <TD> tag.

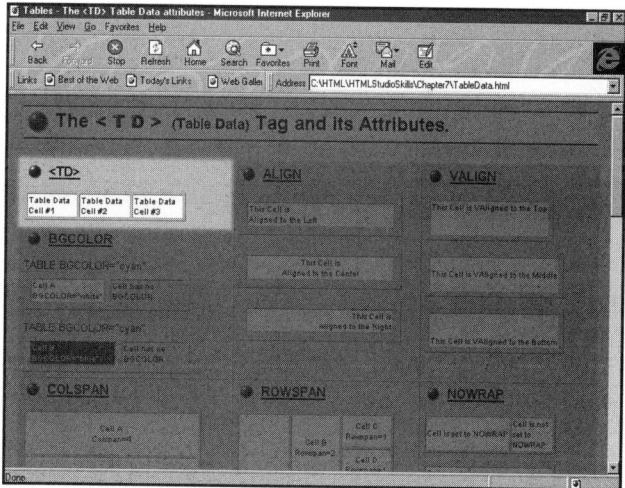

ALIGN Attribute

<TD ALIGN="##">

Here, ## is the horizontal alignment of the text within the following cell; left (default), center, or right. Using ALIGN within the <TD> tag aligns all of the text and data in that single cell horizontally.

Using <TD ALIGN="LEFT"> in the first data cell aligns all of the cell text to the left (see Figure 6.20). The second cell is centered with <TD ALIGN="CENTER">, and the third is aligned to the right.

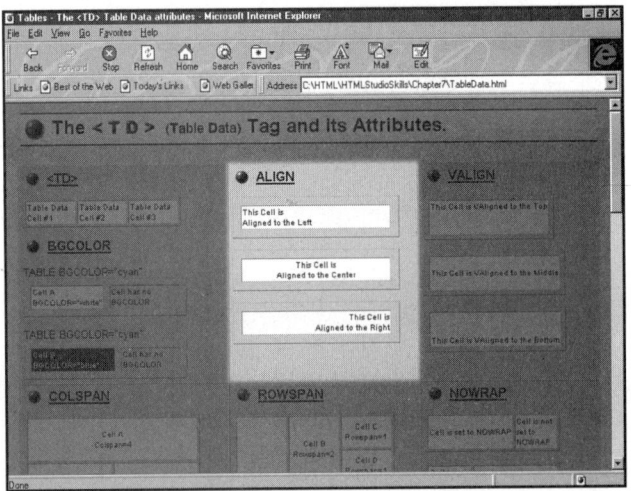

Figure 6.20

<TD ALIGN>.

The great thing about the ALIGN attribute is that it can be used either to align the whole row within the <TR> tag, or as we're using it in the <TD> tag, to control alignment within a single cell. Using ALIGN within the <TR> tag can be advantageous for large portions of a table that need the text aligned; aligning the entire row can be quite a time saver.

VALIGN Attribute

<TD VALIGN="##">

With this attribute, ## is the vertical alignment of the text within the following cell; middle (default), top, or bottom. Using VALIGN within the <TD> tag aligns all of the text and data in that single cell vertically (see Figure 6.21).

Using <TD VALIGN="TOP"> in the first data cell aligns all of the cell text to the top. The second cell is centered with <TD VALIGN="MIDDLE">, and the third is aligned to the bottom.

Chapter 6 The Fine Art of Tables

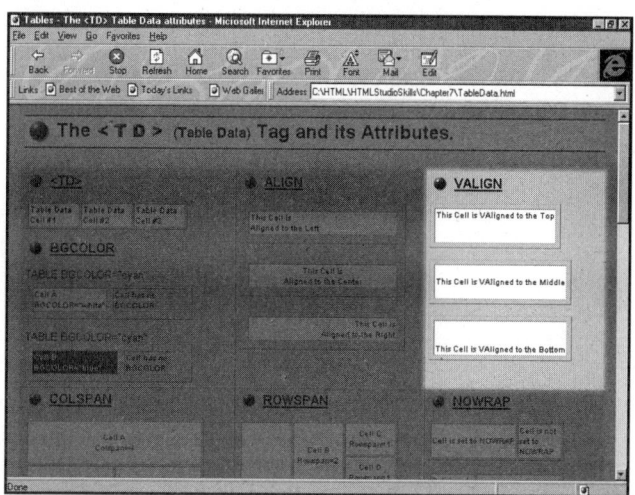

Figure 6.21

`<TD VALIGN>`.

Like the ALIGN attribute, the VALIGN attribute can be used either to align the whole row, within the <TR> tag, or as we've used it in the <TD> tag, it can align each cell individually. For large tables that need all of their cells vertically aligned, aligning it within the <TR> tag can save some time.

BGCOLOR Attribute

`<TD BGCOLOR="##">`

Here, ## is the number (in hex) or name of the color to be used as the following cell background. This attribute changes the background color of a single data cell.

If used within the <TABLE> tag, it colors the entire table, and if used within the <TR> tag, it colors the background of an entire row of cells. This tag is useful in presenting certain types of information, as colorful and easier to comprehend.

Let's take a look at this attribute in action (see Figure 6.22).

Figure 6.22

BGCOLOR.

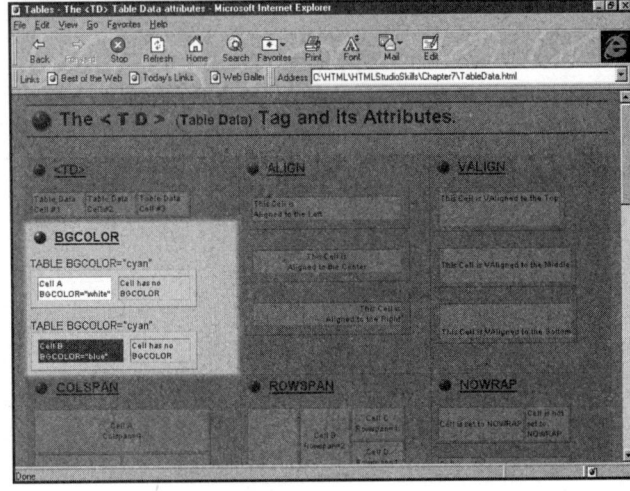

> **Note**
>
> Although you can see the outer TABLE BGCOLOR (cyan) in Explorer, it is not visible in Netscape because Netscape doesn't color the space between the table and the cells. This is known as CellSpacing space, and it is only colored in the Explorer browser.

There are two rows of two cells, and the table color has been set to cyan within the <TABLE> tag.

The first cell in the first row has been set to white, or BGCOLOR="#FFFFFF", which overrules the <TABLE> and <TR BGCOLOR> tags. Because the second cell hasn't been set to anything, it makes <TR> or <TABLE> BGCOLOR the active background color.

The second row's first cell has been set to blue, or BGCOLOR="#0000FF". Because the second cell hasn't been set to anything, it enables the TABLE BGCOLOR to set its background.

COLSPAN and ROWSPAN Attributes

<TD COLSPAN="##">

Here, ## is the number of columns you want the data cell to span. COLSPAN="1" is the default.

Tables are great for presenting lots of data in little boxes, but what if you needed to create a title bar that spanned only six data cells or columns, or you needed to create a total column that spanned several rows? That's why two attributes were added to tables: ROWSPAN, which enables you to create a data cell that

Chapter 6 The Fine Art of Tables

spans multiple rows vertically, and COLSPAN, which enables horizontal spanning of several columns. Columns are the cells that create a line vertically, one after the other, in separate rows. Rows are the cells that create a line horizontally, one after the other, in a single row.

There are only a couple of rules to remember, at least with COLSPAN:

- ▶ COLSPAN can only span complete columns; it doesn't do percentages or fractions of a column. If, for instance, you create a cell that spans 3 columns, and the columns are all 150 pixels each, you will be creating a 450-pixel-wide cell.

- ▶ You can only span as many columns as the maximum amount of columns in the table. Setting a cell to span 5 columns, when you only have four columns in your table, won't work.

A good way to find out how many columns you have in the table is to look at how many <TD> data cells you have in a single row. When you find the row with the most <TD> data cells, that is how many columns you have in a table (see Figure 6.23).

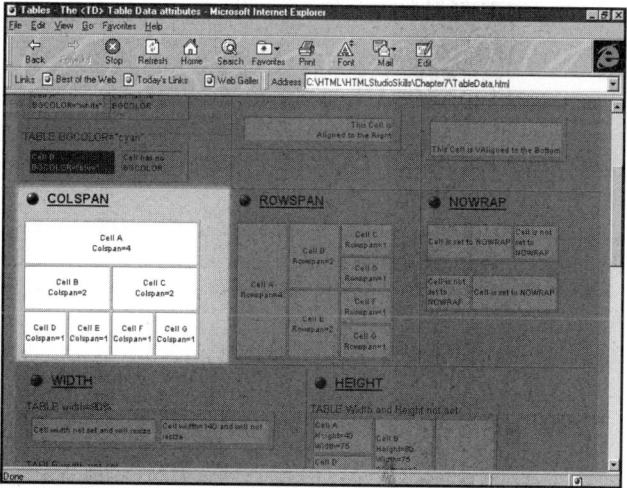

Figure 6.23

COLSPAN.

> **Note**
> The way that cells fall into place with COLSPAN and ROWSPAN within the table is rather important. Cells must be created from top to bottom, left to right. (This rule becomes even more important in the ROWSPAN attribute, so read on.)

In the example, we created a single data cell within a row and set its COLSPAN="4". Next, we created a second row and put two data cells in it, both with COLSPAN="2". In the third row, we created four separate data cells, (the largest number of columns in the table).

If you consider the number of data cells in your table, and how you would like them laid out, it should help you in deciding when and where to use your COLSPAN and ROWSPAN attributes. The cells should just fall into place, at least in your head.

With ROWSPAN, ## is the number of rows you want the data cell to span. ROWSPAN="1" is the default.

ROWSPAN is just like COLSPAN, except it works in rows, rather than columns. Although this sounds simple, its layout differs slightly from COLSPAN. To determine the maximum number of columns, you count the maximum data cells, <TD>, in a row. To determine the maximum number of rows in a table, count the <TR>s, or table rows, in a table; that number becomes your maximum (see Figure 6.24).

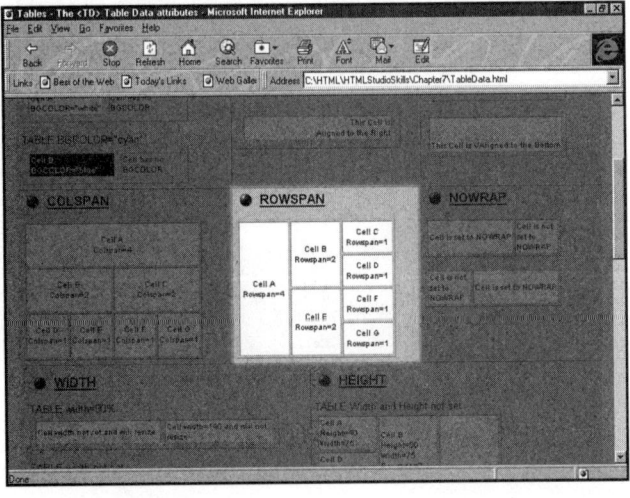

Figure 6.24

ROWSPAN.

Chapter 6 The Fine Art of Tables

In this example we created the same table as COLSPAN but sideways. Notice the difference? Although we achieved the effect of a four row, two row, and a single row spanning series of cells, the way the cells layout is different.

Instead of the cells being laid out as cell a in the first column, then cells b and c in the second, and cells d, e, f, and g in the third, we have what looks like a disorganized series of cells. Let's break it down step by step.

1. Remember that cells must be laid out top to bottom, left to right. That means the first row was cell a (ROWSPAN="4"), then cell b (ROWSPAN="2"), then cell c (ROWSPAN="1").

2. Now that we are at the end of our columns, we need to start a new row. But where will the next cell go? Well, because this is a table with four rows, we need to start with the next row, which would be to the right of cell b and below cell c. This becomes cell d (ROWSPAN="1").

3. Once again, we need to start at the next row, which is now below cell b and to the right of cell a. We now create cell e, which is two rows high (ROWSPAN="2"), but we still have space on this row to the right of cell e.

4. Next, we create cell f (ROWSPAN="1"), and we are at the end of our row. We create another row that becomes our final fourth row. Finally, we create the data cell g (ROWSPAN="1"), and we are done.

The rows should be set up as follows: the first row should have three data cells (a, b, c); the second should have one data cell (d); the third should have two data cells (e, f); and the fourth should have one (g).

NOWRAP Attribute

`<TD NOWRAP>`

This attribute has no options or commands; it controls whether the text will wrap in the following cell or not (default). NOWRAP enables a single data cell to show the text in that cell without wrapping to the next line when space runs out. It creates more space for the text by expanding the table size (see Figure 6.25).

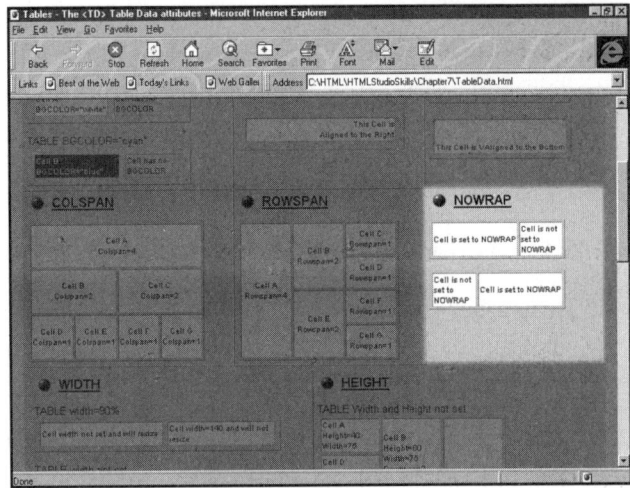

Figure 6.25

NOWRAP.

Here we have two cells in two tables. In the first cell in the first table, we have set the data cell to NOWRAP, or <TD NOWRAP>. In the second cell, we have not set the NOWRAP attribute, and as you can see, the text does not wrap in the first cell, but it does in the second. In the second table, we have done exactly the opposite: We have set the NOWRAP attribute to the second cell instead of the first, and again, you can see that it will not wrap.

WIDTH and HEIGHT Attributes

<TABLE WIDTH="##" HEIGHT="##">

Here, ## is the size in either pixels or percentages.

WIDTH and HEIGHT within the <TD> tag enable you to do any type of page layout for any type of resolution—making it the most powerful of all the things you can do with tables.

It's very important to understand what makes a data cell resize and what doesn't. Setting a table or a data cell to a fixed number (not percentage) of pixels, provided there is enough space around it, will make it completely non-resizeable. If, for instance, you create a 300 pixel-wide and 300-pixel-high table, and you are at 640×480, 800×600, or 1024×768, the size of that table will remain 300×300 pixels.

Chapter 6 The Fine Art of Tables

That is why you only use a fixed pixel size on things that cannot be resized, no matter what you do—namely images. But, if you are mixing images with text or data, then you need to mix your table settings. Sometimes you will use fixed sizes, and sometimes you will use percentages. This enables you to create a nice balance between the things that can be resized and the things that cannot.

Also, when a table has a fixed size, the data cells (even though they use percentages) will not alter the size of the table; it will still be the same fixed size. If the table was set in percentages and the data cells were all set in pixel sizes, then the opposite occurs: the data cells' pixel sizes are ignored, and the table becomes resizeable, treating the data cells as if they were sized in percentages (see Figure 6.26).

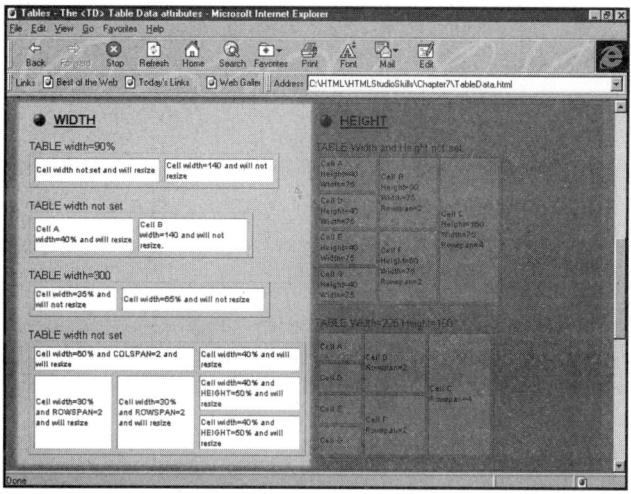

Figure 6.26

WIDTH.

In the first table, you can see that we have set the table to <TABLE WIDTH="90%">, and it fills 90% of the space that it is in. If it were the only table on the page, then it would fill 90% of the width of the page. We didn't set any width on the first data cell and we set a fixed pixel width <TD WIDTH="140"> on the second data cell, which makes the first data cell resizeable because the second data cell has a fixed width. The first data cell resizes to whatever is left of the 90% table width minus the size of the fixed data cell. If, for example, the table was using 600 pixels of space, then the first data cell would be 460 pixels wide because 600–140 (the second cell's width) = 460.

If we resized the page, then the first data cell would resize to the appropriate amount, while the second data cell would remain the same width. If the table after the resize was 400 pixels in width, then the first data cell would be 260, or 400–140.

In the second table, we have not set the table width, but in the first data cell we have set the width to 40%. We set the second cell to 140 pixels.

Because we've made the first cell a percentage (and there is nothing set in the <TABLE> tag), then that must mean that the first cell is resizeable. The second cell is not because it has a fixed size.

In the third table, we have created a cell that is non-resizeable, or fixed, by setting its width to pixel size. Then we set the first data cell's width to 35% and the second to 65%. Even though this sounds like it is resizeable, it isn't. The size of the table will remain at 300 pixels wide, but the first data cell will be 35% of 300 pixels, and the second will be 65% of 300 pixels.

The fourth table is just for fun, and it needs some labeling. There are three rows with six cells. Try to label the cells as they were placed, from cell A to cell F. Then try to determine what cells went into which rows.

HEIGHT behaves basically the same way WIDTH does, so we won't repeat what we've just done, but let's take a look at an interesting feature or problem with sizing tables (see Figure 6.27).

We've created two tables with several cells each that essentially are supposed to be the same size.

The first table has three columns across at 75 pixels each, or 225 pixels wide. It also has four rows at 40 pixels each, or 160 pixels high. So why does the second table, set at 300 pixels wide and 160 pixels high, looks smaller?

In the top table, we have the cellspacing set to five. The space between the three columns and the outside border is actually an extra 20 pixels, and the space between the four rows is actually an extra 25 pixels. The second table has been sized within the <TABLE> tag, which means it will size itself to the exact pixel size, including whatever the cellspacing adds. Therefore, when you're creating your tables to be an exact pixel measurement, make sure your cellspacing is either compensated for or set to 0.

Chapter 6 The Fine Art of Tables   123

Figure 6.27

HEIGHT.

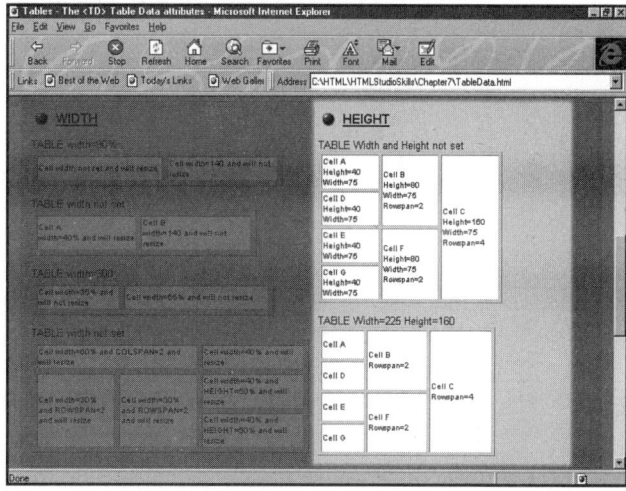

BORDERCOLOR Attributes (Explorer Only)

```
<TD BORDERCOLOR="##" BORDERCOLORDARK="##"
BORDERCOLORLIGHT="##" BORDER="1">
```

Here, ## is the number (in hex) or name of the color you want.

There are two parts to the border. BORDERCOLORLIGHT is the bottom and right of each cell border. BORDERCOLORDARK is the top and left of the cell border. BORDERCOLOR changes the entire border to the same color.

In the Figure 6.28 notice that under the BORDERCOLOR attribute there is no BORDERCOLOR attribute set in the first table; as for the second table, the first data cell is set <TD BORDERCOLOR="#FF0000">, or red; in the third table, the first data cell is set <TD BORDERCOLOR="#0000FF">, or blue. It is the same as we've used it before—in the <TABLE> tag and in the <TR> tag—but this time it only affects a single data cell.

> **Note**
>
> The BORDER attribute must be set larger than 0 for this attribute to work.

> **Note**
>
> If the BORDERCOLOR attributes are used within the <TABLE> tag, they affect the outer border as well as each cell border, but if used within the <TD> or <TR> tags they only affect each cell border.

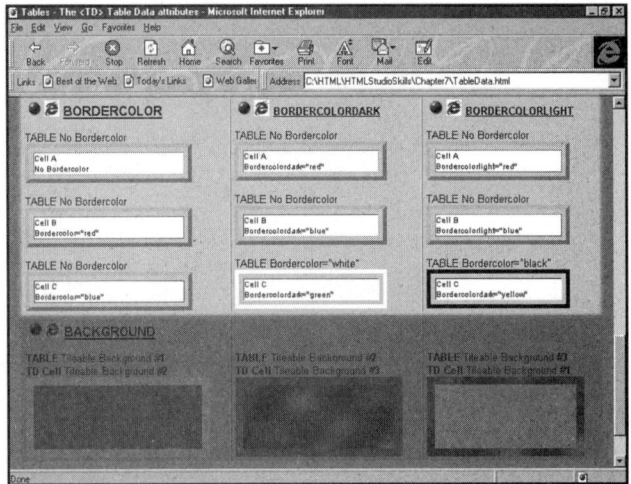

Figure 6.28

The BORDERCOLOR attributes.

Under BORDERCOLORDARK, we've set it the same way, except in the third table we've set the <TABLE> tag to <TABLE BORDERCOLOR="#FFFFFF"> and we've set the <TD BORDERCOLORDARK="#00FF00">, or green so that just the top left side of the cell border is green.

Under BORDERCOLORLIGHT we've again set it the same way.

BACKGROUND Attribute (Explorer Only)

<TD BACKGROUND="##">

With this attribute, ## is the URL or location of the image that you would like tiled as the background of the cell.

This BACKGROUND attribute, much like the attribute used in the <BODY> tag, enables you to load a background (<TD BACKGROUND="images/gfx1.gif">, for example) that will then tile inside a single cell.

Because you can tile a background in a table and tile a background within each and every data cell, this effect can get overused. Please use it sparingly.

Take a look at the background example (see Figure 6.29).

Chapter 6 The Fine Art of Tables   125

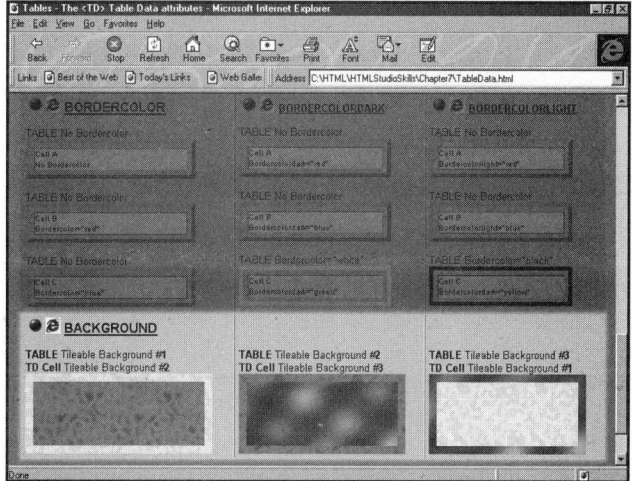

Figure 6.29

BACKGROUND.

In the three tables, we've loaded backgrounds in each <TABLE> tag, and then we've loaded different backgrounds into each data cell. We've kept the cellspacing quite large so that you can see the table background as well as the data cell backgrounds.

<THEAD>, <TBODY>, and <TFOOT> Tags

The <THEAD>, <TBODY>, and <TFOOT> tags are essentially placeholders for the <TD> data cells. Their main purpose is to give you a place for repetitive headers and footers within a Web site.

If, for example, your site had the same button bar in the header, the same email address in the footer, and just the body of the document changed, then you could put the fixed data cells that are in the header between the <THEAD> and </THEAD> tags, and the fixed data cells for the footer between the <TFOOT> and </TFOOT> tags, and only change the data cells between the <TBODY> and </TBODY> tags for all the Web pages.

Let's take a look at what we mean (see Figure 6.30).

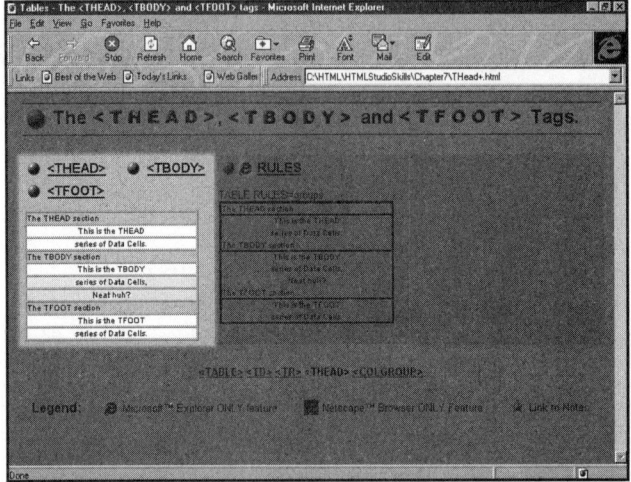

Figure 6.30

<THEAD>, <TBODY>, and <TFOOT>.

We have placed two data cells (in two rows) between the <THEAD> and </THEAD> tags as the header; then we've put three data cells (in three rows) in the <TBODY> section as the body; and finally we've placed two data cells (in two rows) as the <TFOOT> footer. Here's the HTML.

```
<TABLE>
<TR><TD BGCOLOR="#CFCFFF">The THEAD section</TD></TR>
<THEAD>
        <TR ALIGN="CENTER">
        <TD BGCOLOR="WHITE">This is the THEAD</TD>
        </TR>
        <TR ALIGN="CENTER">
        <TD BGCOLOR="WHITE">series of Data Cells.</TD>
        </TR>
</THEAD>
        <TR><TD BGCOLOR="#CFCFFF">The TBODY section</TD></TR>
<TBODY>
        <TR ALIGN="CENTER">
        <TD BGCOLOR="#FFFFFF">This is the TBODY</TD>
        </TR>
        <TR ALIGN="CENTER">
        <TD BGCOLOR="#F8F8F8">series of Data Cells,</TD>
        </TR>
        <TR ALIGN="CENTER">
        <TD BGCOLOR="#EFEFEF">Neat huh?</TD>
```

```
                </TR>
        </TBODY>
                <TR><TD BGCOLOR="#CFCFFF">The TFOOT section</TD></TR>
        <TFOOT>
                <TR ALIGN="CENTER">
                <TD BGCOLOR="WHITE">This is the TFOOT</TD>
                </TR>
                <TR ALIGN="CENTER">
                <TD BGCOLOR="WHITE">series of Data Cells.</TD>
                </TR>
        </TFOOT>
        </TABLE>
```

Although these tags seem somewhat useless, they can come in handy when you're doing repetitive work or using headers and footers.

RULES="GROUPS" Attribute

`<TABLE RULES="GROUPS"> <THEAD> DATA CELLS </THEAD> <TBODY> DATA CELLS </TBODY> <TFOOT> DATA CELLS </TFOOT>`

This attribute affects how borders or rules look after you've created THEAD, TBODY, and TFOOT data groups. After you've created some THEAD, TBODY, and TFOOT groups, RULES=GROUPS within the <TABLE> tag will show the borders only between those groups of data cells.

We've put two rows of data cells in the THEAD section, three in the TBODY section, and two in the TFOOT section (see Figure 6.31). As you can see, the border (in black) is only dividing the table between the cell groups within the <THEAD>, <TBODY>, and <TFOOT> tags.

<COLGROUP> and <COL> Tags

The COLGROUP and COL tags, as with the <THEAD> series of tags, are also something of an anomaly, never quite finding their places within most tables. These tags pre-align and set up data cells to be placed in column groups.

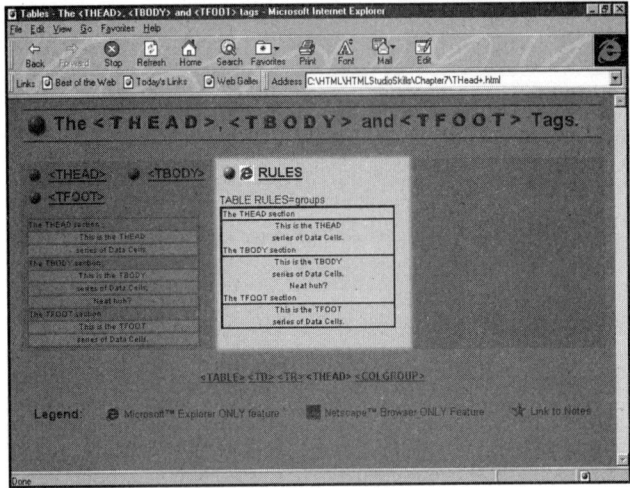

Figure 6.31

`<TABLE RULES="GROUPS">`.

<COLGROUP> Tag

```
<COLGROUP>
<COLGROUP>
    <TD></TD>

    <TD></TD>
```

The <COLGROUP> tag needs to be set up at the beginning of the table—before the data cells are added. The number of COLGROUPs you create should be the same number of <TD> data cells you create (two columns, two data cells, for instance). Also, this tag doesn't need to be closed.

Using the ALIGN attribute, the COLGROUP can then pre-align the data cells.

We have created three COLGROUPs, all aligned separately. The code looks like this:

```
<TABLE>
<COLGROUP ALIGN="LEFT">
<COLGROUP ALIGN="CENTER">
<COLGROUP ALIGN="RIGHT">
    <TD>This is Column Group #1 and is left aligned</TD>
    <TD>This is Column Group #2 and is center aligned</TD>
    <TD>This is Column Group #3 and is right aligned</TD>

</TABLE>
```

Chapter 6 The Fine Art of Tables

Let's take a look at the example (see Figure 6.32).

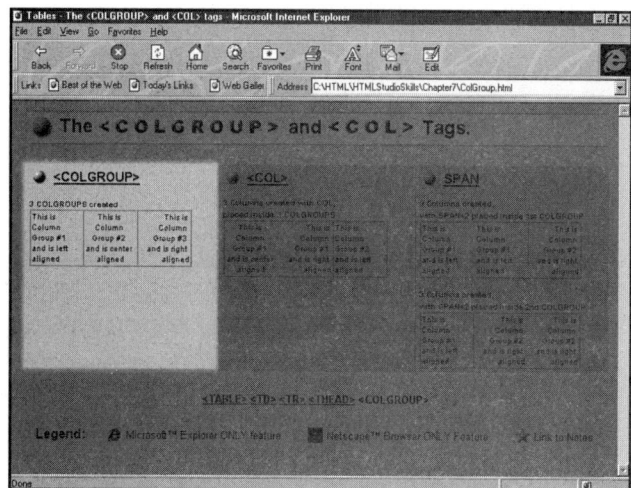

Figure 6.32

<COLGROUP>.

Notice that we now have three columns, aligned differently, as set up in the <COLGROUP> tags.

SPAN Attribute

Using SPAN within the <COLGROUP> tag enables you to create multiple columns within the same single column group. If you add the RULES="GROUPS" to the table, you'll be able to see the column groups more clearly. First, let's look at the code, then the example (see Figure 6.33).

```
<TABLE RULES="GROUPS">
<COLGROUP ALIGN="LEFT">
<COLGROUP ALIGN="RIGHT" SPAN="2">
        <TD>This is Column Group #1 and is left aligned</TD>
        <TD>This is Column Group #2 and is right aligned</TD>
        <TD>This is Column Group #2 and is right aligned</TD>

</TABLE>
```

HTML Studio Skills

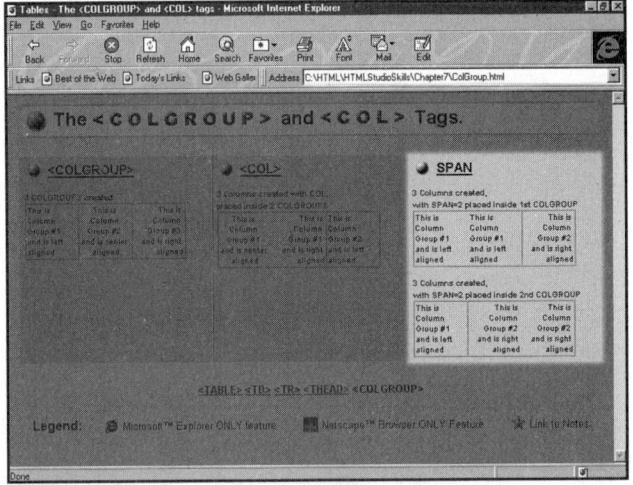

Figure 6.33

`<COLGROUP SPAN>`.

We know there are three columns of text, but only two have been divided with the borders. This is because part of the RULES="GROUPS" attribute affects not only <THEAD> tags, but also the <COLGROUP>s. We have created two <COLGROUP>s and two columns within a single <COLGROUP> with the SPAN=2 attribute. Both columns within the single <COLGROUP> are aligned the same. You can align them separately using the <COL> tag.

<COL> Tag

```
<COLGROUP>
    <COL>
    <COL>
<COLGROUP>
    <COL>
    <TD></TD>

        <TD></TD>
```

The <COL> tag can create multiple columns in a single <COLGROUP>. Once again, the number of data cells should match the number of columns and column groups created.

Chapter 6 The Fine Art of Tables

We have created three columns using three `<COL>` tags and two `<COLGROUP>` tags. All cells are aligned separately, and the code looks like this:

```
<TABLE RULES="GROUPS">
<COLGROUP>
        <COL ALIGN="CENTER">
        <COL ALIGN="RIGHT">
<COLGROUP>
        <COL ALIGN="LEFT">
        <TD>This is Column Group #1 and is center aligned</TD>
        <TD>This is Column Group #1 and is right aligned</TD>
        <TD>This is Column Group #2 and is left aligned</TD>
</TABLE>
```

Let's take a look at the example (see Figure 6.34).

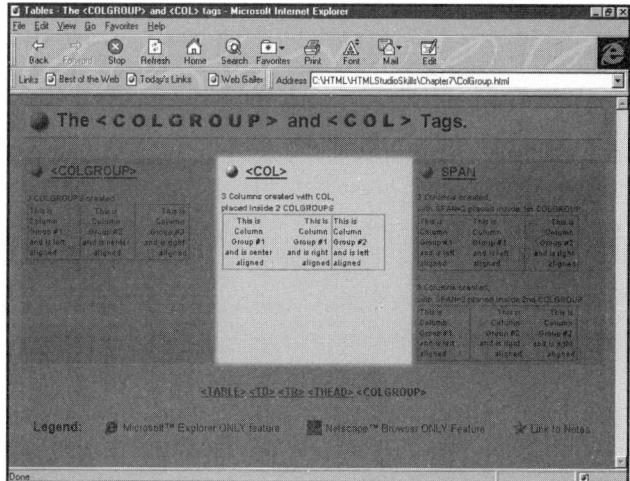

Figure 6.34

The `<COL>` tag.

We still have three separate columns, but because we added the RULES="GROUPS" attribute within the table, we only have two columns or `<COLGROUP>`s because there is only a border between two of the columns.

These tags enable you to create multiple columns, combine them into other columns, and align each column however you want. Using the borders, gives you more control over the look of the table.

Conclusion

The objective of this chapter was to not only familiarize you with tables, but to leave no stone unturned as far as tags, attributes, and options, and how they react and look within a table. You learned the basic structure of a table and its cells, and you learned how width and height, both in percentages and pixel amounts, can dramatically effect your page. You dealt with columns and rows and the table head, body, and footer tags. With the knowledge you've gained about tables, you are now ready to tackle your next HTML task: forms.

chapter 7

Getting Interactive with Forms

A form is a way for the user to communicate with the person or organization responsible for a Web site. Forms come in many shapes and sizes; you can design a form for reservations on an airline (see Figure 7.1) or even design a form that enables users to select (one by one) an entire box of chocolates (see Figure 7.2). Whatever type of feedback you can think of requesting from a user, you can get it with forms.

Forms are not for the squeamish or inexperienced; they greatly depend on scripting languages. But in their simplest form (for lack of a better word), forms add a whole new dimension to your Web site. They enable users to interact with you, purchase products, give their opinions, or whatever you can possibly dream up for the user to do.

Forms are also a wonderful way to gain information for your specific market. If you create a Web site for a stereo company, you might want

- ➤ Getting Started
- Understanding <INPUT> and Its Attributes
- <SELECT> and Its Attributes
- ➤ <OPTION> and Its Attributes

to create a form that asks customers about what type of stereo they own, what they are planning to buy, or even what they want in a new stereo.

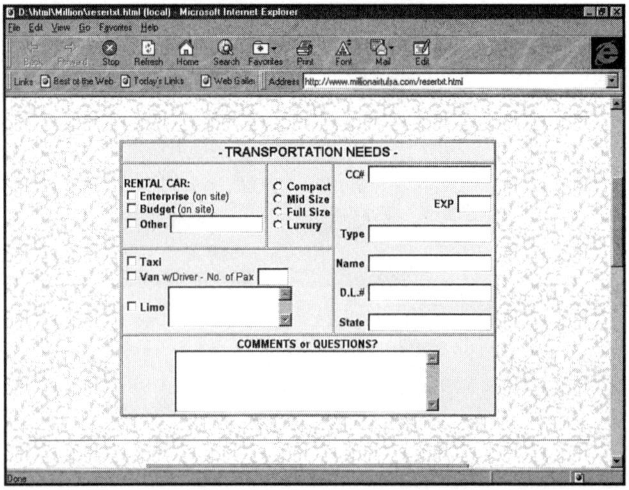

Figure 7.1

Intense forms, with lots of interaction.

Figure 7.2

Fun forms, making the interaction less noticeable.

Chapter 7 Getting Interactive with Forms

If you know (or are willing to learn) Java, VBScript, ActiveX, C, C++, Perl, or any of the other great programming languages that enable your forms to live and breathe, then you are definitely headed in the right direction. Even if you're not a programmer, or if you know nothing about Java, you can still use forms to create a truly interactive Web experience. Without at least some of these programming skills, you can still use a form to email someone with the forms information (using the `mailto:` command we learned in Chapter 3).

In this chapter, we will deal only with forms (including the tags and attributes) because it is important to have a basis for what we will discuss in later chapters. You will eventually learn how to add programming and CGI programs to your forms to make them self-correcting, self-checking, and entertaining.

Getting Started

Use the `<FORM>` tag to create a form. (Like tables, you will need to close it.) You need to include ways of inputting information. This is done by adding some `<INPUT>` tags. A form without inputs has no function, just like a table without data cells.

The following is the simplest form you can create uses just two tags:

```
<FORM ACTION="test.html" METHOD=post>
     <INPUT TYPE=submit VALUE="Submit Form">
</FORM>
```

This form is useless because all it does is submit itself; the document it's passing information to does not process or take any information from the form, rendering it useless. Essentially, it acts as a link.

To better understand forms, let's start with the `<FORM>` tag.

<FORM>

Syntax: `<FORM> </FORM>`

If a form is opened, it also must be closed with the closing `</FORM>` tag. Unlike the `<TABLE>` tag, the `<FORM>` tag really doesn't do much without using some of its attributes; the first one we need to look at is `ACTION`.

To be functional, a form needs input. This enables the user to interact with the form. Use the <INPUT>, <SELECT>, and <TEXTAREA> tags to give the user something to interact with. The form also will need a submit button, which enables the form to be sent to the processing program. In addition, it is a good idea to include a reset button, which enables the user to clear the form and input her answers again.

Let's begin by breaking down all of the attributes within the <FORM> tag and then work our way through all of the corresponding tags and their attributes.

ACTION Attribute

Syntax: <FORM ACTION="##">

is the URL of the program that will process the form, or just a URL link. If nothing is placed within the quotes, then it goes to the base URL.

ACTION is interesting because it requires a program or script to process the form, but the choices of what type of program to process with are numerous.

The processing of a form has traditionally used Common Gateway Interfacing, or CGI. CGI scripts can be built in many programming languages, such as Perl, C, C++, or AppleScript, which process on the server side, whereas newer languages such as VBScript, Java, or JavaScript process the information before sending it to the server (or client side, as it is known) or to another application.

These programming languages, when turned into a CGI script, can perform a multitude of tasks such as:

- Error checking
- Accessing catalogs and databases
- Online shopping

METHOD Attribute

Syntax: <FORM METHOD="##">

is the form action to take place, either GET or POST.

This attribute either sends the information to the processing program (POST) or goes to a URL and appends the values to the end of the URL (GET). What does all that mean? Well, most of the time you will use POST because you will almost always be sending the form to be processed or read, usually to a CGI or scripted program. There will be some occasions, however, when you will want to send the information via the GET option because it treats the ACTION URL as if it's an anchor. It also appends the input information onto the end of the URL, something you will often see on search engine Web sites, using an HTML file instead of a program to process or at least read the information.

TARGET Attribute

Syntax: <FORM TARGET="##">

is the name of the target frame, or window. The default is the current frame.

When you are making a framed Web page with the use of the <FRAME> tag, you will have to name each frame—these become named targets.

Because forms activate a program or go to a specific URL, you can tell them which frame the URL will show up in, or which frame the contents of the form will be processed in. This is, of course, only useful if you are using frames in your document.

ONSUBMIT Attribute

Syntax: <FORM ONSUBMIT="##">

is the action of the script that you want to activate. This can be a Java or VBScript; it can even activate an ActiveX control. Creating ActiveX controls and dealing with ActiveX is well beyond the scope of this book. It's important, however, that you know all of the tags and attributes that belong to the forms family.

An advanced attribute, ONSUBMIT enables you to preprocess your form before it goes to the processing program or URL. For example, if your processing program doesn't error check, you could create a script that error checks the form before it's sent to be processed.

To get more experience with all of these attributes and the many inputs, let's take a look at the input, its attributes, and how each attribute can be used in a form.

ENCTYPE

Syntax: `<FORM ENCTYPE="TYPE/SUBTYPE">`

When sending a form, you can also determine, depending on what type of browser you are using, how you want the information encoded. This attribute is still being bantered about among the browser companies, the World Wide Web Consortium, and the NCSA, and it isn't used much.

But the default for the encoding type is `application/x-www-form-urlencoded`, and it converts the name/values or form information this way:

- The name/value pairs are shown/sent in their order of appearance in the document.

- The name fields are separated by the & (ampersand).

- All space characters are replaced with + (plus).

- Non-alphanumeric characters are replaced with a % (percent) followed by two hex digits that represent the ASCII code value of the character.

- Line breaks are now represented as control/line feed which is %0D0A.

Understanding how the data is sent will help you in parsing (converting/filtering) the data, should you get more involved in programming.

Understanding <INPUT> and Its Attributes

You can't create a form without inputs. You need to create boxes, checks, and buttons for the user to interact with. This is done with the `<INPUT>`, `<SELECT>`, and `<TEXTAREA>` tags, and these tags have a lot of attributes.

Two attributes within the `<INPUT>` tag are `TYPE="SUBMIT"`, which enables the form to be sent to be processed, and `TYPE="RESET"`, which clears the form of all answers/inputs so that the user can answer/input from scratch. This appears as a clickable button that is recognizable on any platform.

NAME Attribute

Syntax: `<INPUT NAME="##">`

`##` is the unique name of the input type that you are using. All input types require a name or the processing program won't understand what to process.

If forms process the information without names, raw information is sent without knowing what information belongs in what sections. It can be confusing to the processing program. So as with databases, all variables, or pieces of information that the user send, need to be associated with a name.

If you use a text input that asks for a person's address, for instance, adding `NAME="ADDRESS"` to the input will help the processing program know where to look for the user's address. If you make a series of checkboxes that enable the user to select what type of radio the user was interested in, then adding `NAME="RADIOTYPES"` to the input would help the processing program know what radio type the user had selected. It doesn't matter what you name the names, but it matters that they are different and easy to understand. When it comes time to make a processing program, you'll need to know the types of answers you were requesting.

If you are giving the user a list of things to choose from using checkboxes, radio buttons, and the `<SELECT>` tag (which all belong in the same category or type), then you can name all of the inputs the same because they all belong to the same category.

VALUE Attribute

Syntax: `<INPUT VALUE="##">`

`##` is the value of the input.

A `VALUE` is the answer to the input. If the user clicks one of five radio buttons that select fruits, the name of each radio button could be `NAME="FRUITS"`. For instance, if the user clicks on the radio button that is beside a picture of an orange, the value could be `VALUE="Orange"`. When it is sent to the processing program, it will see that the user has selected the `"ORANGE"` from the `"FRUITS"` category.

Although every input tag must have a name, it doesn't need a value. Sometimes you will let the user select from a list of values and sometimes the user types his or her own value. The rule is that radio buttons, checkboxes, and buttons must have values.

Although select lists can use values, they don't require them; they pull their values from each `<OPTION>` tag.

`<TEXT>`, `<TEXTAREA>` tags, and their corresponding attributes don't need values, but they can benefit from them. (See the TEXT Input Type section later in this chapter).

TYPE Attribute

Syntax: `<INPUT TYPE="##">`

is the type of input you would like to use. The options are TEXT, PASSWORD, CHECKBOX, RADIO, SUBMIT, RESET, HIDDEN, and IMAGE.

This is the core of the form—the actual input types that you will be using. They are broken down into many types:

- Radio buttons and checkboxes
- Text and password
- Hidden and reset
- Submit and image
- Separate tags
- TEXTAREA and SELECT

These options accomplish everything you could want from a form. Let's take a look at these one by one.

TEXT Input Type

Syntax: `<INPUT TYPE="TEXT">`

This input type uses the MAXLENGTH and SIZE attributes. It doesn't need the VALUE attribute, although by adding one it will appear in the text input line. It creates a text line for the user to enter his own text, which then becomes the value for the input.

Chapter 7 Getting Interactive with Forms

> **Note**
>
> If the size is smaller than the MAXLENGTH, the window will scroll as the user types, until the user reaches the MAXLENGTH number of allowable characters. If the MAXLENGTH is smaller than the size, then the cursor stops at the MAXLENGTH number of allowable characters, leaving a space on the input line.

The great thing about the TEXT type is that you can control the size of it and how many characters the user can type in (with the two attributes SIZE and MAXLENGTH, respectively).

SIZE used within the TEXT type controls how many characters of the input line are visible. For instance, SIZE="10" will show an input line 10 characters wide. If no size is added, the default is 19 characters for Explorer and 20 for Netscape.

MAXLENGTH controls how many characters the user can type in. For example, MAXLENGTH="10" will only enable 10 characters to be typed in. If no MAXLENGTH is added, the user can keep typing forever.

Let's look at the example (see Figure 7.3).

- ▶ In the first text line, we didn't change the sizing of the input line, but we added our own value (VALUE="Hi there"). It shows up in the text line.

- ▶ In the second text line, we added the MAXLENGTH attribute and forced the line to allow only 5 characters (as seen by the cutting off of the word's characters).

- ▶ In the third line, we changed the size to SIZE="35" and the MAXLENGTH to MAXLENGTH="50"; now the user has a longer line and he can type more text.

- ▶ On the last line, we have a long MAXLENGTH (MAXLENGTH="20"), but a short size (SIZE="5"). Although this saves space, the user can barely see what he's typing, so this isn't very practical.

HTML Studio Skills

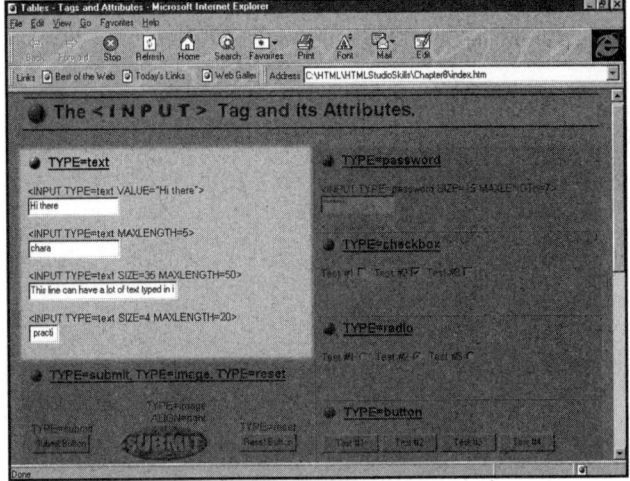

Figure 7.3

The TEXT type.

PASSWORD Input Type

Syntax: <INPUT TYPE="PASSWORD">

This input type uses the MAXLENGTH and SIZE attributes. It creates a text line that hides the characters that the user is typing in by replacing each character with an asterisk (*). Although it doesn't actually replace the characters that the user is typing, it does visually so that no one can see what the user is typing, but the input still remembers what is being typed in.

As the name implies, this is perfect for when the user is typing in a password for access to something, inputting an account number, or any other sensitive and personal information.

In this example, we have used the MAXLENGTH and SIZE attributes (MAXLENGTH="7" SIZE="15"). Some text has been typed in, but all you see are asterisks. This is the PASSWORD type in action. It hides sensitive information. Notice that the maximum number of characters has been reached (MAXLENGTH="7"), but there is still space left on the line (SIZE="15").

Chapter 7 Getting Interactive with Forms   143

Figure 7.4

The PASSWORD type.

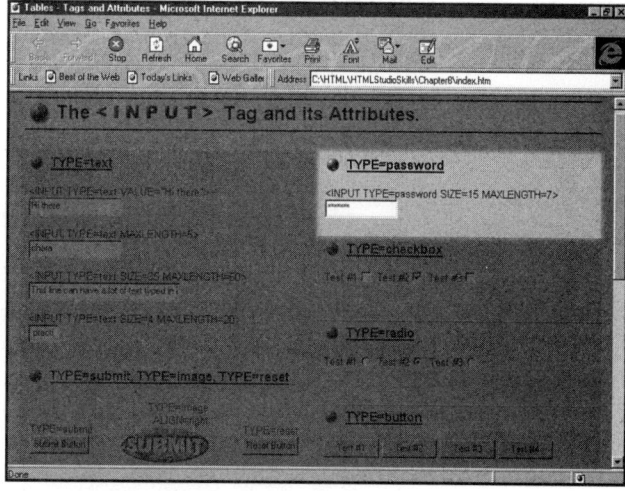

> **Note**
>
> It might be important at this point to understand the difference between a radio button and a checkbox. Checkboxes were created so that multiple simultaneous choices could be made, whereas radio buttons enable only a single choice among multiple buttons.

CHECKBOX Input Type

Syntax: `<INPUT TYPE="CHECKBOX">`

This input type also uses the optional CHECKED attribute, which automatically checks the checkbox. A checkbox can be part of a checkbox section, where all are named the same, but each value is different, allowing the user to check what she is interested in. Checkbox sections are multiple selects—they enable the user to select more than one checkbox. Values are mandatory with this type.

Checkboxes create a small empty box that when clicked on produces a small check mark inside. The value associated with that input becomes the active value. Multiple selecting enables the user to select more than one checkbox.

Of the three checkboxes, two are not checked, and one is using the optional CHECKED attribute within the <INPUT> tag so that the checkbox is pre-checked. This is useful when you are asking the user questions that are obvious, but may or may not be correct.

For example, if the user were filling out a questionnaire and one of the checkboxes asked if she had a computer, she would likely check this box. Therefore, you could pre-check this box by adding the CHECKED attribute to the checkbox input. If the user were borrowing a computer, she could uncheck it.

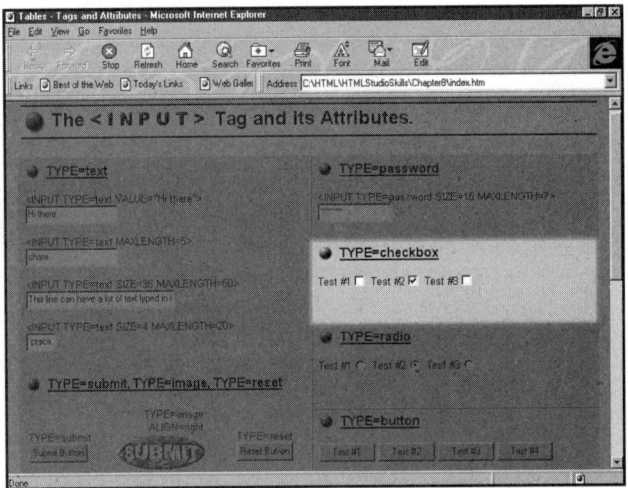

Figure 7.5

The CHECKBOX type.

RADIO Input Type

Syntax: <INPUT TYPE="RADIO">

This input type also uses the optional CHECKED attribute, which automatically checks the radio button. A radio button can be part of a radio button section, where all are named the same, and each value is different, but only one radio button may be selected, enabling the user to check one item that he is interested in. Radio button sections are single select; they enable the user to select only one radio button. Values are mandatory with this type.

Radio buttons create a small circle that is filled in when it is selected. The value associated with that input becomes the active value. Radio buttons can be used in bunches to create section types. For instance, a user could select between a series of cars, software, or pictures that he likes, but unlike checkboxes, he may only select one of the radio buttons in the bunch.

Chapter 7 Getting Interactive with Forms

In this example, the three radio buttons, all named the same, create a group of radio buttons. The one in the middle is pre-checked by adding the CHECKED attribute to the middle input. If you select either of the other buttons, the black circle will move to the one you select because only one radio button in a group may be selected.

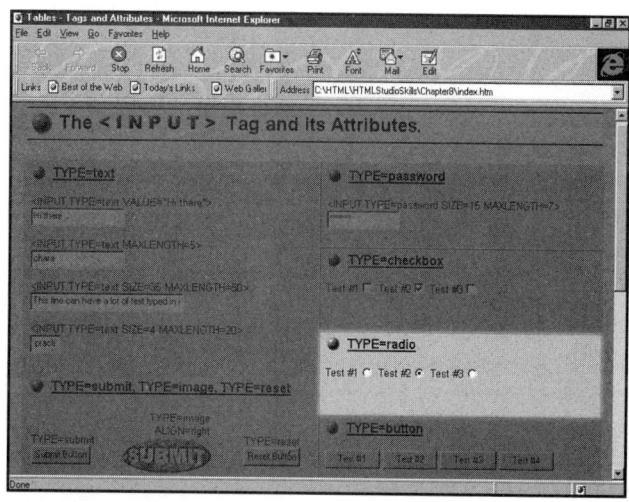

Figure 7.6

The RADIO type.

> **Note**
>
> Although this tag is fairly new, it may not appear properly or at all in some browsers.

> **ADVANCED TIP**
>
> We have added the ONCLICK attribute to each input (Syntax: ONCLICK=""); this attribute waits for the user to click the button before the content in the quotes is executed.
>
> Java, JavaScript, or VBScript can be used within the quotes, either to activate a Java or VB function, or to actually include the script code within the quotes itself (which we have done with JavaScript).

BUTTON Input Type

Syntax: <INPUT TYPE="BUTTON">

This input type creates a button, just like the submit and reset buttons, except that it can pass value information through the form, or it can be used in conjunction with Java or VBScript to achieve other functions.

The four button examples (see Figure 7.7) are straightforward. Click one of them, and that value becomes the active value. Each of the button's values has become the text on the button.

We added a little JavaScript to each of the three buttons; in the first, third, and fourth buttons, we have added ONCLICK="DOCUMENT.FGCOLOR='#------'" where #------ is replaced by our desired color, either by name or RGB.

> **Note**
> document.fgColor only works in the Explorer browser, not in Netscape.

The first button reads:

`<INPUT TYPE="BUTTON" NAME="button1" VALUE="Test #1" ONCLICK="document.fgColor='#0000FF'">`

If you load this chapter from the CD-ROM, and click the first button, you will see the text color (foreground) change to blue.

In the second button, we have added a function that can be viewed in either browser:

`<INPUT TYPE="BUTTON" NAME="button1" VALUE="Test #2" ONCLICK="window.status='Hi there'">`

`window.status` enables us to show something in the bottom corner of the browser window—this is known as the status window.

Figure 7.7

The BUTTON type.

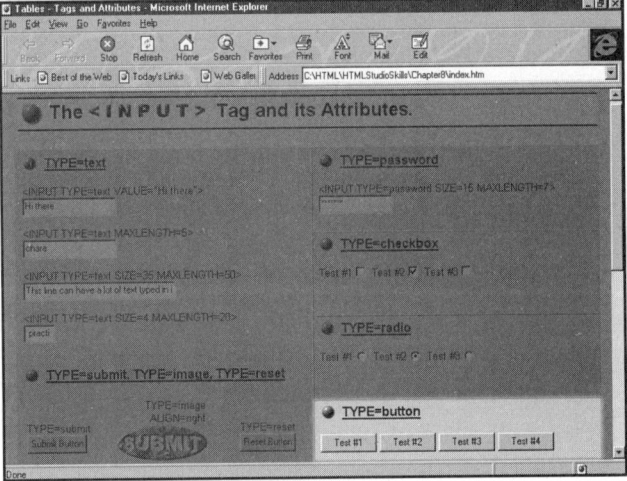

There are some other great mouse controls that work with forms. Check out ONFOCUS, ONBLUR, ONCHANGE, and ONCLICK later in this chapter.

Chapter 7 Getting Interactive with Forms

SUBMIT Input Type

Syntax: `<INPUT TYPE="SUBMIT">`

This input type actually submits the form—there should only be one per form. The value (which is recommended) becomes the text for the button. The NAME attribute shouldn't be used, but if it is, then both the name and value of the submit button are sent.

This type creates a button that submits the form; it is essential to all forms. If a form is created, then it needs to be submitted.

Here's what the code looked like with the submit button we created (see Figure 7.8):

```
<INPUT TYPE="SUBMIT" VALUE="Submit Button">
```

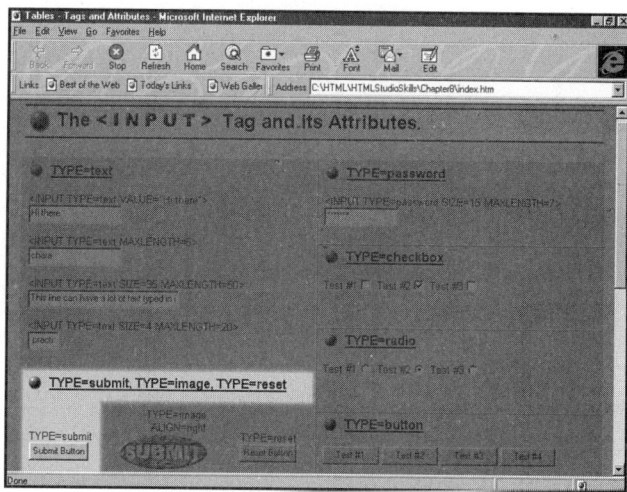

Figure 7.8

The SUBMIT type.

RESET Input Type

Syntax: `<INPUT TYPE="RESET">`

This input type resets all of the input fields in the form—there should only be one per form. The value (which is recommended) becomes the text for the button. The NAME attribute shouldn't be used.

> **Note**
>
> RESET only clears the current form, not all the forms on the page. (In other words, it clears all of the information between the current <FORM> and closing </FORM> tags.)

This type resets or clears all of the input fields to what they were before the user started entering information. The user can start again with a clean sheet of paper, so to speak. It looks just like the submit button (see Figure 7.9). And like the submit button, the only real option it has is the VALUE attribute, which becomes the button's text.

Figure 7.9

The RESET type.

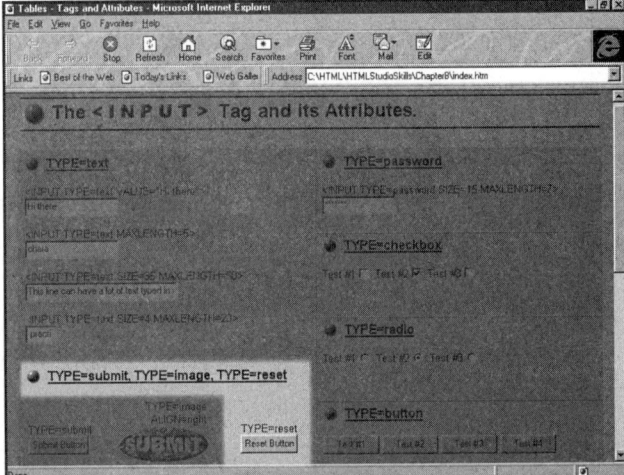

IMAGE Input Type

Syntax: `<INPUT TYPE="IMAGE" SRC="##" ALIGN=##>`

is the location/URL of the image file and ## is the alignment of the text surrounding the image. The X/Y information of where the image was clicked is also sent from the form.

This input enables you to create a graphical submit button. Because it loads an image (SRC), when that image is clicked, the form is then submitted. Remember to treat the SRC just as you would the <IMG> tag.

> **Note**
>
> Netscape demands that you use the BORDER="0" attribute within this tag if you don't want a border to be shown around the image.

Chapter 7 Getting Interactive with Forms

This type can use the ALIGN attribute (for the surrounding text), just like you would use it within the <IMG> tag. If you want it to have no border in Netscape, you need to add the BORDER="0" attribute; Explorer doesn't show a border by default. Let's look at it in action (see Figure 7.10).

Because we added the ALIGN="RIGHT" attribute, the image is aligned to the right and so is the text. If we view this in Netscape, we won't see a border because we added the BORDER="0" attribute.

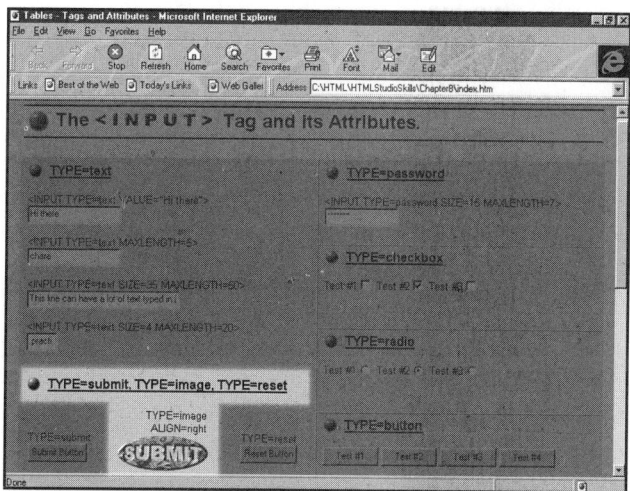

Figure 7.10

The IMAGE type.

HIDDEN Input Type

Syntax: <INPUT TYPE="HIDDEN">

Hidden input type is usually reserved for special commands or parameters for processing programs, and it uses the NAME and VALUE attributes for its parameters.

Occasionally, a form needs to send extra information to the processing program that the user can't fill in. Let's say we were dealing with a mail processing program; it would need to know who we want the form sent to, the mail server used, or what the subject line will be.

We've included some code from a form that sends to mailto.exe program:

```
<INPUT TYPE=HIDDEN NAME="resulturl" VALUE="http://www.smartmax.com/thanks.html">
<INPUT TYPE=HIDDEN NAME="sendto" VALUE="sales@smartmax.com">
<INPUT TYPE=HIDDEN NAME="server" VALUE="mail.smartmax.com">
<INPUT TYPE=HIDDEN NAME="subject" VALUE="SmartMAX software - Order Form">
```

As you can see, its type is hidden, and it uses the NAME attribute to tell the processing program what information it is about to send.

On the first line, we tell the processing program that the 'resulturl' is http://www.smartmax.com/thanks.html, so we can assume that it will send the user there once the form is processed. The next line tells the processing program who to mail the form to. The third line is the mail server. The fourth line is the subject of the mail.

Using the hidden tag for parameters like this brings up some questions: Why is it important to include these parameters in the Web page? Why can't you just add this information to the processing program itself?

If you added this information to the processing program itself, then every time you created a new Web site, or changed who was getting the mail, you would have to rewrite and recompile the processing program. If you allow the processing program to accept some parameters from the form, then you can use this program again and again, without changing it.

ONFOCUS, ONBLUR, ONCHANGE, and ONCLICK Attributes

SYNTAX: `<INPUT ONFOCUS="##" TYPE="TEXT" OR TYPE="PASSWORD">`

`<INPUT ONBLUR="##" TYPE="TEXT" OR TYPE="PASSWORD">`

`<INPUT ONCHANGE="##" TYPE="TEXT" OR TYPE="PASSWORD">`

`<INPUT ONCLICK="##" TYPE="RADIO", TYPE="CHECKBOX" or TYPE="BUTTON">`

is a JavaScript, VBScript, programmed action, or preprogrammed function.

Chapter 7 Getting Interactive with Forms

These attributes activate an action, or function, that is preprogrammed after the applicable effect has happened. All are based on mouse actions.

We have used a small JavaScript action to show how they work, and although we'll explain how each of these actions work, we have included this chapter on the CD-ROM (look for the INDEX.HTML on the CD-ROM, then through your browser select the chapter on Forms). By viewing this chapter in your browser you will see, and be able to interact with, each of these functions. This is important for your understanding of how mouse movements and actions affect each of these functions.

In this example, we wanted some text to show in the status window every time one of the corresponding mouse actions was achieved, so we placed this code into all the attributes. Here's the first attribute, ONFOCUS:

```
<INPUT TYPE="TEXT" ONFOCUS="document.status='You've just found the onFocus feature!'">
```

This calls a JavaScript action that puts some text into the status window. Now for the definitions of what each attribute does.

These attributes only work with text inputs; ONCLICK only works with the button types of input attributes.

The ONFOCUS attribute only activates when the cursor moves onto the text line that has the onFocus attribute in it. If you clicked your mouse on line two (see Figure 7.11) of the onFocus feature, you would have activated it.

The ONBLUR attribute works exactly the opposite. If your cursor is on the text line that ONBLUR is in, and you click to another text line, then the ONBLUR attribute activates.

The ONCHANGE attribute works similarly, but it requires something in the line of text to be changed. For instance, if you change the text in line two (see Figure 7.11) to read "Hi there," instead of "Hi three," and then move your mouse pointer to another text line and click, you'll activate the ONCHANGE attribute because it is now signaling that something in the line has changed.

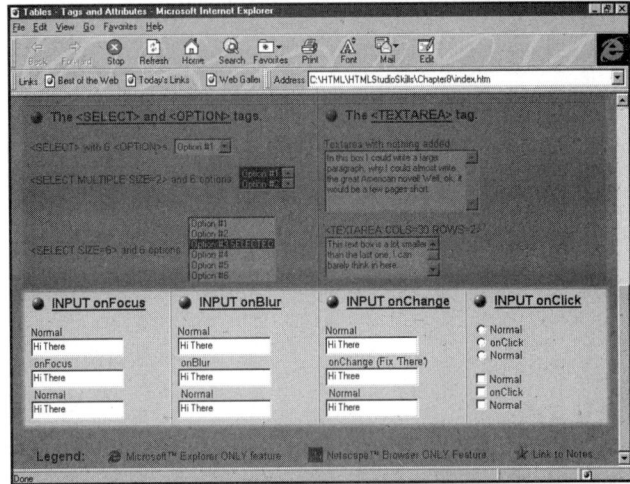

Figure 7.11

ONFOCUS, ONBLUR, ONCHANGE, and ONCLICK attributes.

Although these attributes are somewhat hard to understand, as you learn more about Web design, you will find that using them can make your pages more effective and exciting. You will find novel uses for them, such as error checking and helping the user understand what to type, and where.

CHECKED Attribute

Syntax: `<INPUT CHECKED TYPE="RADIO" or TYPE="CHECKBOX">`

The CHECKED attribute can only be used with either a radio button or a checkbox. There are no options with it, and if it is not included, the default is unchecked.

This attribute if used within the radio button, can only be used on "one" radio button per group. Only one radio button may be checked at one time. If it is used within a checkbox group, it may be used on multiple checkboxes.

`<SELECT>` and Its Attributes

Syntax: `<SELECT>`, closed with `</SELECT>`

The `<SELECT>` tag must contain some `<OPTION>` tags for the different list items to show up. It tells the form that a selection list will be starting.

Chapter 7 Getting Interactive with Forms

This tag has only three attributes.

▶ The first attribute (like all of the input types) is NAME—you must name your selection list.

▶ The next attribute is MULTIPLE, which means the user can make multiple selections from the selection list. If MULTIPLE isn't used, the default only allows for a single selection.

▶ The last attribute is SIZE, and it shows more of the list line by line. If SIZE isn't used, then only one line of the options is shown, with a drop-down menu button added to the right side of the list box.

For example, if SIZE="5", then five lines of options will show. If the size is lower than the number of options, then a scroll bar will show up on the right side, allowing the user to scroll through the options. If the size is higher or equal to the number, the scroll bar either disappears (in Explorer) or becomes inactive (in Netscape).

<OPTION> and Its Attributes

Syntax: <OPTION>## (Not closed)

is the text that will show up in the list box. Also, the text becomes the value for the input.

▶ The <OPTION> tag is used to create each separate selection item that will show up in the list.

▶ It is followed by the text that will appear as one of the selections. This text then automatically becomes the value for the option. However, if you want the value (what is sent with the form) to be different than the text in the selection box, then you can just add the VALUE="" attribute to the <OPTION> tag itself, and it will overrule the text.

▶ The other attribute <OPTION> uses is the SELECTED attribute, which is a lot like the CHECKED attribute used with radio buttons and checkboxes. It can only be used once if the list only allows a single selection (the <SELECT> tag has no MULTIPLE attribute in it), or it can be used multiple times, if the selection box allows multiple choices (the <SELECT> tag has the MULTIPLE attribute added to it).

To understand this better, let's look at the example (see Figure 7.12).

In the first selection box, no options were added to the <SELECT> (except the NAME attribute) or <OPTIONS> tags.

Let's look at the code:

```
<SELECT NAME="select_test1">
     <OPTION>Option #1
     <OPTION>Option #2
     <OPTION>Option #3
     <OPTION>Option #4
     <OPTION>Option #5
     <OPTION>Option #6
</SELECT>
```

<SELECT> produces a list box that enables a single selection, and it enables the user to scroll through the other options.

The next one is not so basic; we've added the MULTIPLE attribute and SIZE=2 to the <SELECT> tag. Because of this, you see two lines of options, and we've highlighted more than one option. Also, a scroll bar has now shown up on the right side.

The third selection box shows all the options by increasing the size to 6 (the same number as options) in the <SELECT> tag. Notice that one of the options is automatically selected. That's because we've added the SELECTED attribute to the third <OPTION> tag.

<TEXTAREA>

The <TEXTAREA> tag creates a text box in which users can type, just like a little word processing window. It's an effective input type; it is used often for comment and question fields on forms. Like all the input types, it uses the NAME attribute—it must be named.

<TEXTAREA> only uses two other attributes: COLS and ROWS, which are in character sizes, not pixels. For instance, COLS="10" means the text box will only be 10 characters wide, while ROWS="10" would be 10 rows of characters, so it would be much higher than it is wide.

Chapter 7 Getting Interactive with Forms

Figure 7.12

Selection lists.

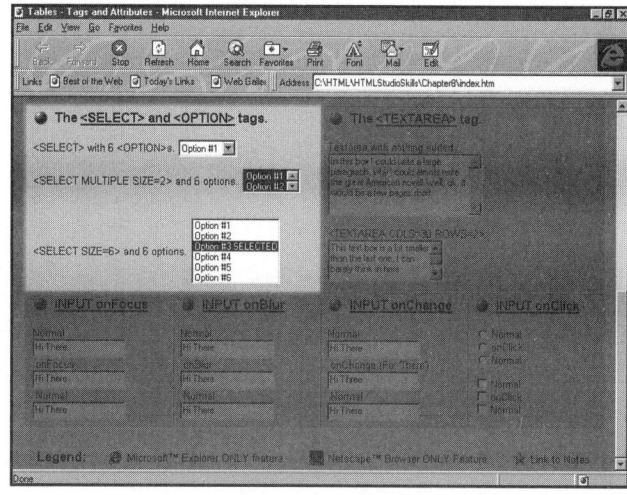

Note

Netscape does a better job than Explorer because its COLS and ROWS are perfectly based on character spacing, whereas Explorer's seem to be based on what size of character you're using, which is the actual character size, and not the character spacing (an '8' being bigger than an 'I') like Netscape uses.

The default for COLS is about 40 wide in Explorer, and 20 wide in Netscape. The ROWS default is five high for Explorer, and two high for Netscape. It's always better to set your own sizes, because the defaults in both browsers are so drastically different.

Let's take a look at the example (see Figure 7.13).

In the first text area box, we haven't added any options—this is the default size. The scroll bar is inactive on the side because the text hasn't exceeded the boundaries of the box.

In the second box, we've set the columns to 30 (COLS="30") and the rows to 5 (ROWS="5"). With more text in the box, the scroll bar now activates.

You will learn much more about the programming side of things in the coming advanced section of the book. We've included many snippets of JavaScript both to learn from and to use yourself. Also, we've included some CGI scripts to get you started right away with forms.

Figure 7.13

The <TEXTAREA> tag.

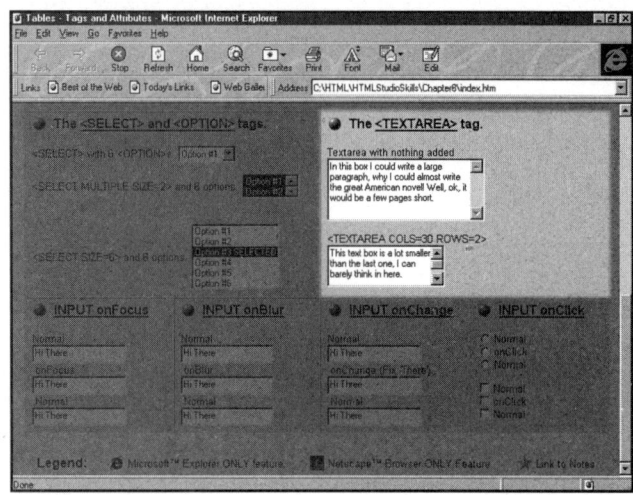

Netscape Note

Netscape uses the attribute WRAP= in the <TEXTAREA> tag (syntax: <TEXTAREA WRAP="##">), where ## is either OFF (default), VIRTUAL, or PHYSICAL.

▶ WRAP="OFF" is the default that provides no text wrapping.

▶ WRAP="VIRTUAL" lets the text wrap, but when the form is submitted, all new lines made in the text box are ignored, and the text area information is sent as a single line.

▶ WRAP="PHYSICAL" lets the text wrap and, unlike VIRTUAL, it sends all of the new lines when the form is submitted.

Because Explorer already wraps the text, yet still sends the information in a single line when the form is submitted (no new line characters are sent), it would be of use to add WRAP="VIRTUAL" to your forms so that they remain consistent between browsers.

Conclusion

In this chapter you learned not only how to create a form and send it, but you also learned how each option reacts with the user and how the user can interact with it. This is by no means the be-all end-all of forms information.

If you deal with forms often, you might think about learning more on JavaScript, AppleScript, Java, CGIs, or ActiveX. All of these languages enable you to do more with forms than just a MAILTO: option. Because these languages enable you to process more information, reroute information, and even error check, they are a necessary tool in becoming a more proficient and skilled Web designer.

Now let's take a look at one of the most overused features of HTML: frames.

chapter 8

Working with Frames

If you're a frequent Internet surfer, you probably have a love-hate relationship with frames. Why? Frames are probably the most frequently abused and overused Netscape-ism on the Web. Now that they're well established in the HTML 3.0 standard, you can look forward to seeing more frames drawing themselves in proliferation throughout your Web browsing adventures.

Frames often represent valuable solutions to problems you might have in organizing information on a site.

Frames enable you to maintain a consistent "shell" under which your users can surf while information changes in different regions of the page. Through the use of frames you can also maintain the interface of your site around other sites so that as you link to outside resources your users always have a simple way to get back (see Figure 8.1).

→ <FRAMESET> Tag

<FRAME> Tag

<NOFRAMES> Tag

<TARGET> Attribute

→ <IFRAME> Tag

As an added advantage, frames can save you development time by enabling you to place and maintain a single menu bar or control panel on your site without having to place it on each page of the site individually.

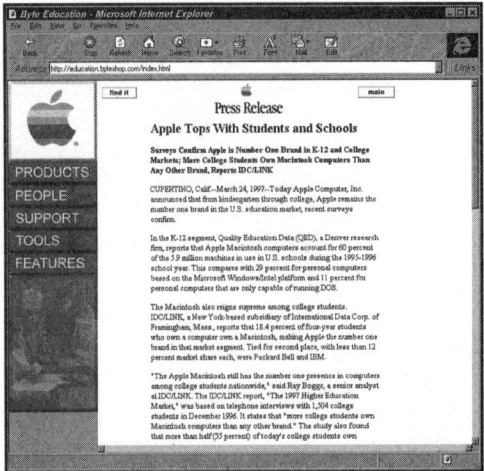

Figure 8.1

"Shelling Out:" The Byte Shop Web site leads users to Apple without sending them away blindly.

The advantages of developing a frames-based site, however, come with a price. Frames can and often do interrupt the visual flow of a page, with their scrolling bars and restricting layout options often forcing you to choose design options that don't fit your initial plans. A further frustration is that, because frames are a relatively recent innovation, you will still end up having to develop pages the old way in order to support non-frames–based browsers and search engines.

There are ways around some of these limitations, through devices and attributes implemented by Microsoft for Internet Explorer. The adoption of these changes to the recognized specifications by Netscape has been slow, not to mention slightly different. As a result of all of this confusion, and the unsightliness caused by having multiple frames on a page, the key to using frames is to use them sparingly and most effectively.

Chapter 8 Working with Frames

Frames can be abused (see Figures 8.2 and 8.3), often to the detriment of the site's visual appeal and user reach. In the case of the Sony site, the 11 different frames actually impede the user's ability to read the information contained on the site. Some frames are scrolling, which occupies some major screen real estate, and those that are non-scrolling are actually concealing pieces of images or text. Is this the best way to reach clients?

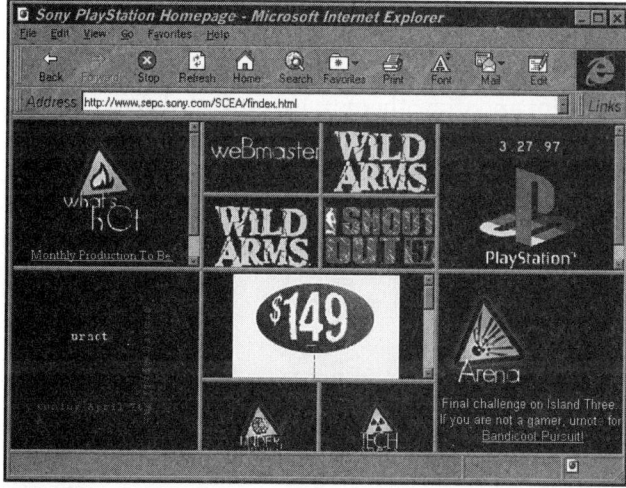

Figure 8.2
Too many frames: The Sony PlayStation site uses 11 frames on one page.

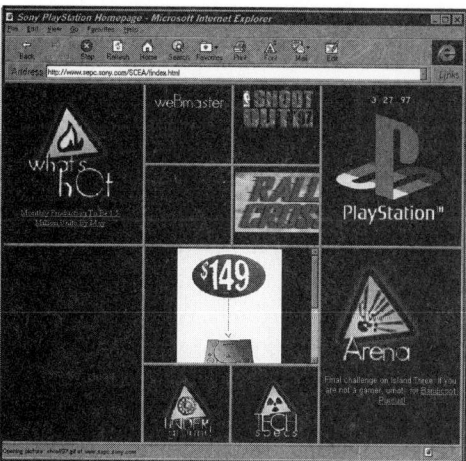

Figure 8.3
The Sony PlayStation site as seen by most users at 640×480 pixels.

In this chapter, we'll show you how to implement frames without ruining the look of your site. Your goal should be to get away with using frames, without your users catching on, through the use of borderless frames and other attributes. On the whole, though, frames-based sites tend to look better on Explorer because it can draw borderless frames without the "seam" that you see in Netscape, and because Explorer enables some extra tags, alluded to earlier, which we'll discuss in detail.

Frame documents consist of two parts: the parent and the child. After the parent has loaded, the instructions are read by the browser, which then proceeds to request each file referenced within the <FRAMESET> element and draw them to the screen. The parent frame's document contains only the information pertaining to the laying out of each individual frame (child) in the browser window. Formatting options such as text or background color have no effect on the final document; therefore, they are unnecessary.

<FRAMESET> Tag

Attributes: COLS, ROWS, FRAMEBORDER, FRAMESPACING, SCROLLING

Contains: FRAMESET (Nested Frames), NOFRAMES, FRAME

A frameset element must be opened and closed, structured like the following syntax, which results in Figure 8.4.

Syntax:

```
<FRAMESET COLS="50%,*">
    <FRAME SRC="foo.html">
    <FRAME SRC="bar.html">
</FRAMESET>
```

A document that uses frames is, in effect, a formatting shell that refers to other documents as elements in much the same way as regular HTML files refer to GIFs. The key to this feature is the <FRAMESET> element, which uses attributes to describe how the parent document window will appear, and implies that the tags contained between the <FRAMESET> and </FRAMESET> elements define the layout of each individual frame. As with all other SRC= attributes, each <FRAME SRC=> tag points to the appropriate file to be loaded.

Chapter 8 **Working with Frames**

Figure 8.4

A simple two-frame document is the result of the previous syntax.

TIP

A frame must touch the "sides" of a window. You can place a frame in the center of the document window, but only by laying out frames along each border, thereby creating a smaller window and a page formatting nightmare.

To add to the possibilities, you can create nested frames. In other words, new <FRAMESET> tags can be embedded within frames themselves, creating such effects as columns, which only appear in specific rows. Why bother? Well, this would enable you, as with nested tables, to define columns within rows, or vice-versa. The syntax for doing this is as follows:

```
<FRAMESET ROWS="15%,*">
    <FRAME SCROLLING=NO SRC=foobar.html>
    <FRAMESET COLS="50%,*">
        <FRAME SRC=foo.html>
        <FRAME SRC=bar.html>
    </FRAMESET>
</FRAMESET>
```

Figure 8.5
A more complicated document that makes use of nested frames.

COLS Attribute

Values: η, %, *

Syntax: `<FRAMESET COLS="230, 30%, *">`

The COLS attribute is used to define columns in the frames document. For each item contained in the value field, a new column is defined. In this particular frames reference, three columns will be drawn. The first column will be 230 pixels wide; the next column will be 30 percent of the remaining window space; and the third column will use whatever space is left (see Figure 8.6).

ROWS Attribute

Values: η, %, *

Syntax: `<FRAMESET ROWS="230, 30%, *">`

The ROWS attribute works exactly the same as the COLS attribute, and it can be used in conjunction with COLS to define a grid pattern (see Figure 8.7). Also, you can embed columns within rows or rows within columns.

Chapter 8 Working with Frames

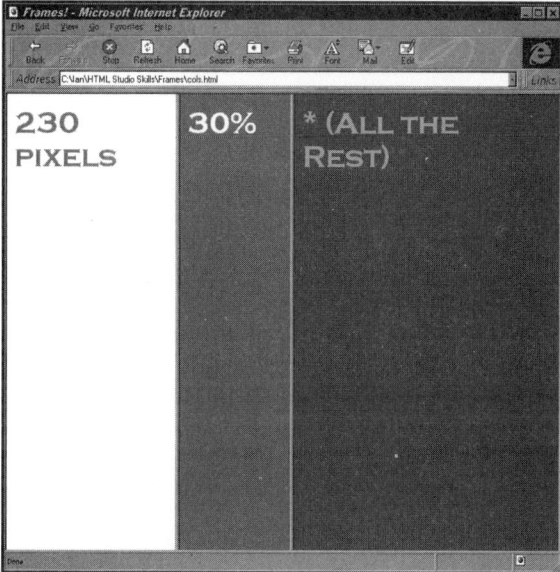

Figure 8.6

Three columns in a frameset.

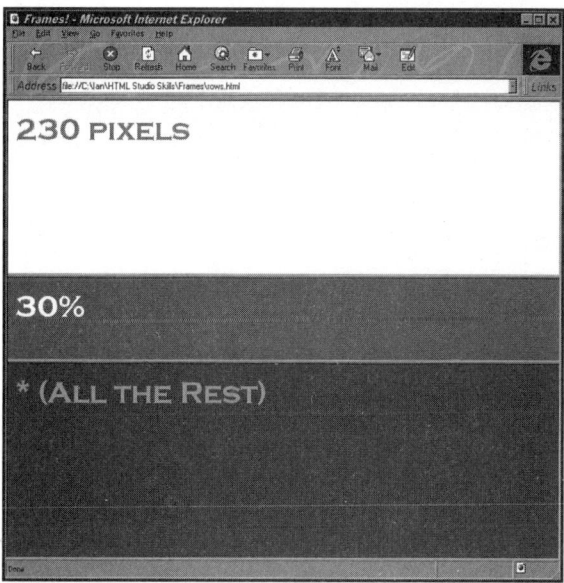

Figure 8.7

Three rows in a frameset.

FRAMEBORDER Attribute

Values: 1 or 0

Syntax: `<FRAMESET FRAMEBORDER="1">`

The default value (one) for this attribute draws a 4-pixel wide, 3D border. Setting the value to 0 turns off this feature. Most commonly, the FRAMEBORDER attribute is used to eliminate the border rather than augment it, resulting in a seamless transition between two frames, as in Figure 8.8.

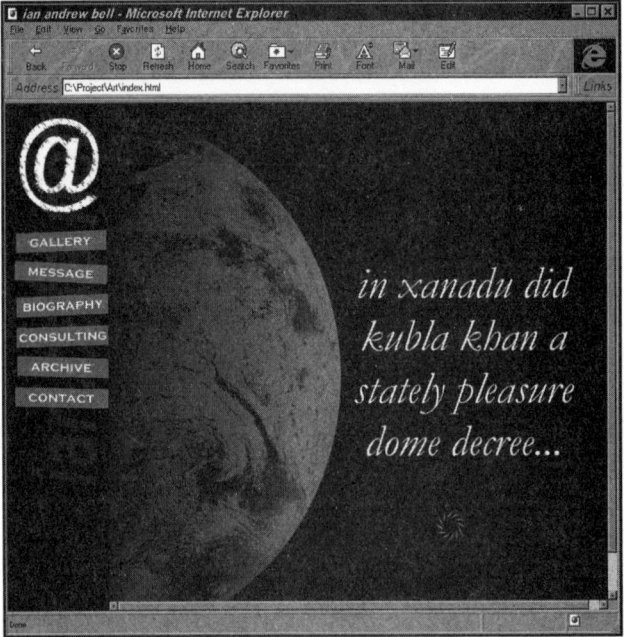

Figure 8.8
A seamless frameset.

FRAMESPACING Attribute

Values: η

Syntax: `<FRAMESET FRAMESPACING="4">`

This attribute uses the background colors of the frames parent to create additional space between frames. This is a useful feature for creating margins between the frames, which is simpler than specifying margin widths for each frame individually.

Figure 8.9

Black spacing separates the three frames.

SCROLLING Attribute

Values: YES, NO, AUTO

Syntax: <FRAMESET SCROLLING="AUTO">

The SCROLLING attribute creates a scrollbar (such as the one that appears on the right-hand edge of your document window) for each frame. When used as a value in the <FRAMESET> tag, SCROLLING defines how all frames will be drawn. The default value for both browsers is AUTO, meaning that a scrollbar will only appear if the text of the page within the frame extends beyond that frame's field of view. If you turn scrolling off, you'd better make sure that the text and graphics don't extend beyond what you expect the size of your users' windows to be (see Figure 8.10).

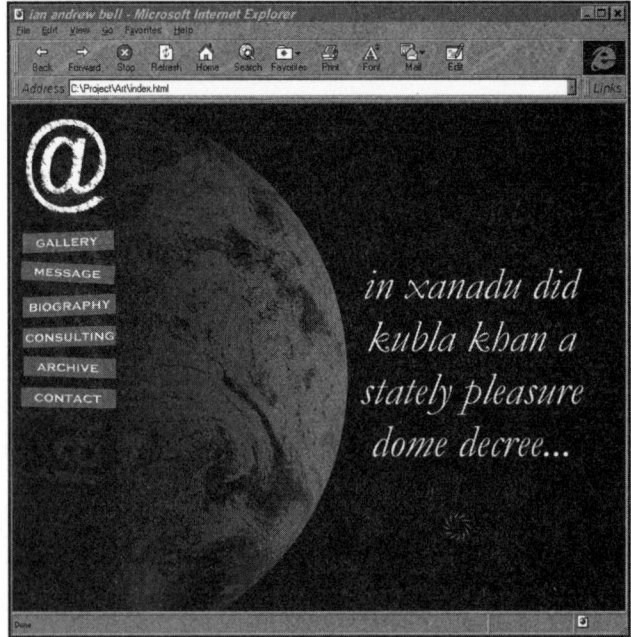

Figure 8.10

Look Ma! No scroll bars!

<FRAME> Tag

Values: SRC, ALIGN, FRAMEBORDER, MARGINHEIGHT, MARGINWIDTH, NAME, NORESIZE, SCROLLING

Syntax: <FRAME FRAMEBORDER="0" SRC="foobar.html" NAME="FooBar">

The <FRAME> tag must be contained within the <FRAMESET> tag. Using values in the <FRAME>, tag you can override attributes of the <FRAMESET> tag for specific frames. In all other aspects they work exactly the same as their values within the frameset parent's attributes. You can also give each frame a name within this tag so that the browser can identify them using scripts, target links, and applets.

SRC Attribute

Values: URL

Syntax: <FRAME SRC="foobar.html">

As with all other SRC references, this attribute specifies where the content file is located—it can be a full path URL or relative to where the referring document is located.

NAME Attribute

Values: User-Defined

Syntax: `<FRAME SRC="foobar.html" NAME="fooBAR">`

This name can arbitrarily refer to each frame, so long as it begins with an alphabetical or numeric character. It can then be specified within the TARGET attribute of links, as discussed with the <HREF> tag.

The following <HREF> syntax, for example, loads a referenced file in another frame, named "FooBAR2," when the user clicks the link:

`<A HREF="/foobar3.html" TARGET="FooBAR2">Click Here</A>`

TARGET attributes are discussed in greater detail later in this chapter.

FRAMEBORDER Attribute

Values: 1 or 0

Syntax: `<FRAME SRC="foobar.html" FRAMEBORDER="1">`

Just as with the same attribute in the <FRAMESET> tag, the default value (one) for this attribute draws a 4-pixel wide, 3D border. Setting the value to 0 actually turns off this feature altogether, whereas implementing this in a <FRAME> statement overrides any statements made in the <FRAMESET> tag.

MARGINHEIGHT Attribute

Values: η

Syntax: `<FRAME SRC="foobar.html" MARGINHEIGHT="1">`

This attribute specifies the vertical margin in pixels, between the frame's border and the text and images contained within the body of the document. The margin creates a buffer zone by using the background color as specified within the individual frame document's <BODY> tag.

MARGINWIDTH Attribute

Values: η

Syntax: `<FRAME SRC="foobar.html" MARGINWIDTH="2">`

This attribute specifies the horizontal margin in pixels between the frame's border and the text and images contained within the body of the document. The margin creates a buffer zone by using the background color as specified within the individual frame document's `<BODY>` tag (see Figure 8.11).

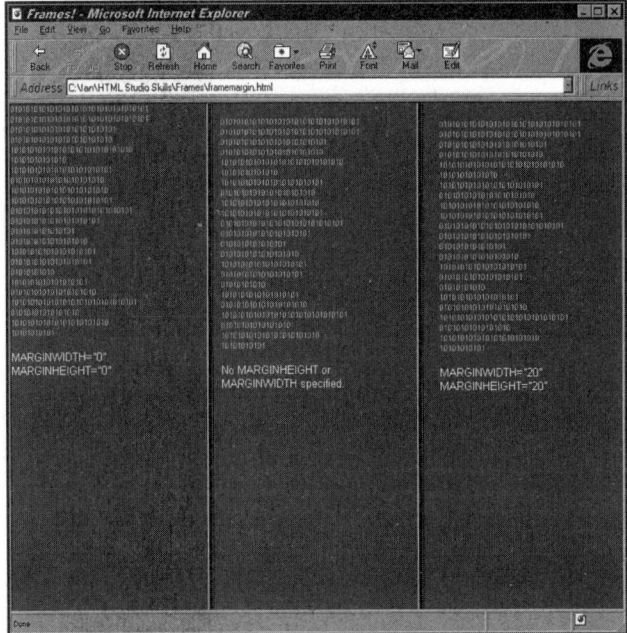

Figure 8.11
Various effects achieved with `MARGINHEIGHT` *and* `MARGINWIDTH`.

ALIGN Attribute

Values: `LEFT, CENTER, RIGHT, TOP, BOTTOM`

Syntax: `<FRAME SRC="foobar.html" ALIGN="CENTER">`

This attribute sets the alignment of the frame or of the surrounding text. As you might expect, the default (when the attribute is not specified) is `LEFT`. The frame alignment options for `ALIGN` are listed in Table 8.1.

Table 8.1
`ALIGN` Attribute Options

Option	Result
LEFT	The frame aligns to the leftmost point of the document, and text flows around it.
CENTER	All surrounding text is aligned with the center of the frame.
RIGHT	The frame aligns to the rightmost point of the document, and text flows around it.
TOP	All surrounding text is aligned with the top of the frame.
BOTTOM	All surrounding text is aligned with the bottom of the frame.

SCROLLING Attribute

Values: YES, NO, AUTO

Syntax: `<FRAME SRC="foobar.html" SCROLLING="AUTO">`

Again, the SCROLLING attribute creates a scroll for each frame. When used as a value in the <FRAME> tag, it overrides how the specific frame will be drawn. The default value for both browsers is AUTO.

NORESIZE Attribute

Values: None

Syntax: `<FRAME SRC="foobar.html" NORESIZE>`

This attribute prevents your users from changing the dimensions of the frame. When they try to resize the window by pulling on the tab at the lower-right corner it simply doesn't budge. NORESIZE can be a useful feature when you have very specific ideas about how you want the document to lay out, but it causes problems if you're expecting your users to have big document windows and they're only running their monitors at 640×480 pixels.

<NOFRAMES> Tag

Values: None

Syntax: `<NOFRAMES>You need A Frames Browser!</NOFRAMES>`

This is a very important tag for backward-compatibility. Web browsers ignore HTML tags they don't understand. Therefore, old Web browsers, such as Netscape 1.1, will skip through all of the frames-related elements and tags until they get to the information within the <NOFRAMES> tag. Simply insert any HTML you want to be loaded by the non-frames Web browser here, and the page will render properly for them. You can either warn users that this page is not viewable without frames or you can develop an alternate non-frames version of the page because frames-capable browsers will ignore any data contained between the <NOFRAMES> and </NOFRAMES> elements.

> **TIP**
> <NOFRAMES> is always contained within the <FRAMESET> container.

TARGET Attribute

Values: Window Name

Syntax: `<A HREF="/foobar.html" TARGET="foobar">`

Now that you have windows scattered liberally around the screen, you need a way of referring to them. The NAME attribute in the <FRAME> tag defines names for each of the frames (also called "panels") in the browser window. This enables you to load files into the frames even when the referring link is not in the same window. Both windows and frames can have names, which means that you can spawn entirely new windows for links.

There are several names reserved for use by the browser, which you can refer to in the TARGET attribute of <HREF>s. They are:

- `TARGET="_BLANK"`—This target will cause the link to always be loaded in a new blank window. This window is not named.

- `TARGET="_SELF"`—This target causes the link to always load in the same window that the anchor was clicked in. This is the default behavior for clicking a link.

- `TARGET="_PARENT"`—This target causes the link to load in the immediate `<FRAMESET>` parent of this document. This defaults to acting like `"_SELF"` if the document has no parent. A parent would be whatever document contains the frameset with the link in it.

- `TARGET="_TOP"`—This target makes the link load in the full body of the window, replacing all of the other frames with the contents of the new document. This, too, defaults to acting like `"_SELF"` if the document is already at the top. It is useful for breaking out of frame sets to start new ones, or to exit a particular interface or move to a new site.

`<IFRAME>` Tag

Attributes: ALIGN, FRAMEBORDER, HEIGHT, WIDTH, SCROLLING, MARGINHEIGHT, MARGINWIDTH, SRC, NAME

Syntax: `<IFRAME FRAMEBORDER=0 SCROLLING=NO SRC="foobar.html"> </IFRAME>`

At the beginning of this chapter you learned that the only way to put a frame in the middle of a document was by defining frames all around the outside borders. This is incredibly complicated and probably not worth the effort. Web designers nearly overflowed with frustration because Netscape did not consider the need for "inline" frames within their original frames proposal to the World Wide Web Consortium.

Microsoft has come to the rescue of Web architects with a set of tags that should have been implemented in the first place. Sadly, as of this writing, the `<IFRAME>` tag has not made its way into Netscape Navigator 4.0, although it is fully implemented in Internet Explorer 3.0 and beyond.

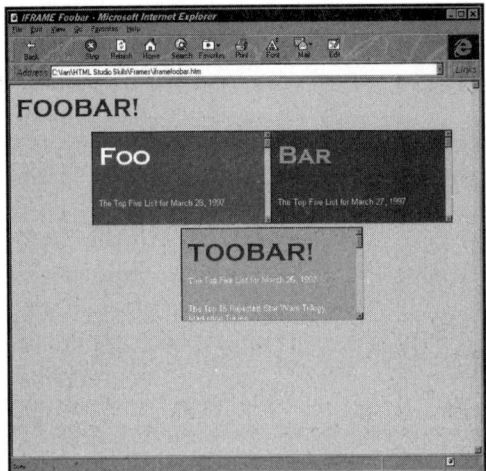

Figure 8.12

An example of <IFRAME> in action: three inline frames within a table.

Although its implementation is still a little buggy, <IFRAME> is probably here to stay. The ease with which it enables the Web designer to add inline frames is significant.

<IFRAME> uses the same attributes in the same way as the regular <FRAME> tag, with the exception of HEIGHT and WIDTH.

HEIGHT and WIDTH

Value: η or %

Syntax: <IFRAME SRC="foobar.html" HEIGHT="50" WIDTH="80%">

These two attributes are simple height and width controls that enable you to scale the size of the frame, which is similar to other tags such as the image inclusion tag, <IMG>.

Conclusion

As you can tell, frames are still a young technology, and they suffer from a poor initial implementation that was not favorable to good Web design. With the introduction of <IFRAME>, we now can build more traditional software-like interfaces on our Web pages, with one possible problem—inline frames look remarkably like the text areas from forms.

Chapter 8 Working with Frames

Only time will tell whether or not people will warm up to frames. The lukewarm reception it received from Web designers caused an unanticipated stumble in the implementation of new tags and elements by Netscape. In the meantime, the most frequent use of frames will probably be the implementation of menu control panels aligned to the left-hand side of the page. This enables the designer to conceal its existence to the user and to provide the best compromise between viewability and usability.

chapter 9

- → Creating Backgrounds
- Working with Transparent GIFS
- Icons
- Graphical Text, Tables, and Lists
- Adobe Photoshop Technigues
- → Using Photographs

Advanced Graphics

This chapter deals with the fun part of HTML and Web design, creating graphics. You will learn many of the skills graphic artists use and employ on their Web site:

► Creating backgrounds and icons

► Making 3D text

► Adding shadows to graphics

Creating Backgrounds

A background is the canvas for your Web site. It provides ambiance, texture, and feel to your pages and gives your site a distinct look and style. This section shows you how to create the different types of backgrounds that achieve many wonderful effects. You will learn how to create vertical tiles that create a horizontal look, as well as horizontal tiles that create a vertical look.

Before You Start

Before you set up a page background, you need to change tools. This section uses Photoshop 4.0 to create the graphics (although you can use 3.0 for everything but the actions). You also need a Web browser, and a blank HTML page ready for editing. (A graphical page editor, such as Adobe PageMill or NetObjects Fusion, is handy, too.)

Setting Up Some Preferences

Before you start designing your tiles, you need to set your Photoshop 4.0 Preferences.

1. Choose File➡Preferences➡Display & Cursors. Set the Painting Cursors to Precise and the Other Cursors to Precise.

2. Choose File➡Preferences➡Units & Rulers. Set the Units to Pixels.

3. Choose File➡Preferences➡Guides & Grid. Set the Gridline to every 5 pixels and the Subdivisions to 1.

4. From the Window menu, select Show Tools and Show Layers. This puts the appropriate palettes in the window.

Vertical Tiling

The effect we are going to achieve is a horizontal pattern that looks as if the Web page is made up of two pieces of recycled paper.

1. First, create a new blank image to serve as the canvas. Choose new from the File menu; then make the Width 60 pixels and the Height 1,024 pixels. Choose RGB color as the mode and make the Contents white (see Figure 9.1).

WARNING

Tiles need to be very long or high if you don't want them to wrap. Make a sidebar-style at least 1,024 pixels high (that is, taller than a high resolution monitor) and a banner-style tile at least 1,240 pixels wide.

Chapter 9 Advanced Graphics

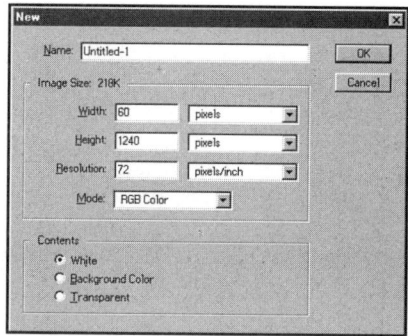

Figure 9.1

Create a blank image.

2. Zoom in on the image so that you have a better view. Choose View→Actual Pixels or double-click the magnifying glass to make sure that all of the pixels are showing onscreen (see Figure 9.2). Scroll to the top of the image.

3. Make the texture. Choose Filter→Texture→Texturizer to get to the Texturizer plug-in. Make the Texture Sandstone; set Scaling at 150% and Relief to 3. Set the Lighting to top-left and click OK (see Figure 9.3).

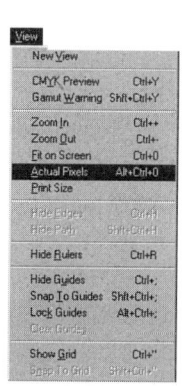

Figure 9.2

Zoom in, scroll up.

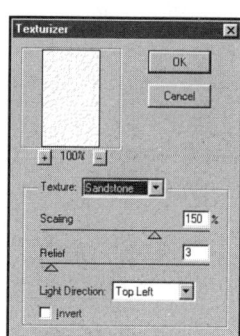

Figure 9.3

The Texturizer dialog box.

4. Create a new layer. Choose New Layer from the Layers palette menu and name the new layer Line Guide. Go back to the image and choose the Line tool (press N). Scroll up or down to the 160 Y pixel mark (the left ruler is the Y value of the pixels, the top ruler is the X value) and draw a horizontal line (see Figure 9.4). The default line tool settings are fine.

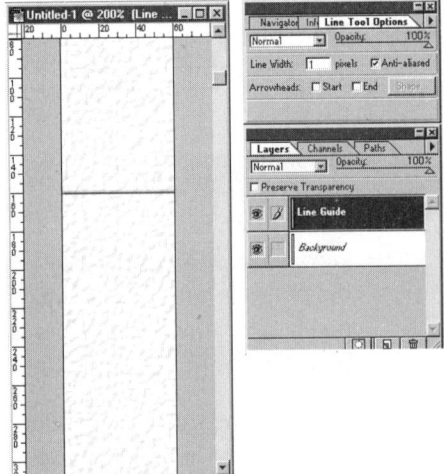

Figure 9.4

Creating a line guide.

5. Create another layer called Jagged Line. Select the Paintbrush tool (press B), then choose Window➥Show Brushes and pick the smallest brush. Draw a jagged line from the left edge of the image to the right, making sure that you start and finish the jagged line *exactly* where the guide line created in Step 4 touches the edges. (see Figure 9.5).

6. Delete the Line Guide layer by dragging it to the Trash Can in the Layers palette. (see Figure 9.6).

7. Click the Jagged Line layer to make it the active layer. Select the Wand tool (press W), and click above the line. Only the area above the line should be selected; if the area below the line is selected, too, choose Select➥None to drop the selection and make sure that your jagged line is unbroken and extends all the way to both edges of the image. Choose Select➥Modify➥Expand and choose 1 pixel (see Figure 9.7).

Chapter 9 **Advanced Graphics** | 179

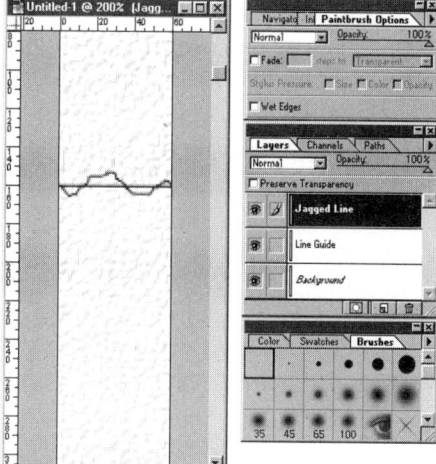

Figure 9.5

Jagged line.

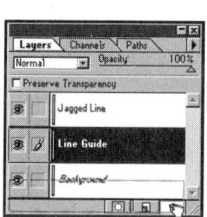

Figure 9.6

Deleting the Line Guide layer.

8. Save the selection. Choose Select➛Save Selection. In the Save Selection dialog box that appears, set Channel to New and Operation to New Channel.

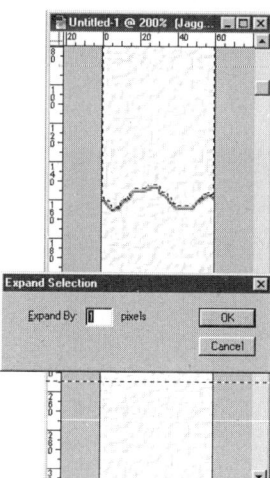

Figure 9.7

Making a marquee or selection.

9. Make the two tone paper. While still in the Jagged Line layer, choose Select➡All. Using the Magic Wand tool and holding down the Option (Mac) or Alt (PC) key, click the top part of the image above the line. This removes the top part from the selection (see Figure 9.8).

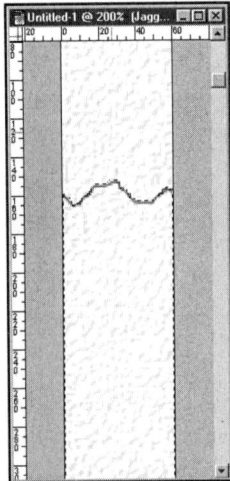

Figure 9.8

Selecting the bottom portion of the image.

10. Fill in the selection. Choose Edit➡Fill, setting Contents to Black, the Opacity to 10%, and the Mode to Normal (see Figure 9.9). Click OK.

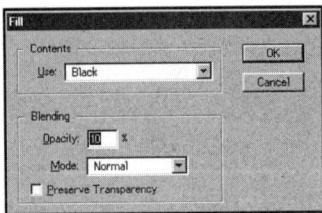

Figure 9.9

Filling in the selection.

This gives the paper an almost two-tone effect; it gives the idea of height, the lighter side being higher than the darker one. Now you need to enhance the effect by making the black line become a shadow.

Chapter 9 **Advanced Graphics**   181

Figure 9.10

Blurring the line.

11. Without dropping the selection, choose Filter➡ Blur➡Gaussian Blur. Set the Radius to 1.3 pixels, and then click OK (see Figure 9.10).

   Notice that after the "blur," the effect of a shaded piece of paper is more prominent. (Remember, you can hide the selection without losing it by choosing View➡Hide Edges so that you can view what you've just done.) The line dividing the two pieces of paper is now fuzzy (it lost some of the definition), so you want to make the jagged line a little sharper.

12. Choose Select➡Load Selection (Channel #4). Set Operation to New Selection (see Figure 9.11).

13. Choose Edit➡Clear, then Select➡None and view your image (see Figure 9.12).

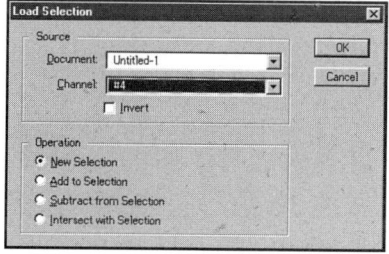

Figure 9.11

Loading a selection.

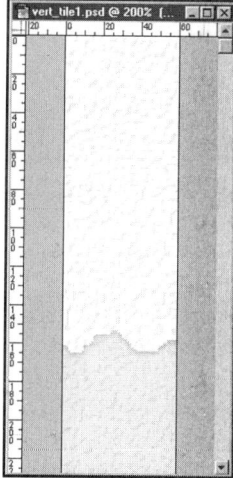

Figure 9.12

Almost finished...

14. Create a new layer and name it Muting Layer. This layer mutes the colors of the background. Fill in the layer with 100% of the image's predominant color, which is white. Choose Edit➡ Fill, setting the Contents to White, the Opacity to

100%, and the Mode to Normal. In the Layers window, move the Opacity slider until the image is mostly white, but the background can still be seen. In Figure 9.13 it's set to 20.

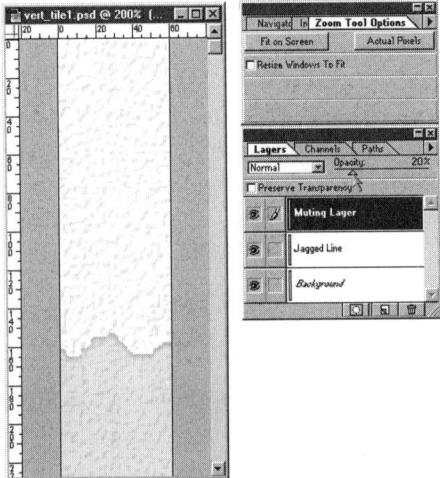

Figure 9.13

Muting the background.

Preparing the Image for the Web

Now that you're almost done, what's left? Well, you could save this image as a JPEG, but because it doesn't have very many complex colors, you should use the GIF compression to give you a smaller image size.

1. Save the image you are working on in Photoshop format so that you can work on it at a later date, should you want to change anything.

2. The image is currently in RGB Color mode, which enables each pixel's color to be set independently to any RGB color you need to convert it to Indexed Color mode, which means that each pixel's color is drawn from a palette of no more than 256 colors. Choose Image➡Mode➡Indexed Color, and when it asks if you want to flatten the layers, click OK. The Indexed Color dialog box appears. Set the Palette to Adaptive, the Color Depth to Other, and the number of colors to 12. Set the Dither to Diffusion and Click OK (see Figure 9.14).

Chapter 9 **Advanced Graphics** | 183

> **Note**
>
> You can experiment with this number of colors to make it lower or higher, which either increases or decreases the file size of the image. This also affects the look of the image; the more colors, the less loss, and so on. The key here is to experiment and achieve the best image with the lowest number of colors.

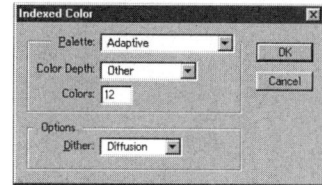

Figure 9.14

Dithering the image to 12 colors.

3. Now you can save the image. Select Save As from the File menu and save your file as a CompuServe GIF. Save the GIF as Normal, rather than Interlaced, when you're using a GIF in a background image.

4. Load up or create a new HTML document. Load the GIF that you just created as the background. Let's take a look at the example (see Figure 9.15).

> **WARNING**
>
> When creating backgrounds, you're better off not using interlacing, which causes longer download times. This can lead to frustrated users who move on instead of waiting around for your background to load.

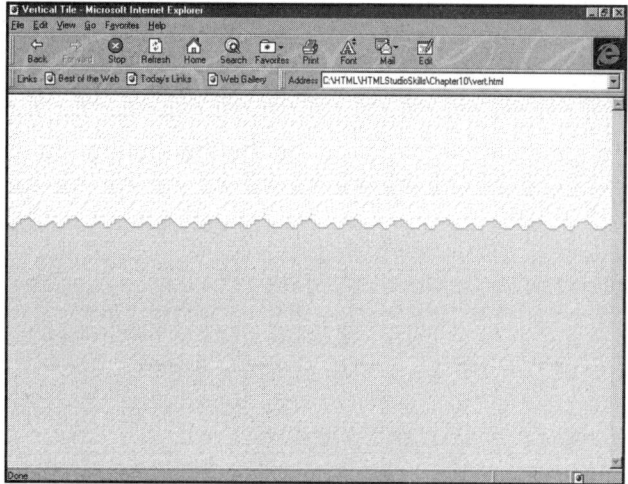

Figure 9.15

The final product.

> **Note**
>
> That little jagged line is now a continuous line across the entire screen because you matched up the line at both edges from the same point. This can also work for patterns. You can use a pattern as a tile, and if it matches at the edges at the same places, it will tile seamlessly (see Figures 9.16 and 9.17).

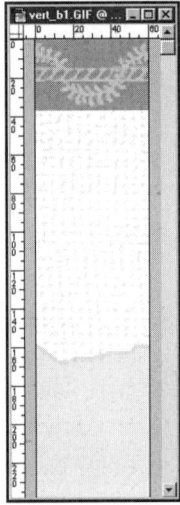

Figure 9.16

The actual patterned tile.

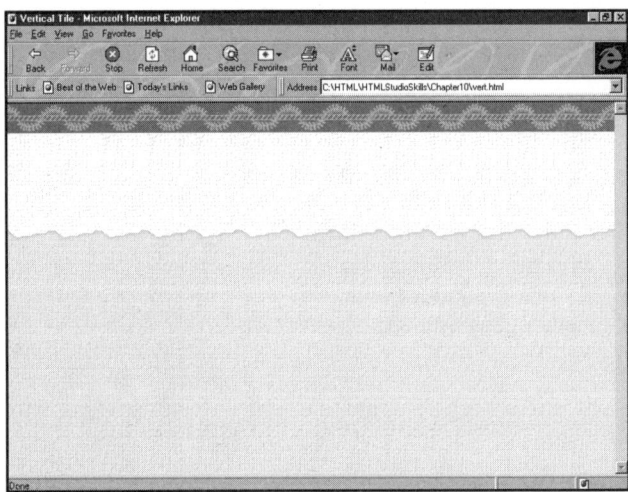

Figure 9.17

The final effect.

You can see there are many things that can be done with vertical tiles, and the effects can be quite pleasing. Just experiment and have some fun. You'll find that experimentation is the best part of Web design.

> **TIP**
>
> One of the greatest features of this type of tile is that you can select Image➡Rotate Canvas➡90° CW or CCW to turn the tile so that it becomes a horizontal tile. You can also rotate horizontal tiles to make them vertical.

Chapter 9 Advanced Graphics

Working with Transparent GIFs

Of all of the graphic types you use, transparent GIFs and transparent GIF animations are the most common. To use these properly, it's important to understand the terminology and the concepts behind them.

There are three important terms you need to know when using transparent graphics on the Web: anti-aliasing, alpha channels, and transparent GIFs. We'll deal with these one by one.

Anti-aliasing

Anti-aliasing is the process of letting one color blend into another. It works by changing pixels between colored areas to intermediate colors to smooth the transition between colors. Without anti-aliasing, colors are solid, lines are jagged, and differences between shapes and colors are extremely visible (see Figure 9.18).

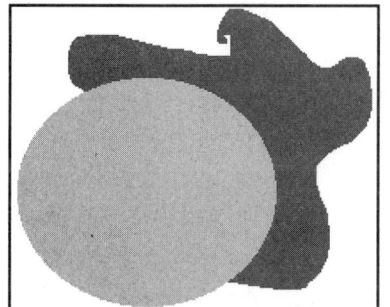

Figure 9.18
Shapes without anti-aliasing.

Notice how the lines are jagged, and if you look closely, you can see that the circle is just made up of several small straight lines. Although this looks very unattractive, it's important to know that there are some shapes that look fine when aliased: Namely, shapes made up of perfectly vertical or perfectly horizontal lines (see Figure 9.19).

The best solution to this problem is to create anti-aliased graphics. Let's take a look at the shapes created using the anti-aliasing option in Photoshop (see Figure 9.20).

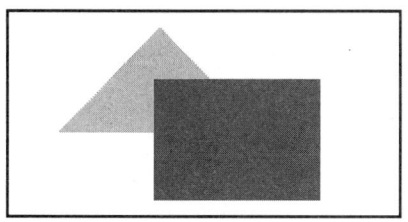

Figure 9.19
Aliased shapes that look okay.

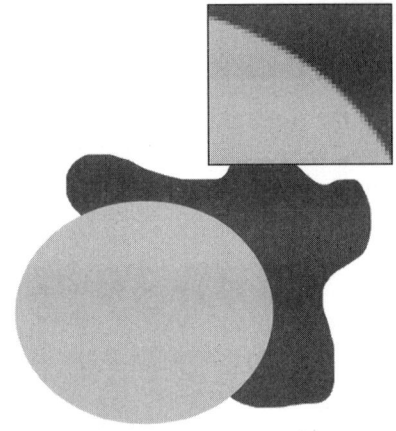

Figure 9.20

Anti-aliased shapes.

The shapes are clearer. If you look at the detailed view of the green circle, you can see that the edges are not the foreground green but rather blends of green with red underneath it.

In Photoshop, anti-aliasing is automatically applied to all the tools, except the rectangular Marquee tool (it uses straight lines) and the Pencil tool.

Alpha Channel Mapping

An alpha channel is just a selection that has been saved in the graphic file. Whether or not the user created and saved the selection, and most importantly, what file format the graphic file was saved in (because only a few can save alpha channels), determines whether or not a graphic has an alpha channel. The file formats that remember alpha channels are TIFF, Photoshop, transparent GIF (GIF89a), and GIF's heir apparent, PNG.

Photoshop stores alpha channels in the Channels palette.

GIF89a (Transparent GIFs)

Transparent GIFs are rather simple. One of the colors in the GIF is designated as transparent, and when the GIF is displayed by a Web browser, any pixels of the transparent color show the Web page background underneath rather than the transparent color.

In versions of Photoshop before 4.0, you used the GIF89a export plug-in to create indexed color images and then export them as transparent GIFs, which let you choose the transparent color (see Figure 9.21).

The GIF89a plug-in enabled you to pick the color directly from the image and also showed you the palette of the image in the bottom of the window. As

Figure 9.21

Photoshop's GIF export plug-in, useful prior to version 4.0.

Chapter 9 Advanced Graphics

you picked colors, the plug-in replaced them with the transparent color and showed you which ones it is removing from the palette.

Although this is a great little plug-in, it still presented some problems. When Photoshop users would make a transparent GIF, they would usually create an image over a background that would hopefully not contain any colors from the image. Then using the plug-in, they would make the background color transparent so that the image would show up seamlessly on the Web page background. Easy, right?

Well, not if the color in the image's background is too different from the background of the Web page. Such mismatches create halos—traces of the background color that seem to crop up.

In the example, we placed an image that uses a dark background on the Web page (see Figure 9.22).

Figure 9.22

The halo dilemma.

Because we created an image with a lot of black, black couldn't be the background color. So we made the background white. The problem is anti-aliasing, which adds transitional gray colors between the black foreground and white background. When we went to export the image as a GIF and made the white background transparent, the light gray pixels created by anti-aliasing stand out clearly against the black background, and it's these pixels that create the "halo."

The workaround for this creates a background color that is almost the same color as the background of the Web page, yet different from any of the image's colors.

1. First, fill the image with black by choosing Edit➧Fill. Set Contents to Black and Opacity to 100%.

> **TIP**
>
> To make the background of your page black, be sure to add the BGCOLOR parameter to the page's <BODY➡ tag, like so: <BODY BGCOLOR = #FFFFFF➡. (See Chapter 3 for more information about background colors.)

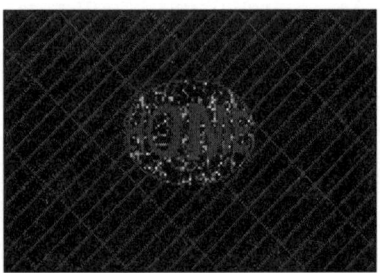

Figure 9.23

Using a similar colored background to solve the halo dilemma.

> **TIP**
>
> You don't need the GIF89a Export plug-in to create transparent GIFs in Photoshop 4.0. All you need to do is make a selection around the image, and then save the selection, which makes the image a channel and places it in the Channels palette. Be forewarned that the alpha channel removes the unselected stuff from the image permanently, so don't try this trick with your only copy of an image.

2. Make the foreground color blue. In the Color Picker, choose the brightest blue possible. Select Edit➡Fill (Contents to Foreground Color and Opacity to 10%).

3. Switch to Indexed Color mode (Image➡Mode➡Indexed Color) and flatten the layers. When the Indexed Color dialog box appears, set the Palette to Adaptive, the Colors to 16, and the Dither to None.

4. Export the image by selecting File➡Export➡GIF89a Export). Choose the color you want to be transparent with the Eyedropper. In this example, we use the same Web page but with the new image (see Figure 9.23).

As you can see, no more halo problem. The image looks as if it fits on this background. But if you place this image on a white background, what would happen then? Exactly the same thing that happened when you used the white background on a dark Web page.

To use this technique in Photoshop 4.0, create an image, create an alpha channel, save it as a GIF, and see what it looks like on both white and black Web pages.

1. Create a new image (60×60 pixels, RGB Color mode, and Contents White).

2. Select the Type Mask tool. Create a new layer by choosing New Layer from the Layers palette and name it Icon.

3. Click anywhere in the image and the Type Tool dialog box appears, which enables you to enter the text, select the font, and select the size you want.

Chapter 9 Advanced Graphics

> **⚡ WARNING**
>
> You can save as many channels as you want with Photoshop, but if an image contains more than one extra channel, the GIF option is disabled in the Save dialog box. To save such an image as a GIF, remove the extraneous channels by dragging them into the Channel palette's trash can.

Select an icon or letter for the experiment. Make the font Wingdings and set the size to 60 pixels. Check the Bold and Anti-aliased checkboxes. In the text area, type in the character "[." Click OK (see Figure 9.24).

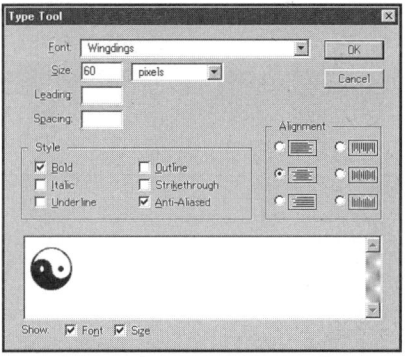

Figure 9.24

Selecting the proper text.

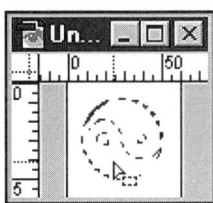

Figure 9.25

Centering the selection.

4. Keeping your mouse cursor over the selection, click and drag it so that it lays over the center of the image (see Figure 9.25).

5. Choose Edit➡Fill. Set the Contents to Black, the Opacity to 100%, and the Mode to Normal. Now switch to the Magic Wand tool (press W). Because this character isn't completely filled in (the white part of the icon is actually transparent), you need to fill in behind it so that it's a solid icon. Click the Wand outside of the icon to create a selection outside the icon. Choose Select➡Invert so that you have a selection of the icon.

6. Choose Select➡Modify➡Contract and contract the selection by 1 pixel. (Because the edges of the icon are already smooth and because you will be filling in some color behind it, you don't want to affect the outside of the icon—that's why you contract the selection.)

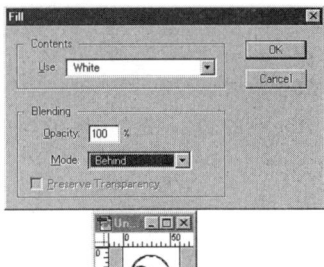

Figure 9.26

Filling in behind the layer.

7. Now fill in behind the icon with white. Choose Edit➥Fill. Set the Contents to White, the Opacity to 100%, and the Mode to Behind (see Figure 9.26). Make sure you are on the Icon layer, and not the Background.

8. Now choose Select➥None. Click the Background layer to activate it. Choose Edit➥Fill. Set Contents to Black and the Opacity to 100%. Click OK.

9. Now click the Icon layer. Load the layer selection by choosing Select➥Load Selection. Pick Icon Transparency for the Channel. Click OK. Save it as a new channel—this is the alpha channel. Choose Select➥Save Selection and set the Channel pull-down menu to New. Click OK. The layer is now the alpha channel or transparency channel.

10. Save the image as a Photoshop file so that you can edit it later. Now convert the image to Indexed Color mode. Click OK when asked to flatten the layers, and in the Indexed Color dialog box set the Palette to Adaptive, the Colors to 8, and the Dither to Diffusion.

11. Save the image as a GIF file. After you name it and click OK, a pop-up window asks if you want to save it as Interlaced or Normal. Interlaced means the image shows up as if it's fading in. Normal means the image shows up from top to bottom. Most graphic designers use Normal, but experiment and see which one you like better.

Figure 9.27

The icon on a white background.

Figure 9.28

The icon on a black background.

Let's take a look at it against a white and black Web page (see Figures 9.27 and 9.28).

As you can see, the black icon on the black background looks clearer than the white one. What does this tell us? That no matter how we create our transparent GIFs, using a similar color background produces more detailed and precise transparent GIFs.

Icons

Ahhh, those lovable icons; little pictures, animations, or bullets that capture your eye's attention. Icons can perform many functions on your Web pages, from being bullets in lists, company logos, titles, even visual anchors, but the most common function is that of a picture of a letter serving as the email anchor.

Figure 9.29 shows a Web page using several visual anchors.

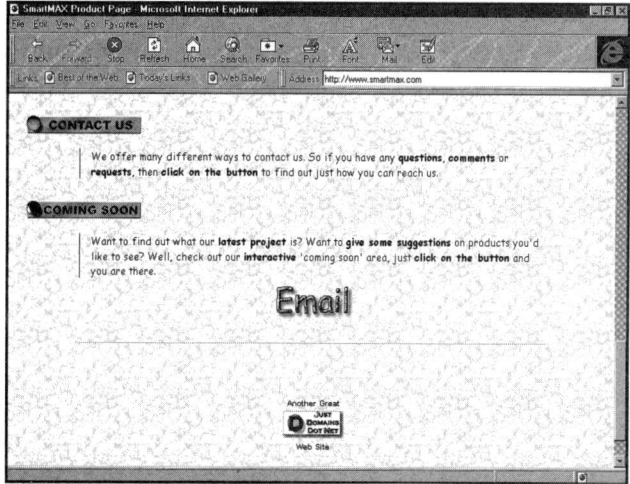

Figure 9.29

Icons as visual anchors.

There are four visual anchors in this example. Two icons lead to different sections of the site: Coming Soon and Contact Us. Also, there is an email icon that when clicked opens up any new email messages. The last icon is a link to the Web provider's site.

If this page was simply text created with the <FONT> tag, it would be very dull. Icons give a Web site more entertainment value, as well as providing an easier and clearer way of recognizing certain places or sections.

The Bullet Icon

1. Create a new image (80×80 pixels; RGB Color; white background). Use the Zoom tool (press Z and click) to zoom in to 200%.

2. Click the Marquee tool and hold it down until you can choose the elliptical Marquee tool. (When you first click the Marquee tool, it is rectangular. If you hold down the mouse button, a menu of four selection tools pops up—choose the circular one.) Hold down the Option-Shift (Mac) or Alt-Shift (PC) keys to create a perfect circle in the middle of the image (see Figure 9.30).

3. Select New Layer from the Layers palette menu and name it Shadow. Fill in the layer with black. Now make another new layer and name it Orange Ball. Fill this one with white.

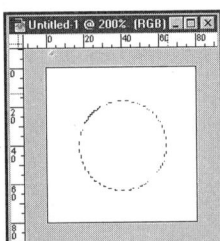

Figure 9.30

Creating a perfect circle selection.

4. Now you need to set up the colors for the orange. Select a bright orange background color. Then select a lighter orange for the foreground color.

5. To make the orange, double-click the Gradient tool to bring up the Gradient Tool Options palette.

In the Gradient Tool Options palette, select Foreground to Background from the Gradient pop-up menu and Radial from the Type pop-up menu. (Linear lets the gradient happen from one side of the image to the opposite side, whereas Radial lets the gradient happen from the center to the outer edge, creating a circular gradient.) You should now see the orange gradient beside the Edit box (see Figure 9.31). Click OK.

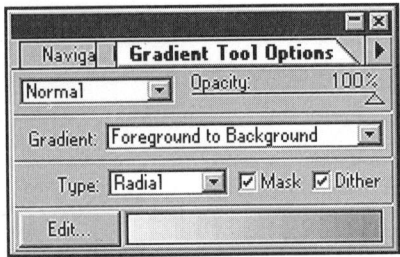

Figure 9.31

Setting up the gradient.

Chapter 9 **Advanced Graphics** | 193 |

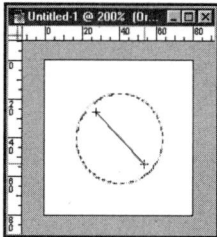

Figure 9.32

Dragging to make the gradient.

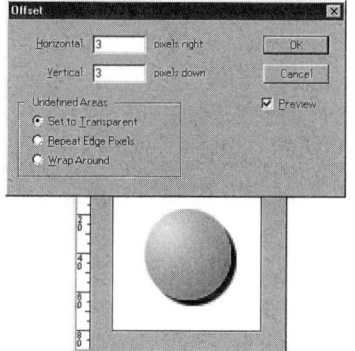

Figure 9.33

Offsetting the Shadow layer.

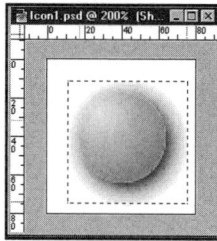

Figure 9.34

Creating a selection to crop.

6. Click and drag the image from the top-left corner down to the bottom-right corner of the circle, and release the mouse button (see Figure 9.32).

7. You should now have something that looks somewhat like an orange—with the light source hitting the top corner of the orange.

   To create the shadow, choose Select➥None and click the Shadow layer. To move the shadow, choose Filter➥Other➥Offset and set the Horizontal distance to 3 pixels, the Vertical distance to 3 pixels, and choose Set to Transparent for the Undefined Areas (see Figure 9.33).

8. This shadow still looks too hard to be realistic, so let's soften it up. Choose Filter➥Blur➥Gaussian Blur and set the Radius to 4.5 pixels.

9. Save this file as a Photoshop file before you alter it anymore.

10. Crop the image so that any extraneous white space is gone. Select the rectangular Marquee tool. Hold down the Shift key (to create a perfect square) and draw a selection around just enough of the orange ball and its shadow (see Figure 9.34).

11. Now choose Image➥Crop.

12. Choose Image➥Image Size. Set the Width to 20 pixels, the Height to 20 pixels, and the resampling method to Bicubic. Click OK.

13. Switch to Indexed Color mode and flatten the layers. Set the Palette to Adaptive, the Colors to 16, and the Dither to Diffusion.

14. Choose File→Export→GIF89a Export, and in the Export window, uncheck Interlace. Use the Magnifying glass in the GIF89a dialog box to zoom in. Then use the Eyedropper to select the white closest to the edge (see Figure 9.35).

15. Click OK and choose a name for the image.

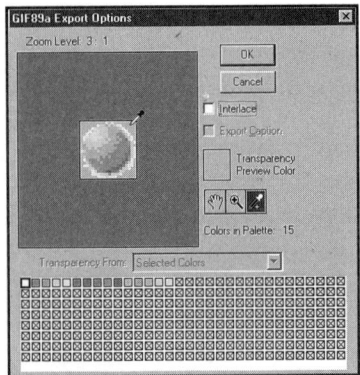

Figure 9.35
Picking the transparency color.

The great thing about this technique is that you can substitute other colors (in Step 4) for whatever you like. Just remember to have a bold color for the background and a much lighter color for the foreground. Here's what the bullets look like on a Web page (see Figure 9.36).

Sizing and Spacing

Two important considerations to remember with icons, or any images for that matter, are spacing and sizing.

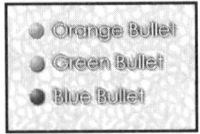

Figure 9.36
The bullets in action on a Web page.

For spacing, it's best to be objective—you don't want to clump your images, yet at the same time, the perfect spacing is really what's pleasing to the eye. There are two attributes with the <IMG> tag that you learned about earlier—the VSPACE and HSPACE attributes. Use them whenever you need a little more space either beside or above your image, but base your spacing on what you find pleasing and organized. Constantly refer to your Web page to see how the spacing looks.

Chapter 9 Advanced Graphics

For sizing, smaller is better. Icons should be large enough to see, yet small enough that they load *quickly*. When you create your icons, start with a large image or canvas, then resize your image; after you're done, you need to remember a couple of things. If you are working with a large canvas, all the effects you use, such as shadowing, glowing, or textures, need to be much larger because when you resize the image, a lot of the detail and definition is lost. So remember, if your image is larger, your effects should be too.

Graphical Text, Tables, and Lists

Getting good at using HTML text, tables, and lists is important, but sometimes that doesn't always produce the WOW! reaction from people who visit your site. One way to get greater impact is to use type-based images instead of HTML-specified text.

Using Graphical Text

Although the <FONT> tag can produce some nice effects, it is limited. Not only does the text look very bland, but choosing typefaces for the fonts can prove pointless if the user doesn't have them on her computer. So what do you do?

Create important text in Photoshop or a similar program and then save it as a transparent GIF.

Important text consists of titles, subjects, or links to other areas. This section teaches you how to put basic text onscreen, as well as some advanced tricks to produce some very cool effects.

Let's start with the basic text.

1. Create a new file (400×200 pixels, RGB Color Mode, and Background White).

2. Choose the Type Mask tool from the Toolbox. Create a new layer and name it White text.

3. Click the image, and the Type Tool dialog box appears. Choose a font that you can play with (this example uses Funhouse—with the words "Graphic Text" split so that Graphic is on one line, and Text is on the next). Then we set the type at 60 pixels (this may be

> **TIP**
>
> The best way to master duplicating and moving layers is in the Layers palette. The layers from top to bottom are laid out in order of appearance—the top layer is in front of all the layers, and the layers that fall below it are behind the layer above. There are three icons at the bottom of the palette (see Figure 9.38).
>
> ► Add Layer Mask—Creates a mask on the current layer.
>
> ► Create New Layer—Doubles as the Copy Layer button.
>
> ► Delete Layer—Works when you drop the layer onto it or select the layer and click the Delete Layer button.

different for your font, but experiment until the words fill in the middle of the image) and the Leading (which is the space between each text row) to 60 (see Figure 9.37).

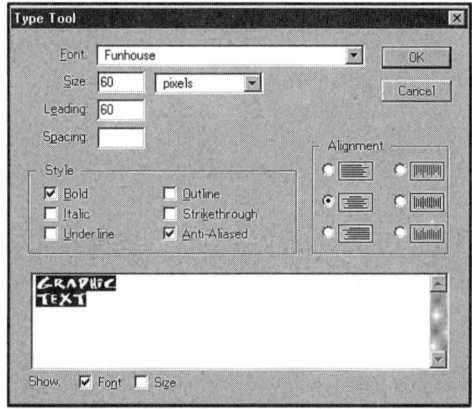

Figure 9.37

Making some text.

4. Choose Edit➥Fill and set Contents to White, Opacity to 100%, and Mode to Normal. Then duplicate the layer by choosing Layer➥Duplicate Layer. Name the new layer Black text and choose Image➥Adjust➥Invert. Then choose Select➥None.

5. Move the White text layer to the front by moving it above the Black text layer (see Figure 9.39). Move the layers by clicking and dragging them either up the layer list (which brings the layer forward) or down (which sends the layer back).

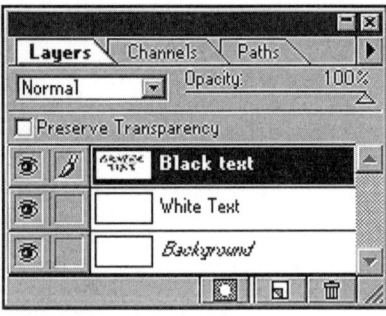

Figure 9.38

The Layers palette.

Chapter 9 Advanced Graphics

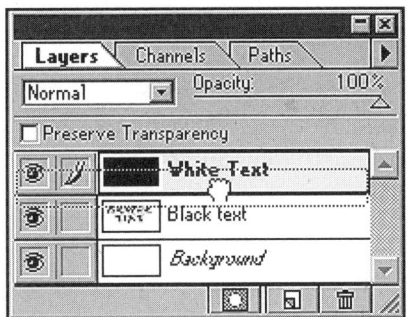

Figure 9.39
Moving layers.

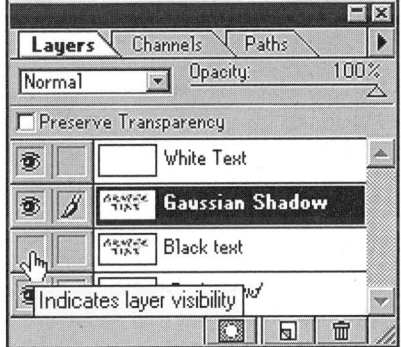

Figure 9.40
Making the "Black text" layer invisible.

> **Note**
> The Eye icon is either on or off. If the Eye icon is visible (on), then the layer is visible; if the icon is does not appear, then the layer is invisible. It's also important to remember that the layer you are working on must be selected in the Layers palette to be active. If you can't make any changes to a layer, this might be your problem—always click the layer you are working on.

6. Click and drag the Black text layer to the Create New Layer icon. Double-click the new layer and name it Gaussian shadow. To make the Black text layer invisible, click the Black text layer's Eye icon (see Figure 9.40).

7. One of the first effects you learn is the drop shadow effect. Here's what the image looks like after rearranging the layers (see Figure 9.41).

As you can see, the text isn't visible at all...the window is completely white. Make a shadow so that you can see the text. Click the Gaussian shadow layer and make sure there is nothing selected (Select➥None). Choose Filter➥Other➥Offset (Horizontal 2, Vertical 2, and choose Set to Transparent for the Undefined Areas). Now look at the image (see Figure 9.42).

Figure 9.41
The unaltered image.

Figure 9.42
Offsetting the shadow layer.

Figure 9.43

The Gaussian shadow gives the text visibility and depth.

Figure 9.44

Copying, moving, and making layers invisible.

Figure 9.45

The Motion shadow effect. The key word is "funky."

10. Although the text is more visible, it still doesn't have much depth. Give it some depth by choosing Filter➥Blur➥Gaussian Blur and set the Radius to 3.5 pixels. Now the image has a lot of depth—from 2D to 3D in one filter (see Figure 9.43).

    This effect is called a drop shadow. In fact, without using the Gaussian Blur, it was still a drop shadow, just not a very good one. You'll find that the Blur filters create a lot of neat effects.

11. Now let's try the Motion Blur effect. First, you need to copy the Black text layer again and name the copied layer Motion shadow. Set the Gaussian shadow layer to invisible (see Figure 9.44).

12. Now that you've created another new layer and you are just dying for another effect, go up to Filter➥Blur➥Motion Blur and set the Angle to −45 and the Distance to 30. As you can see, the effect is somewhat funky. It has stretched the shadow across a 45 degree angle, creating a rather tall shadowing effect (see Figure 9.45).

 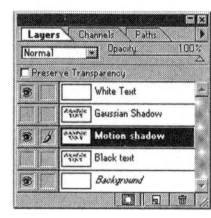

13. The last effect in the shadow category is the Radial or zoom shadow effect. Once again, copy the Black text layer and name the new layer Radial shadow. Make sure this layer is below the Motion shadow layer and make the Motion shadow layer invisible.

14. Now choose Filter➡Blur➡Radial Blur Set the Amount to 50, the Blur Method to Zoom, and the Quality to Best. This creates an almost curved background effect, where the outer part of the background is lower than the middle (see Figure 9.46).

Figure 9.46

The Radial shadow creates a curved background effect.

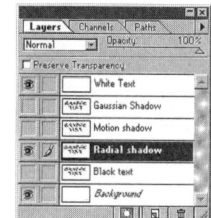

Beveled Text

Let's move on to a different type of effect—the beveled text effect. Although we touch on this later in the Photoshop Techniques section, some of the steps are unique to this text effect—achieving a colorful 3D text effect.

1. First, you need to copy the White text layer and name this new layer Beveled text. Make sure it's at the top of the layer list and make the White text and Radial Shadow layers invisible.

2. Make sure nothing is selected (Select➡None) and choose Filter➡Render➡Lighting Effects. Now change the Light Type to Directional and make sure it is turned on. Set the Intensity to 23, the Gloss and Material to 15, the Exposure and Ambience to 0", and the Texture Channel to Beveled Text Transparency. Make sure the White is high checkbox is checked and the Height is 20. Now align your light from the top-left corner of the image to the middle. Click Save and name the new effect bevel. Check all of these settings against Figure 9.47 and then click OK.

Figure 9.47

Creating a bevel.

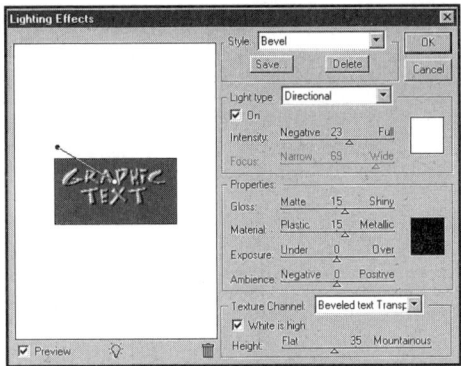

3. Once again, copy the White text layer and name the new layer Colored text. Move it to the top of the layers list and remember to keep the Beveled text layer visible (the Eye is on). Click the Colored text layer (make sure it is the active layer) and select the layer by choosing Select➤ Load Selection. Set the Channel to Colored Text Transparency.

   Now select a bright foreground and background color—we chose blue and red, respectively. Double-click the Gradient tool. In the Gradient Tool Options palette, select Foreground to Background from the Gradient pop-up menu and the Type pop-up menu to Linear (see Figure 9.48).

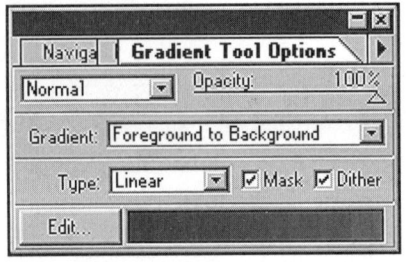

Figure 9.48

Setting up the gradient.

4. Drag a gradient across from the top of the selection to the bottom (see Figure 9.49).

Figure 9.49

Making the gradient.

Chapter 9 **Advanced Graphics** 201

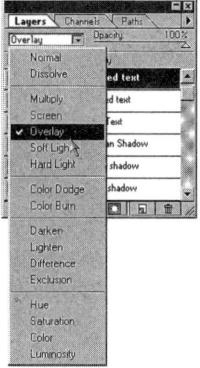

Figure 9.50

Changing the layer's transparency.

5. Choose Select➡None. Click the Blending Modes pop-up menu in the Layers palette and select Overlay (see Figure 9.50). This enables the colors of the layer to show through, but it blends in the layers below it—in this case, letting the bevel effect show through.

6. Add a little Gaussian shadow by making the Gaussian shadow layer visible. Let's have a look at the final effect (see Figure 9.51).

Figure 9.51

The completed 3D beveled effect with color added.

The great thing about this technique is that you can change the color of the entire effect by changing the color of the Colored text layer.

Let's take a look at a Web page with all of the images as transparent GIFs (see Figure 9.52).

Figure 9.52

All of the text effects.

You probably recognize most of the effects we discussed, except the one on the bottom right. Just for fun, try and reproduce this effect with the techniques you've learned

Using Graphical Tables and Borders Instead of Tags

This effect is seldom used well, but when it is, it can look amazing. Basically, all you are doing is taking an image with a lot of empty space in the middle, slicing up the image, and reassembling it as pieces in a table. This enables you to create an area in the middle of this image where you can place HTML text or other images—it becomes a frame for whatever you want to place inside it.

For this example, we're going to create an area that looks as if it's above its background.

1. Create a new blank white image (200×270 pixels, Background White, Color Mode RGB).

2. Using the Lasso tool (press L), draw a jagged square on the inside of the image about 5 pixels from the edge (this is the hardest part because you will need to keep the mouse button down while drawing the selection). This may take a few attempts because you want to keep a somewhat square shape, and you have to do this in one motion. Take your time and draw slowly (see Figure 9.53).

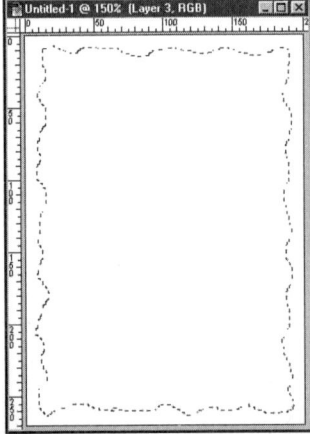

Figure 9.53

Drawing a jagged square using the Lasso tool.

3. Create a new layer by either clicking the Create New Layer button in the Layers palette, or by choosing Layer➡New➡Layer. Name this new layer White. Now fill this layer with 100% white. Copy the White layer (Layer➡Duplicate) and name the new layer Black. Choose Select➡None and choose Image➡Adjust➡Invert. Now the layer is black.

4. Now move the White layer to the top of the layer list and click the Black layer to make it the active layer. Choose Filter➡Other➡Offset Horizontal 2 pixels, Vertical 2 pixels, and choose Set to Transparent for Undefined Areas. This will move the Black layer, preparing it for the shadow effect (see Figure 9.54).

Figure 9.54

Offsetting the black layer.

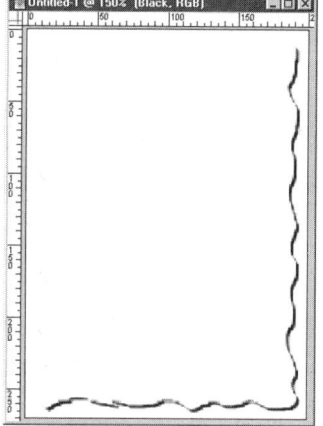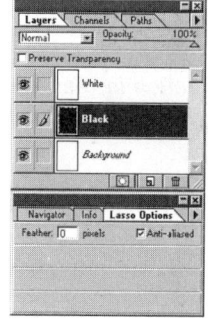

5. Choose Filter➡Blur➡Gaussian Blur and set the Radius to 3.5 pixels. Click OK.

6. Save the transparency selections for both layers as a new channel by clicking the White layer and then choosing Select➡Load Selection, and click OK. Do the same for the Black layer, but set the Operation to Add to selection, choose Select➡Save Selection, and click OK. Choose Select➡None.

7. Set up the grid so that you can cut up the image. Under File→Preferences→Guides & Grid, make sure the Gridline is set to 5 pixels, with 1 subsection. Create a new layer and name the new layer Blank Space. Move it to the top of the list.

8. Choose View→Show Grid and make sure the Snap To Grid option in the View menu is checked. Choose the rectangular Marquee tool (press M) and draw a rectangle on the inside of the square, using up as much space as possible but without any of the lines crossing any part of the image, not even a pixel (see Figure 9.55).

9. Now fill it with 100% black. Jot down how big this selection is for later use. Look at the Info palette and jot down the size of the selection—165×240 in the example (see Figure 9.56).

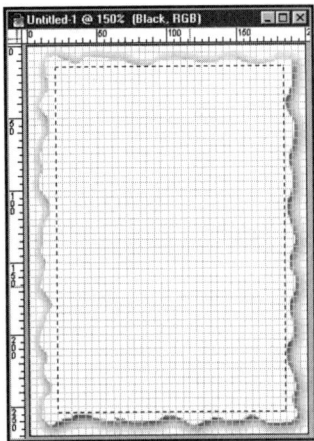

Figure 9.55

The selection in the middle of the image becomes the blank space in the table.

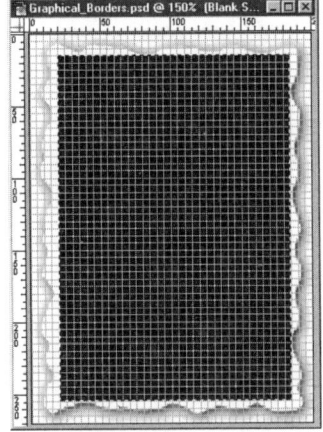
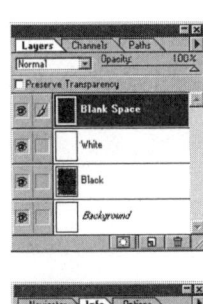
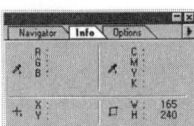

Figure 9.56

Keep a record of how big this selection is (bottom-right corner).

10. Save this image as a Photoshop file.

11. Copy the image so that you can cut it up. Choose Image→Duplicate, but make sure Merged Layers is unchecked. On the newly created image, draw

Chapter 9 **Advanced Graphics** 205

a rectangle around the top part of the image, but stop before you cross over into the black rectangle (see Figure 9.57).

Figure 9.57

Getting the top selection ready for cutting.

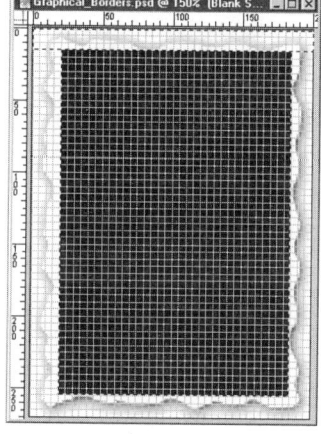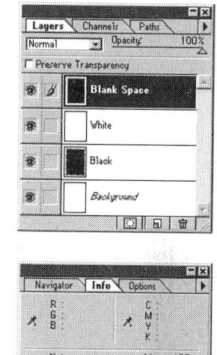

12. Jot down this selection size, shown in the Info palette, and name it "The top piece." Set the Blank Space layer to invisible and choose Image➡Crop. Now you can turn off the grid (View➡Hide Grid) and convert the image to indexed color. In the Indexed Color dialog box, set the Palette to Adaptive, the Colors to 8, and the Dither to Diffusion. Save this as a CompuServe GIF, name it "gbtop.gif," and close the window.

13. Now you need to cut up the left side of the frame. Go back to the original image and duplicate it again, making sure Merged Layers is unchecked. This time, on the duplicate image (with the grid on) draw a rectangle on the left side of the rectangle, starting where the rectangle starts at the top, and ending where it stops on the bottom (see Figure 9.58).

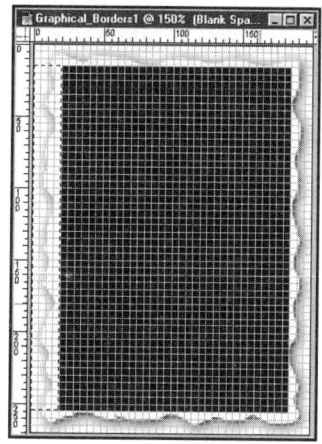

Figure 9.58

Getting the side selection ready for cutting.

14. Now repeat Step 12, except change the name of the selection size—call it "The left side piece." The file name should be "gblside.gif" (for Graphics Border Left Side).

15. The right side is done exactly the same as the left side. Repeat Step 13, but do the same on the right side.

16. Now repeat Step 12, except change the name of the selection size—call it "The right side piece." The file name should be called "gbrside.gif" (for Graphics Border Right Side).

17. Now you need to do the bottom. Repeating Step 13, draw your selection at the bottom.

18. Repeat Step 12, except change the name of the selection size—call it "The bottom piece." The file name should be called "gbbottom.gif" (for Graphics Border Bottom).

The HTML Document

Now you should have four images and five selection sizes.

The images should be "gbtop.gif," "gblside.gif," "gbrside.gif," and "gbbottom.gif." The selection names you should have are "The blank space," "The top piece," "The left side piece," "The right side piece," and "The bottom piece."

Now you need to create a table based on the same size as the original image. Placing that information in the <TABLE> tag will mess up Netscape Navigator and the way it views the table, so the best way for the table to lay out is to include all width and height dimensions in the data cells. The <TABLE> tag should look like this:

```
<TABLE  CELLPADDING="0"  CELLSPACING="0"  BORDER="0">
```

Notice how the cellpadding, cellspacing, and border are set to 0; you don't want anything between your images.

To create the "The top piece," you need the numbers you jotted down for its selection size. Those numbers will be the width and height of the data cell and the image size. Also, you need to remember that this first row in the table will span three rows: the left side, the blank space, and the right side. Here's what the first data cell looks like:

```
<TD WIDTH="200" HEIGHT="15" ROWSPAN="3"><IMG SRC="images/gbtop.gif" WIDTH="200" HEIGHT="15"></TD>
```

Now you want to create the next row and add the next three data cells. The next data cell is the left side, so you need the numbers from the sheet for "The left side" numbers, then the "Blank Space" numbers, and finally, the "The right side" numbers. The next line should look like this:

```
<TR><TD WIDTH="20" HEIGHT="240"><IMG SRC="images/gblside.gif" WIDTH="20" HEIGHT="240"></TD><TD WIDTH="165" HEIGHT="240"> </TD><TD WIDTH="15" HEIGHT="240"><IMG SRC="images/gbrside.gif" WIDTH="15" HEIGHT="240"></TD>
```

Although this looks a little confusing, Navigator will add a tiny bit of space between the table cells if we add carriage returns between the tags. Let's look at each tag.

`<TR>` is the new row.

`<TD WIDTH="20" HEIGHT="240"><IMG SRC="images/gblside.gif" WIDTH="20" HEIGHT="240"></TD>` is the left side data cell.

`<TD WIDTH="165" HEIGHT="240"> </TD>` is the blank space data cell; this is where you will add any and all information into the middle of the frame.

`<TD WIDTH="15" HEIGHT="240"><IMG SRC="images/gbrside.gif" WIDTH="15" HEIGHT="240"></TD>` is the right side data cell.

The next row will look like the top row:

```
<TR><TD WIDTH="200" HEIGHT="15" ROWSPAN="3"><IMG SRC="images/gbbottom.gif" WIDTH="200" HEIGHT="15"></TD>
```

The only difference is the image name used, and a row is added at the beginning. Now all you need to do is finish the table with the `</TABLE>` tag and look at it (with some information added to the blank cell) in a suitable setting. Rocco's Radios (our example site) happens to use this technique (see Figure 9.59).

Figure 9.59

The effect in action.

Experiment with this technique to come up with some amazing ideas. Try doing this with an image of a television or a watch, or placing information in the middle of a picture frame.

Spacing with Transparent GIFs

Sometimes text doesn't space exactly where you want, or you'll find that you've been adding so many <BR> lines for spacing that it has become impossible to read the code. Or you may just get finicky with the spacing and want to space things ever so slightly. So what's the best way to space things, besides creating tables? By creating a small 1 pixel transparent GIF and using it in conjunction with VSPACE, HSPACE, WIDTH, and HEIGHT to create invisible spaces on your page. This enables you to space even the smallest pieces of text and images—just the way you want.

1. First, you need to create the GIF. In Photoshop, create a new 1 pixel by 1 pixel image. Make it an RGB image with a White background.

2. Choose Select➡All and then Select➡Save Selection. Click OK. Switch to Indexed Color mode and click OK.

3. Now save the image as a CompuServe GIF. Give it a short name—this example is called t.gif (see Figure 9.60).

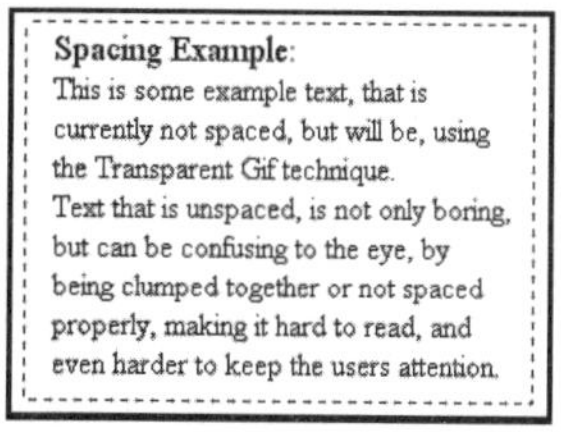

Chapter 9 Advanced Graphics

Figure 9.60

Some sample text without any spacing.

In Figure 9.60 you can see some text that obviously uses <BR> tags, but nothing else. The code looks like this:

```
<TABLE><TD WIDTH="250">
<FONT SIZE="4">Spacing Example:</FONT><BR>
This is some example text, that is currently not
spaced, but will be, using the Transparent Gif
technique.<BR>
Text that is unspaced, is not only boring, but can be
confusing to the eye, by being clumped together or not
spaced properly, making it hard to read, and even
harder to keep the users attention.
</TD></TABLE>
```

Using the <FONT> tag, the first line ("Spacing Example:") is bigger than the rest. Then a new line is created with the <BR> tag. Another line break was added one sentence down. Other than that, there's not really any spacing. It doesn't look bad, but it could look better.

Space the first line by adding a space character between each letter. Because no browser supports more than one space character in normal text, use the transparent GIF at the space between the two words—Spacing and Example. The <IMG> tag is used in conjunction with the HSPACE attribute so that you can set how much blank space it will keep on either side of it.

The code for the first line should now look like this:

```
<FONT SIZE="4">S p a c i n g<IMG SRC="images/t.gif"
HSPACE="6">E x a m p l e :</FONT><BR>
```

Then for a break between the first line and the sentences, use the transparent GIF again to create a vertical space. Use the VSPACE attribute this time. You'll need to add a <BR> after the image so that the following text or information will start on the next line.

The next line should read:

```
<IMG SRC="images/t.gif" VSPACE="6"><BR>
```

Add a small space in front of the first words in each of the sentence lines so that it creates an indented book style look. You need to use the HSPACE attribute with the image. To make the first letter stand out, increase its size with the <FONT> tag. The next line should look like this:

```
<IMG SRC="images/t.gif" HSPACE="10"><FONT SIZE="5">
T</FONT>his is some example text, that is currently not
spaced, but will be, using the Transparent Gif
technique.<BR>
```

Use another transparent GIF to create another vertical space—this time, between the two paragraphs. Because it's between the paragraphs you can make the space a little smaller than the last one. The line should read:

```
<IMG SRC="images/t.gif" VSPACE="4"><BR>
```

Once again, you'll create a lead space for the next paragraph, and you'll increase size of the first letters.

The last line should look like this:

```
<IMG SRC="images/t.gif" HSPACE="10"><FONT SIZE="5">
T</FONT>ext that is unspaced, is not only boring, but
can be confusing to the eye, by being clumped together
or not spaced properly, making it hard to read, and
even harder to keep the users attention.
```

If you place this in the table, on the Web page, the text will look like this (see Figure 9.61).

Figure 9.61

Same text, with spacing and font changes.

Adobe Photoshop Techniques

With all the great graphic techniques on computers comes the obvious question: What software program was used? In the case of this book, it was Adobe's Photoshop version 4.0; the most amazing graphics tool a Web designer can use, in our opinion.

Not only are there numerous plug-ins (helper programs) that you can purchase, but the number of books, online support, and users out there using this program are massive. Remember, popularity wins. And around here, that's Photoshop. So fire up that software, and let's get you up to speed on some basic Photoshop 4.0 graphic techniques.

Working with Actions

One of the most useful functions included with Photoshop 4.0 are the actions.

Actions are recorded events that can be played back. Almost everything you do in Photoshop, aside from anything using the drawing tools, can be recorded and played back at a later time. Some of your more painful repetitive procedures, such as shading, indexing colors, resizing, and copying can all be automated.

To see or use the actions, you'll need to open the Actions palette by choosing Window➜Show Actions (see Figure 9.62).

How to Use Actions

Actions have two modes: the Default mode, which enables you edit the actions as well as run them, and the Button mode, which enables you to color code your actions and run them with one click. To access the Button mode, use the Actions palette menu. It's a small arrow on the right side of the panel; when you click it, a menu pops up (see Figure 9.63).

> **Note**
>
> There are only a couple of rules you need to remember when using this technique. First, when you use HSPACE and VSPACE, the space being used is double +1 of whatever you type. That means, HSPACE="5" is actually 11 pixels of space. Why? Because HSPACE and VSPACE put that number of pixels on either side of the image. In this case, the image is 1 pixel, with 5 pixels on the left of the image and 5 pixels on the right—this makes 11 pixels. If you ever need to create a space that *must* be even, use the WIDTH and HEIGHT attributes.
>
> The other rule to remember is that if information (text/image) falls after the transparent GIF, it should be placed right after the image, not on the next line. If you want to create a vertical space, you should always use the <BR> tag after your GIF.

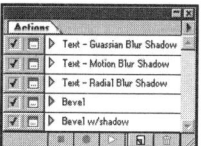

Figure 9.62

The Actions palette.

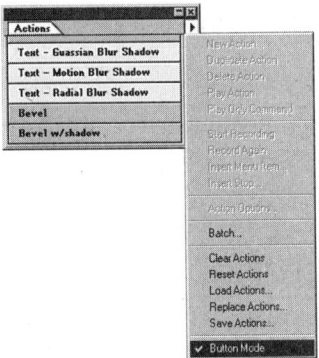

Figure 9.63

The Actions palette menu.

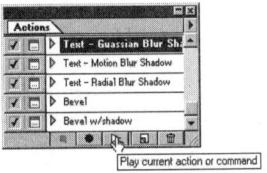

Figure 9.64

Playing an action.

Not only does this figure show you what the Actions palette menu looks like, but this is also what the Button mode looks like. And as you can see, some of the actions have been color coded. Yellow is used for your text effects and Blue is used for beveling (these are some of the actions included on the CD-ROM).

Using an action in Button mode is simple—just click the appropriate button. If it is not in Button mode, highlight the action you want to use by clicking it, and then press the Play button (see Figure 9.64).

Before you start using the actions, load the ones you'll be using off the CD-ROM. Look for the actions in the proper folder (look for the Photoshop folder, then the Actions folder) on the CD-ROM. Choose an action file; in this example, we've chosen the "textbev.atn" (text and beveling actions). This will load and append the actions onto your current ones.

If you scroll down, you'll see the new actions added to the bottom of the actions list. (If you want to start off fresh with the loaded actions, save your current ones and select Clear Actions from the Actions palette pop-up menu, then load in the new actions.)

Let's try one of the actions.

1. First, create a new image (400×150 pixels, RGB Color mode, and Contents White).

2. Choose Button Mode from the Actions palette again to turn off Button Mode. Click the action to see what it says. Highlight the Text—Gaussian shadow action and click Play. A dialog box appears; it asks you to create a selection on the background layer. Make sure the background is white and no other layers are created (see Figure 9.65).

Chapter 9 Advanced Graphics 213

Figure 9.65

Message window.

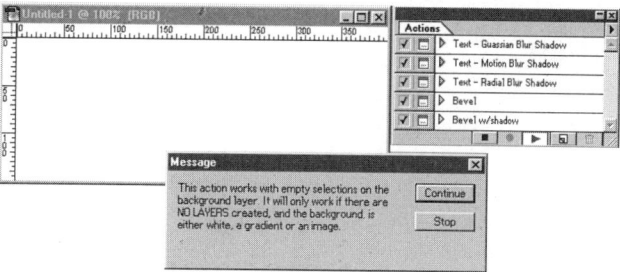

3. You have a white background and no other layers were created, but you haven't made a selection. Using the Type Mask tool, enter some text. Your text should look like the text in Figure 9.66. Note the only layer is Background and the text mask is selected.

Figure 9.66

The selection.

4. Then highlight the action again and click Play. This time when the message pops up, click Continue. You should see the completed effect in a few seconds (see Figure 9.67).

Using actions is quite simple, but there are often rules to using them. The last example required you to make a selection on a blank layer—that's easy. But some actions will require more instructions. All of the actions included on the CD-ROM have message windows explaining exactly what you'll need to do.

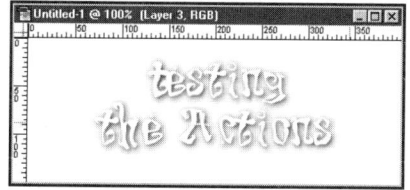

Figure 9.67

The completed action.

> **Note**
>
> None of the drawing actions are recorded. They are user related actions, which require you to design or draw something. The only actions that are recordable are linear actions, or ones that have specific options or variables associated with them, such as copying, indexing, making new layers, copying layers, loading selections, and so on.

How to Record, Edit, and Copy Actions

The recording process is simple. From the Actions palette menu, select New Action and give it a name (now or later). Then choose Record. Now all of your actions will be recorded.

When you've stopped recording your actions, click the Stop button (see Figure 9.68).

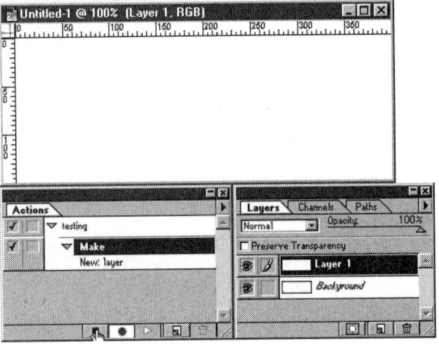

Figure 9.68

Finished recording.

To edit these commands (the actions within the action), open the specific action you want to edit, find the command, and double-click it. (This activates the command—you cannot edit a command without activating it.) To open an action that is ready for editing, click the little arrow beside the name of the action (see Figures 9.69 and 9.70).

Double-click the command you want to edit. This example only has one command, Make—New: layer, but most actions include many commands.

Notice at the bottom of the Actions palette there are five icons: Stop, Record, Play, Create/Copy an action or command, and Delete action/command.

To copy a command or action, drag it from the list to the Copy icon—the same goes for deleting.

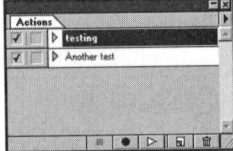

Figure 9.69

The closed action.

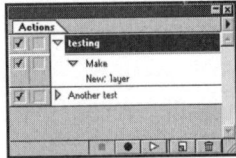

Figure 9.70

The open action (ready for editing).

Chapter 9 Advanced Graphics

> **Note**
> If you need help with actions, there is some online help that goes into detail, or you can really get advanced and pick up the *Photoshop Complete* book from Hayden Books. (If you're into graphic design, this book is highly recommended. It's the perfect companion for this book.)

To move an action or a command around in the list, drag it up or down the list, and let it go where you want.

Working with Layers

Layers are the most powerful tool Photoshop has to offer. They enable you to create masks or selections, place them on their own layers, and make them as transparent as you want. You can also control what mode the layer is in, such as only letting the luminosity through, and not the color.

To understand layers, let's take a look at the Layers palette (see Figure 9.71).

At the top of the palette, there is a drop-down menu on the left—this is the Blending Modes pop-up menu. To the right of it is the Opacity slider; this controls how transparent the layer is—it can range from 1% to 100%.

Below is the Preserve Transparency checkbox, which if checked, maintains the transparency (or non-transparency) of the layer no matter what you do; it's almost always unchecked.

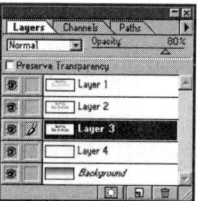

Figure 9.71

The Layers palette.

Below the Preserve Transparency checkbox are the actual layers. Each layer name has four parts to it. On the far left is the Eye icon; beside that is the Paintbrush icon; if this icon appears beside a layer, then that is the active layer. That means anything you do affects this layer. To the right of the Paintbrush icon is the thumbnail, a tiny picture representation of the layer's image. To the right of the thumbnail is the layer name.

Below the layers are the Add Layer Mask, the Create New Layer, and the Delete Current Layer icons.

The Layers palette works a lot like the Actions palette. To move layers around you can click and drag them up and down the list. Where the layers are placed is important—the layer at the top is the most visible or closest layer, and the layer at the bottom (usually the background) is the least visible or farthest back.

You can also move layers up and down by choosing Layer➥Arrange➥Bring Forward and Layer➥Arrange➥Send Backward, respectively.

Layers are deleted when clicked and dragged to the Trash Can, and layers are copied when they are clicked and dragged on the Create New Layer icon.

Using the Opacity slider on layers is very important. If you created a drop shadow that you felt was too dark, and it was on its own layer, you could use the Opacity slider to lower its opacity so that it's not so dark.

You can also use the Blending Mode menu to create transitions or blends. You used the Blending Mode menu when you created the bevel. You had a gray bevel and a colored layer of text. The text was placed above the bevel and the mode was set to Overlay so that the color mixed with the bevel of the next level. Here's what each layer looked like before the mode was changed (see Figures 9.72 and 9.73).

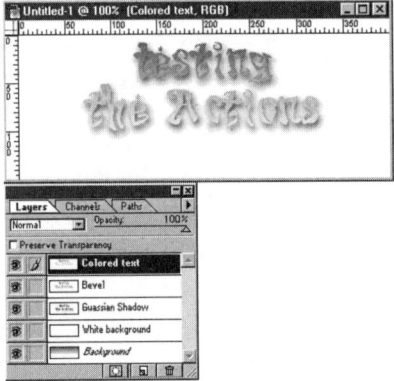

Figure 9.72

Colored text layer in Normal mode.

Chapter 9 Advanced Graphics

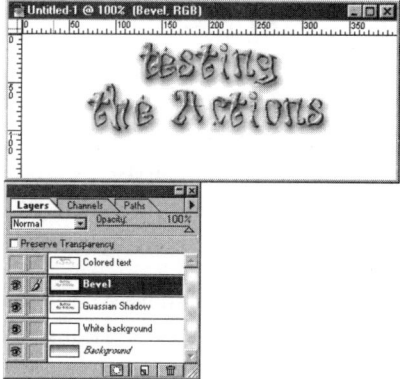

Figure 9.73

Bevel layer.

And now the blending mode on the colored text layer is changed to Overlay (see Figure 9.74).

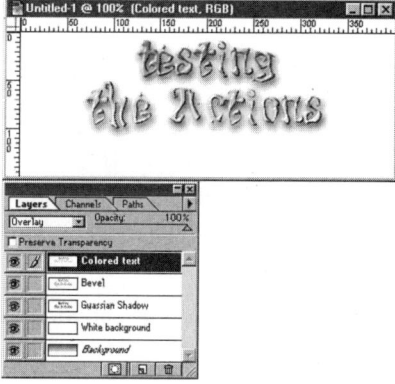

Figure 9.74

Colored text in the Overlay mode, which lets the colors blend with the Bevel.

This is the kind of control that layers enable.

To master these techniques, don't forget to read your Photoshop manual. You may also consider picking up some Photoshop books, such as *Photoshop Studio Skills* because these books not only deal with graphic design techniques, but also the understanding of each and every command in Photoshop.

Shadowing Effects

All shadow effects that we've used are based on drop shadowing, or creating a shadow below the image. Shadowing on the object itself is closer to shading and requires a very artistic touch. Although shading requires more talent, anyone can learn the shadowing techniques we use.

The best way to achieve a drop shadow is to have an image that is on a layer. That means that the background is not part of the image. It's either a photo image, an icon, or some text, but with no extraneous information around it. This is the best way to deal with layers and shadowing.

All of the techniques we have discussed place everything on their own layer(s). This is a practice you should get in to.

1. To give a layer its shadow, load its selection (select the layer, choose Layer➥Load Selection, and click OK). Now click the layer below the one you are working with (if there is only one layer, then click the background layer) and create a new layer. Name the new layer Shadow Base.

2. Choose Edit➥Fill with Black and the opacity at 100% in Normal mode. Now you can create a drop shadow with just a black layer, but you need to offset the shadow layer. Choose Filter➥Offset to set the undefined areas to transparent.

3. Play around with the Horizontal and Vertical pixel amounts and see what happens to the image. (It will preview automatically in the image.) Try –2 horizontal and 2 vertical; this moves the shadow layer to the left and down whereas setting horizontal and vertical to 2 moves the shadow layer to the right and down. Keep this setting and click OK (see Figure 9.75).

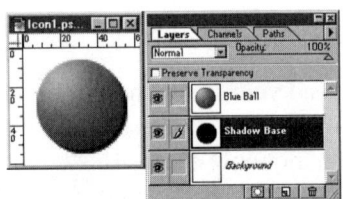

Figure 9.75

Creating the shadow base.

Chapter 9 Advanced Graphics

If you leave the shadow as is, it's not a bad effect. In fact, if you find the shadow is too dark and you need a more subtle shadow, move the Opacity slider down on the Layers palette. But you may find that this shadow is too hard edged, not subtle like real shadows. Well, all good shadows are created by blurring their edges.

There are three blur effects you can use: Gaussian, Motion, and Radial. The one you'll use the most is Gaussian Blur, simply because it is a clean blur.

Let's try the other two first, starting with Motion Blur.

1. Copy your shadow layer and name it Motion Blur shadow. Then make the Shadow Base layer invisible.

2. Choose Filter➡Blur➡Motion Blur and set the Angle to –45 and the Distance to 20. This creates an effect of smearing the shadow in one direction as shown in Figure 9.76.

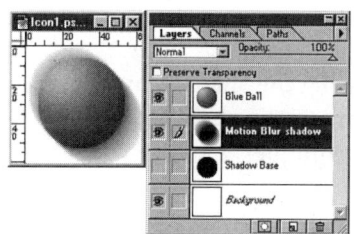

Figure 9.76

Motion Blur shadow.

Now we can make a Radial Blur shadow.

1. Copy the Shadow Base layer again and name it Radial Blur shadow. Make the Shadow Base and Motion Blur layers invisible.

2. Highlight the Radial Blur shadow layer and choose Filter➡Radial Blur. Set the Amount to 60, the Method to Zoom, and the Quality to Best. This blur smears the shadow from the middle to the outside, as shown in Figure 9.77.

The final blur we want to try is the most effective and the most used. Gaussian Blur effectively smears the pixels any amount you set and does it cleanly, creating the most accurate blur.

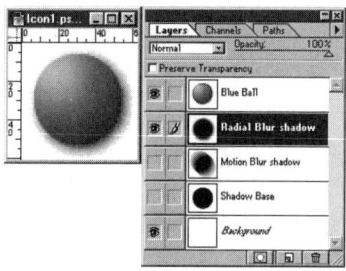

Figure 9.77

Radial Blur shadow.

1. Copy the shadow base layer again and name the new layer Gaussian Blur shadow. Make the other shadow layers invisible.

2. Highlight the Gaussian Blur shadow layer and choose Filter➥Blur➥Gaussian Blur. Set the Radius to 1.5 pixels (see Figure 9.78).

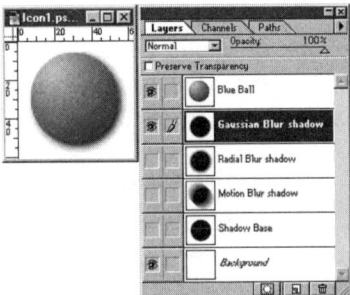

Figure 9.78

Gaussian Blur shadow.

As you can see, this is a subtle, yet effective blur that creates a more realistic shadow than the others.

What you set the radius of the blur to, how big the shadow layer is, and what side you make your offset can all dramatically change your shadow effect, so experiment with these techniques.

Resizing and Reducing the Palette

The most important thing to remember when working with images on the Web is to keep your images small. We don't just mean image size, but also image color depth. The process of changing an image's size is called resizing, and the process of changing an image's color depth is called changing the bit depth, or reducing the palette.

Resizing

When you are working on image effects in Photoshop, you almost always create a larger image than what you will use. This will help you make small adjustments to the image, and the image will retain a greater amount of detail, even after it has been sized down.

When the image is larger, any effects or alterations need to be larger also, or they will be missed when it's sized down. Also, if you need to make an image that is exactly a certain pixel size, then create a new image. Make it the exact size you need, then resize it with the Image➡ Image Size option. Change the width and height from pixels to percentages, and then set the width and height to 200% or 300%. When you need to resize it down, you can switch back to pixels and reduce it to the exact size you had it before and it will keep its perspective.

When you are resizing, make sure you have the Resample Image checkbox checked and that it's set to Bicubic (see Figure 9.79).

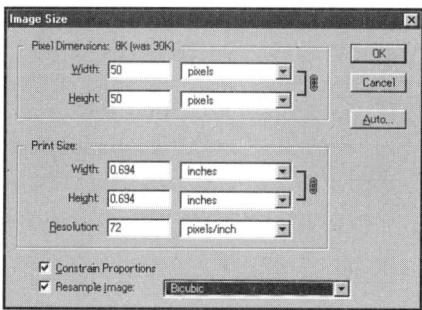

Figure 9.79

Resizing properly.

Bit Depth

When you create images in Photoshop you almost always create them as RGB images, and then change them to Indexed Color mode after you're done. This is done because none of the Photoshop filters work on an image in Indexed Color mode. As general rule of thumb, you should change things in RGB Color mode and use them in Indexed Color mode on the Web.

With certain images, however, you will find that JPEGs are the best way to save your images. The JPEG format enables you to save your images with in RGB mode, with all of its original colors; unfortunately, JPEG can also introduce distortion, especially in images that contain large areas of flat color or areas of high-contrast. JPEG is well-suited for detailed photographs, intricate art, anything that cannot be dithered to a lower palette without losing too much detail. JPEG should never be used for images that contain type or line art.

When dithering an image, choose Image→Mode→Indexed Color. A dialog box appears asking if you want to flatten the image and discard the hidden layers. (It only asks this if your image has more than a background layer. Also it is a good idea to save your image as a Photoshop file before indexing your image(s).) Clicking Yes brings up the Indexed Color dialog box. There are four options (see Figure 9.80).

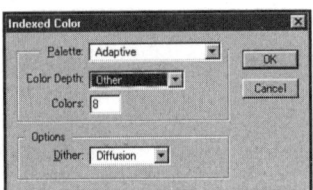

Figure 9.80

The Indexed Color window.

The Palette choices are Exact, System (Macintosh), System (Windows), Web, Uniform, Adaptive, Custom, and Previous. The ones you will use most are Adaptive for all your transparent GIFs, and Custom and Previous for your animated GIFs.

If you choose Adaptive, the Color Depth option can be used. It offers the choice of how many colors to dither to, either 3 bits/pixel (8 colors), 4 bits/pixel (16 colors), 5 bits/pixel (32 colors), 6 bits/pixel (64 colors), 7 bits/pixel (128 colors), 8 bits/pixel (256 colors), or Other.

If you choose Other, you can pick how many colors you want to dither to by typing in the number in the Colors option. This is the one we use the most.

The last option is Dither type. You can choose None, Diffusion, or Pattern; you will almost always want Diffusion for photorealistic images, and None for illustrations and type.

When dithering an image, always start with an Adaptive palette and choose Other as the color depth. When choosing how many colors you want it to be, start with the lowest number of colors (such as 4) and click OK. If the image dithers badly, choose Edit→Undo and try it again, moving up a couple of colors until you find the perfect medium, a low color depth with a clear image.

Chapter 9 Advanced Graphics

If things seem to be dithering badly no matter how many colors you choose as the depth, you may want to try drawing a selection around important parts of the image and then indexing the image. The selection will dither the image based on the pixels inside the selection, rather than looking at all of the pixels in the image.

Using Photographs

In most cases, photographs are easily added to Web pages. Sometimes all you need to do is crop the image, resize it, dither it, and voilà—it's done. This is the perfect scenario, however. Many times you will find that the images you are sent, or must scan, need to be enhanced because they aren't good quality; or sometimes the client will want the pictures enhanced artistically to make them stand out.

Although dealing with photographs can be a book in itself, we will show you a wonderful technique that enables you to cut out exactly what part of the image you want to alter and turn it into a layer.

1. Load your image and make sure it's in RGB Color mode by choosing Image➡Mode➡RGB Color. Resize the image to the size you want it to be on the Web page by choosing Image➡Image Size. You may even want to crop the image by making a rectangular selection around what you want to keep and then choosing Image➡Crop. Now copy the background layer once by choosing Layer➡Duplicate Layer and name the new layer Cut out.

2. Create a blank layer and place it between the Cut out layer and the Background layer. Name it Colored background (see Figure 9.81). Now you're ready to work on it.

Figure 9.81

Preparing the image.

3. Choose Image→Image Size and change the Width to 300 percent instead of pixels. Make sure that the Constrain Proportions checkbox is checked.

4. For the colored background layer, choose a foreground color that is bright and different than the colors in the image. Click the Colored background layer and fill it in with the foreground color. In the Fill dialog box, set the Contents to Foreground Color, Opacity to 100%, and Mode to Normal.

5. To make the Jeep in the foreground green, you will have to cut the Jeep out of the picture so that you can alter its color. To do this, click the Cut out layer. Double-click the Eraser tool to bring up the Eraser Options palette. Choose Paintbrush from the Eraser mode pop-up menu (see Figure 9.82).

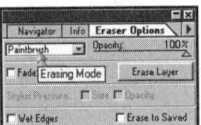

Figure 9.82

Erasing mode.

6. Bring up the Brushes palette (Window→Show Brushes) and choose a brush to start erasing with. Because you are starting to cut out directly around the Jeep, you will want the smallest brush possible. These are the finest cuts you will make, so you need something tiny, but with smooth edges (see Figure 9.83).

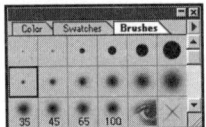

Figure 9.83

The tiniest scalpel.

7. Now draw around the outside of the Jeep, as if you were tracing it, but don't go *onto* the Jeep. Be certain that you are only cutting away outside of the Jeep (see Figure 9.84).

8. Using a bigger brush, clear some more space around the outside of the Jeep (see Figure 9.85).

9. Keep using larger brushes and clear out the space around your cut out. You should now only have your selection left on the screen (see Figure 9.86).

Figure 9.84

Drawing around the selection.

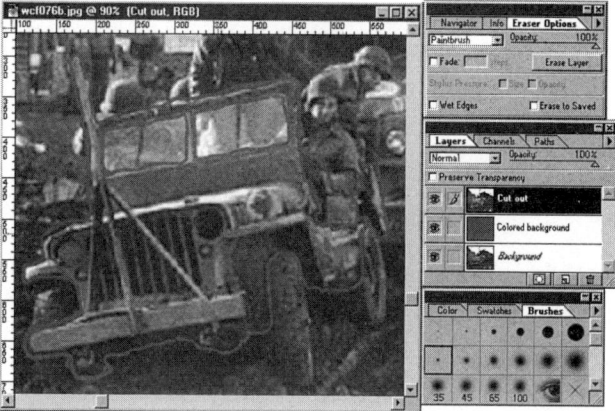

Figure 9.85

Clearing more space.

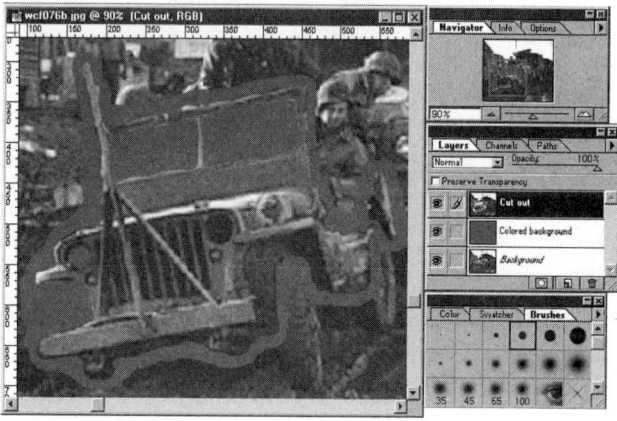

Figure 9.86

The cut out completed.

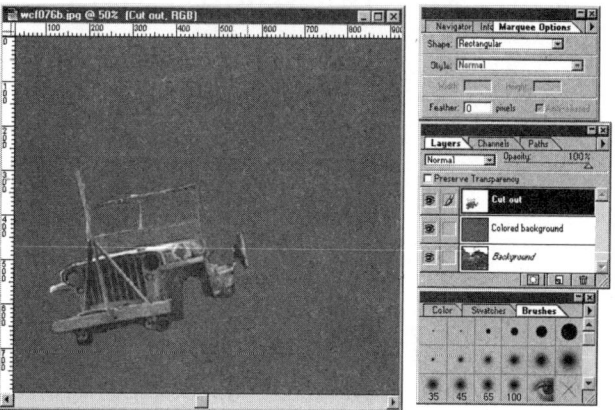

10. Delete the Colored background layer. Save your image as a Photoshop file, in case you want to do some altering to it later.

11. Before you alter the image, you should resize it down to what you want on your Web page.

12. To colorize the Jeep, highlight the Cut out layer and choose Image➞Adjust➞Hue/Saturation. Then click Colorize. Set the Hue to 108, the Saturation to 20, and the Lightness to –12.

You should now have a green colored Jeep (see Figure 9.87).

Figure 9.87

The green Jeep.

This technique is limitless in its possibilities. Use your imagination and experiment. The images you can come up will be amazing. Good luck.

Conclusion

We have covered a multitude of graphics techniques in this chapter, and these are by no means all of them. You have learned how to create properly tiled backgrounds, how to create beveled and shadowed text, how to use graphical borders around your tables, and how to space with transparent GIFs.

You've also learned about anti-aliasing, the concepts and execution of making transparent GIFs, and even alpha channel mapping.

We've taken you into the depths of Photoshop 4.0 and taught you how to use and create actions, layers, blending, and transparency effects.

Chapter 9 Advanced Graphics

We've also discussed the concepts behind shadowing, resizing, and dithering properly so that your images will always be detailed and small in file size. We've even showed you how to deal best with photographic images.

This chapter has been quite a mouthful, and if you didn't absorb everything on the first pass, then read it again later—it will open up more ideas as it's repeated.

Now, we move on to another great topic—animation.

chapter 10

Animations

You've probably seen many animations while surfing the Internet. You may even make animations yourself, and probably noticed that many animations take a long time to download, or are slow on your system because they are too large or contain too many frames. Animations can be overused, and they can be used incorrectly. This chapter not only covers the basics of creating the animations, but also the advanced side of animations. By the end of this chapter, you should be able to create faster loading, properly used animations that will make your Web pages come alive.

Animations are not just eye candy. Interface designers long ago learned to use motion to direct the eye of the reader to important or enriching information. Your primary motivation for adding an animation to a Web page should be to enhance the page's readability, not just show off your skills. Therefore, by proper use we're referring simply to making sure that your pages aren't overwhelming end users with too much animation.

- Creating Animations
- Importing Images into the Animation Programs
- Size Reduction Issues
- Animation Effects and Techniques

Although a jumping cartoon character can add that special eye-catching appeal to a page, it can also be distracting. And more than a few animations on a page are bothersome.

Even other media, such as television, keep as few objects moving on the screen as possible. Although it's ironic to think that a medium such as TV, whose entire existence is based on movement, tries to keep things still, it suddenly makes sense when you consider that the director's objective is to keep you focused on one character, one activity, or one object. Watch your favorite sitcom this week and count the number of moving objects in a particular camera shot. I'll bet you won't run out of thumbs. What you do count, though, will be exactly what the director intends for you to be watching. Consider this when evaluating where to put an animation on a page.

Creating Animations

You've learned that to create transparent GIFs you need a piece of software to help you. Unlike JPEGs, transparent GIFs need to be created by either choosing a color as the transparent color before saving it, or by creating an alpha channel and saving it as a GIF.

Animated GIFs are treated the same way. You need a program to help you arrange the images, set the timing, and work with palettes and backgrounds. Then you can save the file as an animated GIF.

With animated GIFs, you can control the following:

- Image
- Palette
- Transparent color
- Timing
- Background removal type

> **Note**
> You may want to read Chapter 9, "Advanced Graphics," which gives a good run-through on some great Photoshop techniques. This will help get you up to speed on how to prepare the images before you create these animations.

Chapter 10 Animations

> **Note**
>
> As with all GIF types, palettes affect size directly, but animated GIFs enable you to create a palette that is used by the entire animation. Global paletting, as it is called, helps reduce the size of the animation. Many Web designers, however, still insist on creating animations with local palettes (or palettes for every image in an animation), which increase the size of an animation dramatically. In this chapter, we'll teach you the golden rule of animations—create a global palette for every animation!

- Width and height
- Alignment of each image
- Number of times the animation should loop

Choose your own graphics program to create and then export your images for the animation program. We've pointed you to two example programs in this book, and several others from the Studio Skills Web site. Because most of the animation programs allow importing of almost any format, save the images you create in JPG, TIF, or BMP.

Exporting to GIF is always the best idea because GIF creates a 256-color (8-bit) palette or less. If you use another image format, the animation program will have to dither the image on the fly, creating a palette that may not look so great and giving you less control over the image. If you have saved the images as another format, you can use Photoshop to index the colors and save them as GIFs.

You might also want to consider the fact that you'll have problems when attempting to use 16- or 24-bit images as animation frames. When the animation software dithers the palette on the fly you'll see that the latticework of color combinations used to make what used to be solid color blocks frequently change position. This becomes a very ugly effect.

Importing Images into the Animation Programs

For the Mac, we will use the GifBuilder program. Written by Yves Piquet, it is a companion product to his image manipulation application Clip2GIF. In the spirit of most Mac OS tools, both GifBuilder and Clip2GIF are full-featured shareware. You'll find GifBuilder is especially easy to use, although it lacks the pizzazz of similar applications for Windows.

For the PC, we will use the Microsoft GIF Animator program (available for download at http://www.microsoft.com/imagecomposer/gifanimator/gifanin.html) and Alchemy Mindwork's GIF Construction Set (available at http://www.mindworkshop.com/alchemy/gifcon.html). Both of these programs have their positives and negatives, but they are straightforward in the way they enable you to lay out our frames of animation.

GifBuilder (Mac Application)

GifBuilder makes the process of creating animated GIFs into a drag-and-drop affair, and the interface is embarrassingly simple. Start by dragging and dropping each frame of your animation, in the form of individual GIFs, into the frames window as illustrated in Figure 10.1.

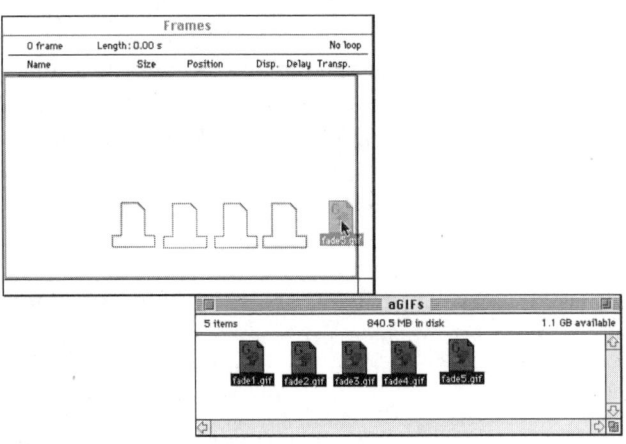

Figure 10.1

Dropping the files into place.

Using the Options pull-down menu, you're now free to play with the animation settings to your heart's content (see Figure 10.2). As an added bonus, you can save your options settings, which will replace the default settings with your own; the next time you use the application you will not find yourself making the same settings changes you always have to make whenever you use GifBuilder.

Figure 10.2

The Options menu features palette options under Colors.

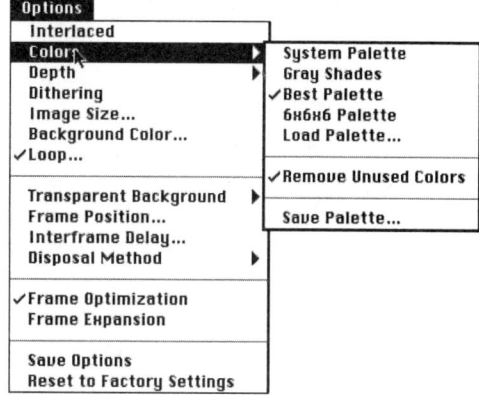

> **TIP**
>
> Using different palettes will help you to optimize file size. You can load a palette from an external GIF, or in one of five different modes. Best Palette will give you optimized graphical clarity without risking too much loss of quality. Try tinkering with the 6×6×6 Palette or System Palette to see how this affects your output image.

Through the Options menu you can set background color and transparency; this will give you an idea of what the final product will look like on the Web page.

The Loop command is simple to use; it enables you to specify never, infinite, or a specific number of times for the animation to repeat.

The Interframe Delay represents how long the GIF will stop between frames of the image. You can rescale the image up or down using Image Size. The Interframe Delay can be set differently for each frame of the animation, by clicking on each frame in the construction window. This is a powerful feature that can yield some dramatic effects if used creatively.

Frame Position enables you to take a static frame and reposition it within the final product. It also enables you import a single image multiple times so that you can make it jump around the viewable area.

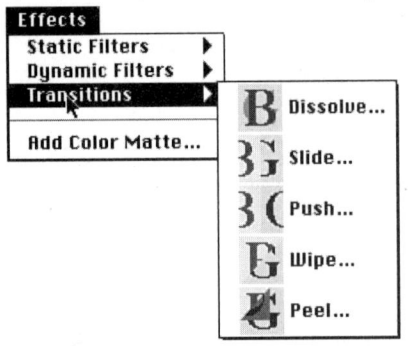

Figure 10.3
Transitions effects to save you time.

Version 2.0 of GifBuilder includes some handy transition effects for you to replace one GIF with the next as seen in Figure 10.3. The Effects menu also enables you to add a background matte for individual GIFs and to apply filters both to individual frames and to the global image.

GifBuilder is more than adequate to handle your most complex GIF animations. It features good size optimization and even has a nifty feature that will copy the appropriate <IMAGE> HTML tag to the clipboard so that you can paste it into your Web documents. After you're done tweaking your images, simply select Save from the File menu and you're finished.

Microsoft's GIF Animator, GIF Construction Set (Windows Applications)

Microsoft's GIF Animator and GIF Construction Set have drastically different interfaces, but they essentially produce the same results. GIF Animator is a no frills, straightforward GIF animation program, whereas GIF Construction Set is the "tons O' bells and whistles" animation program with many more effects and transitions. Both achieve the same end, but the path taken to that end is a little different. Let's take a look at one of the differences.

Say, for example, that you start a new animation by loading in your first image. When loading it, GIF Construction Set will ask you if you want to use it as your global palette or as a local palette. For the first image, you would choose "Use this image as the global palette," which means that the same palette is applied to all frames within the animation (see Figure 10.4). This has two potential effects:

Chapter 10 **Animations** 235

> **Note**
> One way to make the best use of global palettes is to make sure that your first image has all of the colors (or more) that are found in subsequent images.

▶ If the first image is black and white and subsequent files are color, GIF Construction Set will attempt to dither all frames to the same palette as the black-and-white frame.

▶ If the first effect doesn't scare you off, you'll save a great deal of data, making the file size significantly smaller.

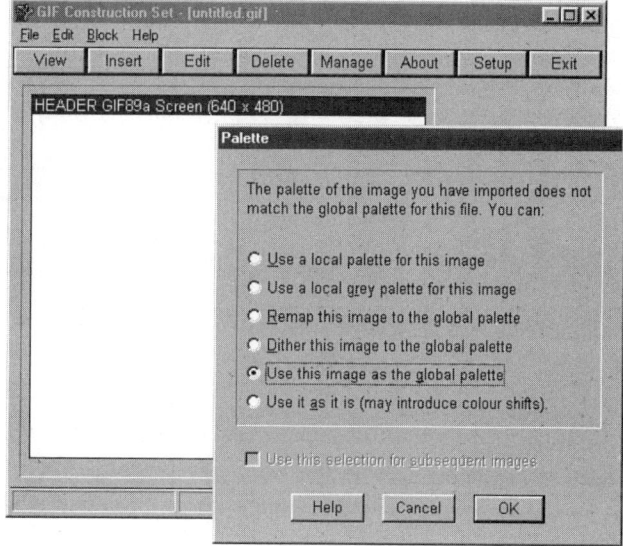

Figure 10.4
Would you like your image loaded globally or locally?

GIF Animator will ask nothing, assuming your palette is local. (If you index all of your frames in Photoshop to the same palette, then they are automatically global—this is what we will be doing.)

Now if you add a second image to the animation (if that image uses the same palette), it will load without any questions in both programs. After the images are in the program, you can then change things such as timing, placement, and other options. These are handled differently in each program.

In GIF Animator, it's a matter of choosing the image from the left side of the window, and then choosing the appropriate tab on the right to change what you want (see Figure 10.5). This makes the changing of timing and placements for a single image easy.

Figure 10.5

Changing animation parameters in GIF Animator.

To alter an image's timing or transparency color with GIF Construction Set, insert a control option and then edit it (see Figure 10.6).

Chapter 10 Animations

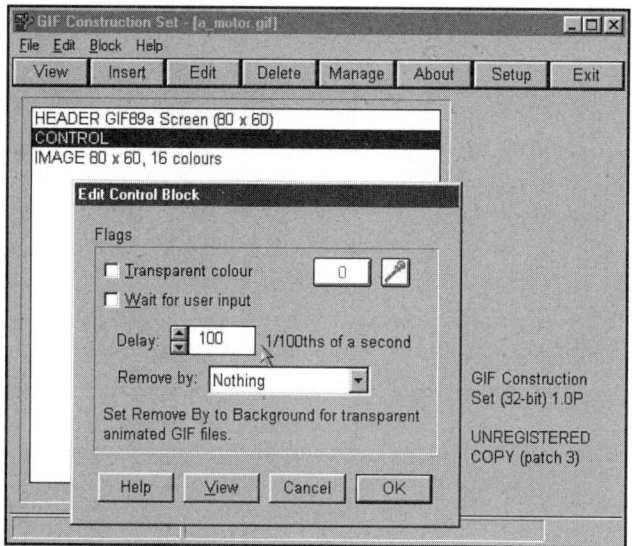

Figure 10.6

Inserting a control into GIF Construction Set and editing it.

This makes it a little more complex to use than GIF Animator because you also need to insert a loop command if you want your animation to loop. But unlike GIF Animator, when you want to move the placement for the entire image step-by-step for just a few frames or for the entire animation, GIF Construction Set lets you "manage" your frames with more control. Like all competing software, there are pluses and minuses to each.

For almost all of our examples in this chapter we'll be using Microsoft's GIF Animator because it is a good tool for creating animations, and it doesn't have too many options to confuse you. It leaves the designing up to you, and it does all the work of creating the animated GIF.

Size Reduction Issues

There are three things that affect file size in animated GIFs: palettes (global and local), size (width and height), and the number of frames in the animation.

> **Note**
>
> Remember just because you create a large image that has a small animated part doesn't mean you have to use the entire image in the animation. You can chop an image and put it back together using tables (review the section on graphical tables). Then you can animate just the piece that needs it, not the entire image.

The rules pertaining to file size economy are simple:

- Keep the palettes global—one palette for all the images in an animation. We'll touch on this in great detail later on in this chapter.

- Keep the number of frames down. Remember making a 300-frame animation may give it the Ben Hur feel, but it will also take forever for your user to see and download. If you've got a great animation that you just know is too big, delete every second frame and double the timing "duration" on all the other frames. This may help the situation greatly.

- Keep the size small to shorten page loading times. All animations should be as small as possible, but for animations of around 50×50, you should be shooting for around 20–45K; more for larger (physical) images.

Look what we did for Rocco's Radios (our site that shows off the techniques being taught in this book). Notice the van and the neon sign? At one time this was a single image. It was cut up, indexed, and the neon sign was then turned into an animated sign, apart from the other pieces of the image (see Figures 10.7 and 10.8).

But these are things that need to be experimented with, and most of all perfected. Sizes and frame counts can never be exact, so experiment. Always save the original images, just in case you need to go back and make changes.

Chapter 10 Animations 239

Figure 10.7

The van (looks as though it's one image).

Figure 10.8

The van was assembled piece by piece.

Working with Palettes

Creating a global palette for an animated GIF is the same as creating a palette for a transparent one, although the process of how you do it is a little different.

Remember that when indexing a color for a transparent GIF, you drop the color amount as low as possible, and then you save it as a GIF. With animated GIFs, you could do that to every image, but if you were importing images into a GIF animation program, all the images would have local palettes, or palettes for each image. This is not what you want to do. Instead you want to create a single palette for all the images.

You only create the global palette after you have created every one of the frames. Creating the palette should be the last thing you do before moving into the animation program.

Creating a Global Palette

First, you need to assemble the images into Photoshop by loading them or by duplicating them frame by frame (if they are Photoshop files). Then you should create a new image, one big enough to hold all of the frames (see Figure 10.9).

Next, one by one, copy each image and paste it into the big empty image. When you're done, every image in your animation should be present (see Figure 10.10).

Now, index the colors from lowest to highest. Try the lowest number of colors when you are prompted to pick a number of colors. Look at the result. If it loses too much detail, try again, but this time increase the number of colors. Find a color amount where all the images still look okay. (Remember to index your graphics by choosing Image➡Mode➡Indexed Color and setting the Palette to Adaptive in the Indexed Color dialog box, set the number of colors to whatever looks good, and set the Dither to Diffusion).

Figure 10.9

The new, big, empty image and all of the small images.

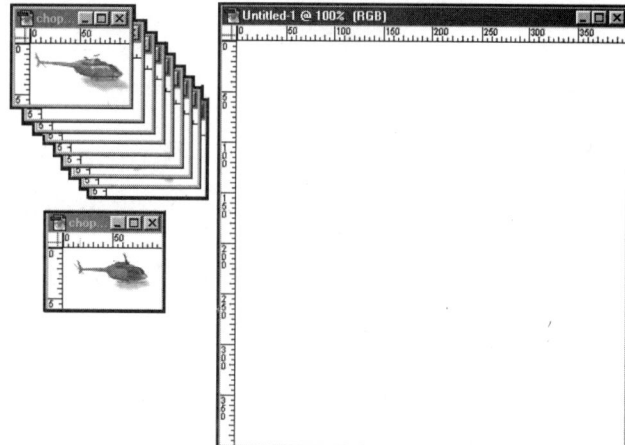

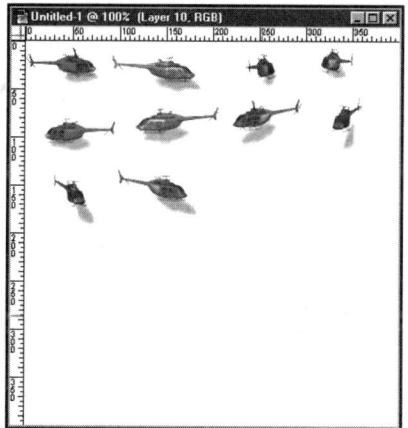

Figure 10.10

All of the images have been copied and pasted.

If you set the palette to Custom, you can save your palette just in case something happens when switching to Indexed Color mode (you would not want to do this whole process over again). This will bring up the Custom palette window; it will let you either save the current palette or load another one. You want to save this one, so click Save. You can save it either as an .ACT palette or as a Microsoft .PAL palette. Choose either one because Photoshop only needs to know what kind it is. If you already have an indexed image and you want to save its palette, in Photoshop 4.0, choose Image➡Mode➡Color Table to bring up the palette window for the indexed image. There you can save the current palette.

Now you can start saving your images as GIFs by indexing them to this global palette, and then saving them to disk. To index them to the previous palette (which is the perfect global palette), choose Image➡Mode➡Indexed Color and set Palette to Previous and Dither to Diffusion. Save them as GIFs.

> **Note**
>
> Many Web designers and graphic artists use advanced products such as DeBabelizer from Equilibrium Software to optimize palettes for the Web and other media. DeBabelizer, in particular, can analyze a series of images and determine the best palette to use for all of them, and will enable you to save it for loading into Photoshop by choosing Image➡Mode➡Color Table. Debabelizer does a much better job than Photoshop because it analyzes the whole series of images rather than one at a time.

> **Note**
>
> Videotape is shot at 30 frames per second; animation is shot at 12 (24 frames shot twice); and film is shot at 24 frames per second. Why is this important? Well it's not, but it's good for trivial pursuit!
>
> Actually, it's important to remember that you should never try to achieve either an animation or film ratio. Try and keep your animations between 1 and 10 frames a second; otherwise, your file size will grow beyond belief.

After you've completed your last image, move to your animation program and start loading the images. They now all use the same palette between them.

Timing, Frame Rates, and Clear Background Options

Changing the timing or duration of an animation is simple. Timing is based on look and feel and is best perfected by experimenting with each animation. Most hand-drawn cartoons animate at around 12 frames per second, which means a frame every 7/100ths of a second. Movies shot on 35mm roll at a frame rate of 24 frames per second, whereas most video rolls at just a smidgen under 30 frames per second. It's easy to see how you could burn up a lot of data for a short animation, so your aspirations should probably be limited to a cartoon-like effect at best. Changing interframe delays (which is just a backward way of referring to frame rates) can change the entire feel of an animation, so most designers choose to see how much they can get away with, and if it looks good, they leave it!

Timing

In GIF Construction Set, you change the time (called Delay) in the Control command, which you place before each image.

In GIF Animator, you change the time (called Duration) by clicking on the image on the left and clicking on the Image tab on the right. You can change the time from 0 to 10,000 (actually higher, but I didn't want to get carried away). It is in 1/100ths of a second (although it's not very accurate). That means 100 would be one second, 1,000 would be 10, and so on.

Chapter 10 Animations

Background

After you show an image or a frame in a GIF animation, you must remove it, or clear it. In both GIF Construction Set (in the Control command) and GIF Animator (in the Image tab), there are two removing types with which you need to concern yourself. If you are creating an animation that uses no transparent GIFs, choose Leave As Is as the Undraw, or Remove type. If you are using transparent images, then use the remove method of Remove Background.

Before you start hyperventilating, remember, we are going to show you examples of how to do all of it, so get your fingers and mouse ready, here comes the fun. Also, these steps will be long and arduous, but because taking a break will affect the flow and process of what you are doing, there will be a lot of steps in each effect.

Animation Effects and Techniques

Each of these basic techniques starts with the Photoshop techniques first, then it moves into the animation program. The animation portion of each technique is broken into PC and Mac sections, so you'll be able to follow step-by-step no matter which platform you are using.

The Fading Animation

The fading animation fades in and out from the background. First, we'll create the individual images. Then we'll duplicate each frame, create the global palette, and finally, animate the frames.

So let's begin by opening Photoshop.

Creating the Photoshop Images

Create a new image (File➡New) and make it 80 pixels wide and 40 pixels high, RGB color, with a white background.

Next, create a text selection with the Type Mask tool (press T; the icon you want is the transparent letter "T"). Click on the image, and then choose a font and a word that you would like to use for the effect. I used the Arial Rounded font and the word "Email" for this effect, but you can use whatever you want. Play around with the sizes and spacing until your word fits in the image space. Leave at least three or four pixels of blank space around your text.

Make sure your Actions menu is open (Window➜Show Actions) and that the Actions from the CD-ROM are loaded. (Read the section on Photoshop actions to learn how to load the actions.) Choose the action Text—Gauss. Shadow w/outline and click the play button (see Figure 10.11).

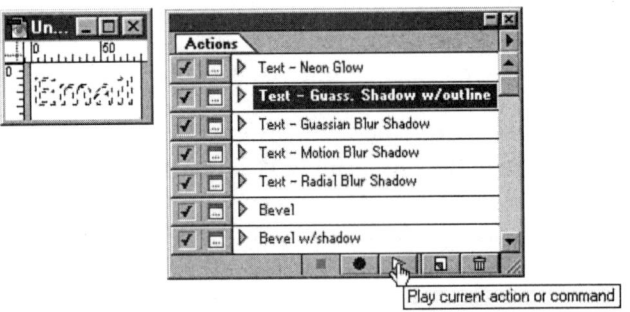

Figure 10.11

Selecting your text, then playing the action.

After the action completes, your image should look like Figure 10.12.

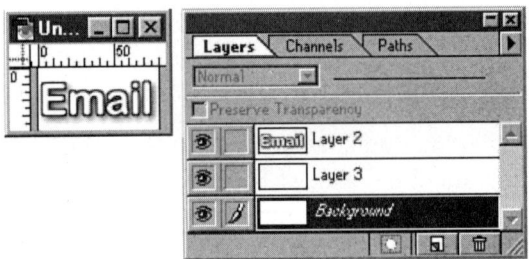

Figure 10.12

The finished image after the action.

Now you can create each animation frame. You may want to save this image now as a Photoshop file, in case you want to edit it later. Also, you may want to crop it (draw a selection around the image, then choose Image➜Crop) if there is too much blank space around the image.

Make sure nothing is selected (Select➜None) and click Layer 2. Next, make five frames for the fade: one at 100% opacity, one of nothing but white, and three of the actual fade. Duplicate the image at 100% opacity

Chapter 10 Animations

and call it fade_frame1. (Image➧Duplicate and make sure the Merged Layers button is checked). Now slide the opacity slider to 75% (see Figure 10.13).

Duplicate the image and name it fade_frame2. (Image➧Duplicate and make sure the Merged Layers button is checked!) Once again, drop the Opacity slider, this time to 50%, and duplicate the image again, naming it fade_frame3. Next, drop the opacity to 25%, duplicate it, and name it. Finally, drop the opacity to 1% (that's as low as the slider goes, but it's the same as 0%, if you want to be sure, you can make Layer 2 invisible by clicking the visibility icon), duplicate it, and name it. You should now have five copied frames and the original image on your desktop (see Figure 10.14).

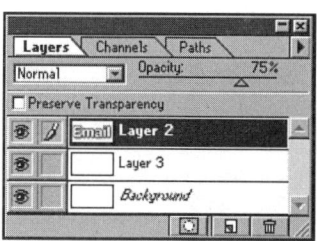

Figure 10.13

Making the image transparent.

> **Note**
>
> The interesting thing about this effect is that any image could have been used. The concept behind this is to make the image, and then use the Opacity slider in the Layers palette to create a fading look. After you alter the transparency, duplicate each frame, index it, and save it. Before you can do any of that, set up the Alpha channel, or transparency channel. (This enables you us to put animation on any background that is almost all white.) Click Layer 2, choose Select➧Load Selection (click OK), and then Select➧Save Selection (click OK). Now you have an alpha channel.

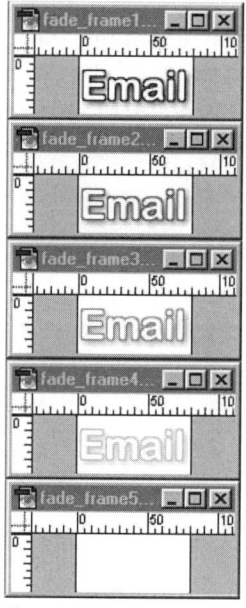
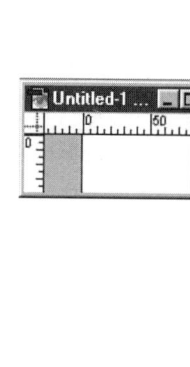

Figure 10.14

All the frames.

Next, you want to create the global palette. Copy all of the frames to a single blank image and then index the colors. Then create a new image (about 300×300 pixels should be fine). Click on the first frame (fade_frame1), making sure the Layers palette is open (Window➡Show Layers) and drag the background layer onto the newly created "blank" image (see Figure 10.15).

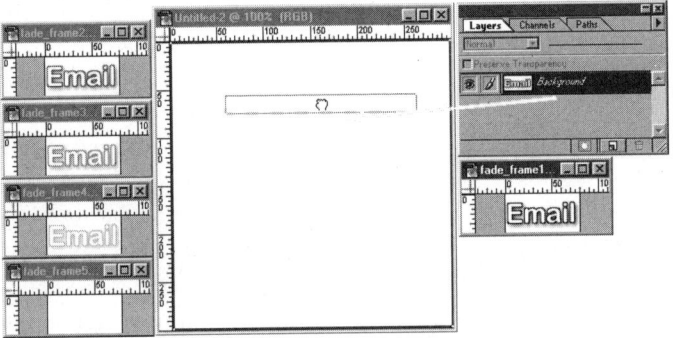

Figure 10.15

Copying the frame layer to the blank image.

Now click on the next frame (fade_frame2) and copy over its background layer to the blank image (make sure to drag and drop it on a blank area, not over top of the other image). Repeat this action for frames three and four. Your blank image should look like Figure 10.16.

Now draw a selection rectangle around the images and crop it (Image➡Crop).

Choose Image➡Mode➡Indexed Colors to index the colors. Choose Yes to flatten. Palette should be set to Adaptive; Colors should be set to 6; and the Dither should be set to Diffusion. (Experiment with the number of colors to see what looks best, this example happened to dither great at six colors.) Then click OK.

Now choose Image➡Mode➡RGB Color and then again choose Image➡Mode➡Indexed Color. Set the Palette to Custom and the Dither to Diffusion. Click OK. This will bring up the Custom Palette window (we had to index our image first and then index it again so that the palette would be remembered). Click Save. Choose the type of palette (either is fine) and name your new palette (for this example, we used Microsoft Palette and named our palette fade.pal).

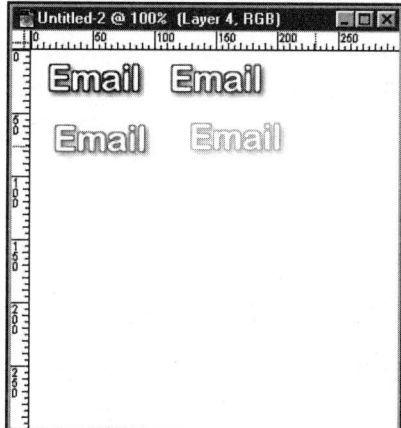

Figure 10.16

The copied frames.

Click the first frame fade_frame1, and choose Image➡Mode➡Indexed Color. Set the Palette to Previous and click OK. Then save this image as a GIF file (File➡Save As). This example is named fade1.gif. Repeat for the second frame, and the third, and so on, until you've saved fade5.gif. You have now indexed all the frames to the same palette. You are now ready for the animation program.

Assembling the Fade Animation

Now that the images have been created, it's time to do the actual animating. Before you open the animation program you should figure out how the images will be shown, so that you can speed up the importing.

In this example, you want the animation to fade from opaque to transparent, and you want the first image to be the 100% opaque image. The order of the fade will go fade1.gif, fade2, fade3, fade4, and fade5. Because the animation loops, it will go from the blank image (fade5) and flash back to the first (fade1)—but you don't want this. You want to fade back to the first frame so that the fifth frame goes backward. Now the frame list looks like this: first fade1.gif then fade2, fade3, fade4, fade5, fade4, fade3, and fade2.gif. You don't need to repeat fade1 because it will loop back to it.

Now that you know how the frames will be placed, you can start the animation program.

MAC Steps

Save yourself some serious time here by opening GifBuilder and then jumping back to the desktop. As in Figure 10.17, make sure you'll be able to drag your files to the Frames window and select them all by holding down the Shift key. Drag them together to the Frames window and they will all appear. If they're not in the proper order, simply select them and drag them up and down within the window to rearrange them.

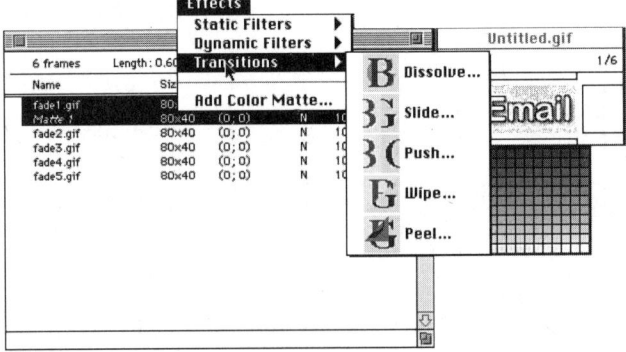

Figure 10.17

Dragging each image into the frames window.

By clicking each frame while holding down the Shift key, you can select them all and set the delay options for the whole bunch. Click the Options menu and select Interframe Delay. You can select any number, measured in 100ths of a second. For our purposes, 20/100ths is fine (see Figure 10.18).

Set the transparency color by selecting Transparency from the Options menu. In this case, you want to tell it to use the first pixel (in the top left-hand corner) to determine what the transparent color will be—a very handy feature indeed. Set the looping to Forever by selecting Loop from the Options menu. Easy! Now select Save As from the File menu and you're done.

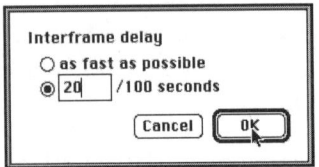

Figure 10.18

Setting the delay.

Chapter 10 **Animations** 249

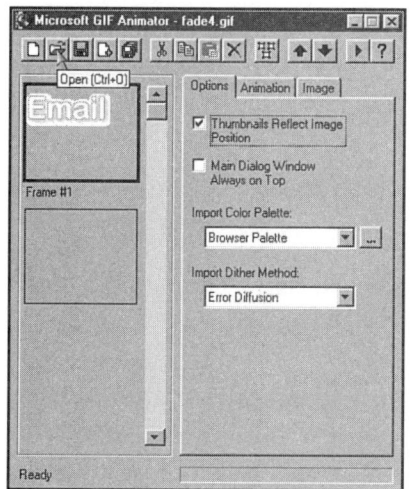

Figure 10.19

Opening the first frame.

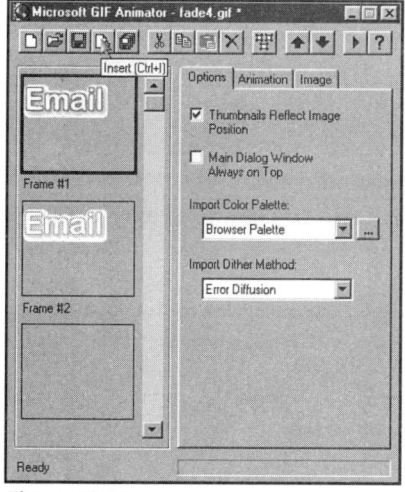

Figure 10.20

Inserting the next frames.

PC Steps

After GIF Animator is loaded, you will want to load the frames one by one. Because GIF Animator loads the images from last to first, the list of frames needs to be reversed. You should open the last frame on the list first. Click the Open button and load fade2.gif (see Figure 10.19).

After the first frame has been loaded, you can add the other frames. Load in the next image by clicking the Insert Image button and adding the next frame on the list, fade3.gif (see Figure 10.20).

Repeat this until all the other frames have been inserted; the order for loading the rest of the frames is fade4, fade5, fade4, fade3, fade2, and fade1.gif.

To set the timing and the removal of the background for the frames, click Frame #1 (on the left) and then click on the Image tab (on the right). Set the DURATION to 300, and then click Frame #2. Scroll down the frame list (on the left) until you see Frame #8; then hold down Shift and click Frame #8. This enables you to edit frames 2 to 8 at the same time.

Now set the Duration to 5. Click Frame 5 and set the Duration to 25. To set the Undraw Method for all the frames, click on Frame1, then scroll down and Shift-Click on Frame8. Set the Undraw Method to Remove background.

Lastly, you want to set the looping for the animation. Click the Animation tab, then click the Looping box and set it to 1,000.

Click the Save As button and save the image as fade.gif. It's now ready to place on your Web page.

You will notice that the way the timing was set up, it stays on for a while, then fades to white, waits just a second, then fades back to the image. By changing the timing, you can change the effect of the animation. Try to time the first frame shorter and the fifth frame longer, and see what happens.

The Glowing Animation

For this example, we're going to create a neon sign type of effect using one of the Photoshop Actions included on the CD-ROM.

Creating the Photoshop Images

Create a new image (File➧New) and make it 80 pixels wide and 40 pixels high, RGB Color, with a white background. Now choose Edit➧Fill and set the Contents to black and the Opacity to 100%.

Switch to the Type Mask tool. Press T (it's the little transparent "T" icon), then click the image and pick a font and some text. We've chosen the Arial Rounded font, with a size of 32 pixels, and typed the text New.

In the Actions panel (Window➧Show Actions), click the Text—Neon Glow action. Before pressing the play button, this action requires that you choose a bright foreground color and a dull background color. We've chosen a bright Red as our foreground color, and a dull Yellow as our background color. Now you can click the action and press the play button.

This is a great action because it not only creates a neon effect, but it creates two separate layers—one layer that is the glowing neon bar effect, and one layer that looks as if the neon is turned off (see Figure 10.21).

Before you go any further you should create the transparent alpha channel. To do this, click the Layer 1 copy layer, choose Select➧Load Selection, and click OK. Then choose Select➧Save Selection and click OK. The alpha channel is now saved. (You may want to save the image as a Photoshop file now.)

Chapter 10 Animations

Figure 10.21

The Neon action.

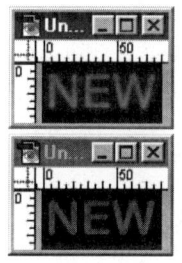
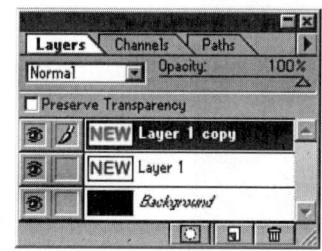

You'll want to duplicate this image into its separate frames. We've decided to use three frames for the glow effect: one with the glow effect on full, one at 50%, and one with the glow turned off. Start by duplicating the first frame, "the glow effect on full." You need to make sure that Layer 1 copy is visible. Now select Image➡Duplicate and name the new layer glow_frame1. (Make sure Merged Layers is checked.)

Go back to the original image and make sure the Layer 1 copy layer and the Layer 1 layer are both active and visible. Set the Opacity slider on both layers to 50%. (You'll have to do this for each of the layers.) Now duplicate the layer (Image➡Duplicate). Make sure Merged Layers is checked and name the new layer glow_frame2.

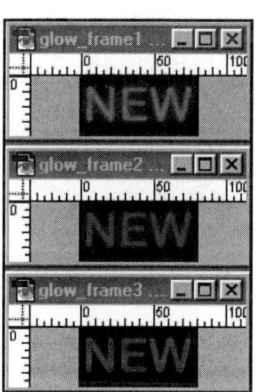

Figure 10.22

The three glow effect frames.

Go back to the original image and make the Layer 1 copy layer invisible. (Turn off the little eye visibility icon.) Click Layer 1. (Make sure to set its Opacity slider back to 100%.) Duplicate it, like you did the last two, and name it glow_frame3. You should now have three frames that look like this (see Figure 10.22).

Next, to create the global palette, you need to copy all of the frames to a single blank image, and then index the colors. Create a new image (about 300×300 pixels should be fine), and then fill it in with black

Figure 10.23

The blank, cropped image, ready for indexing.

Note

Before you index the colors, make sure you are indexing exactly what you want in the image. Draw a small rectangle selection around the bottom the first words "W," then do this for the next "W," and finally the last "W." To draw multiple selections, hold down the Shift key (see Figure 10.24).

Figure 10.24

Drawing multiple selections so that indexing will be perfect.

(Edit➥Fill). As you did in the Fading effect, click the first frame (glow_frame1), making sure the layers panel is open (Window➥Show Layers) and drag the background layer onto the newly created Blank image.

Click the next frame (glow_frame2) and drag and drop its background layer to the blank image (make sure to drag and drop it on a blank area, not over top of the other image). Do this again, for the third frame and move on to the next step.

Now draw a selection rectangle around the images and crop it (Image➥Crop). Your image should look like this (see Figure 10.23).

Choose Image➥Mode➥Indexed Colors to index the colors. Choose yes to flatten. The palette should be set to Adaptive and Colors should be set to 16. (Experiment with the number of colors to see what looks best, this example happened to dither great at 16 colors.) Set Dither to Diffusion, and then click OK. Choose Image➥Mode➥RGB Color and then again choose Image➥Mode➥Indexed Color. Set the Palette to Custom and the Dither to Diffusion. Click OK. This will bring up the Custom Palette window.

(You had to index the image first, and then index it again so that the palette would be remembered.) Click Save. Choose the type of palette (either is fine) and name your new palette (we chose a Microsoft Palette and named our palette glow.pal).

Now click on the first frame glow_frame1, and choose Image➥Mode➥Indexed Color. Set the Palette to Previous and click OK. Save this image as a GIF file (File➥Save As). (We named ours glow1.gif). Repeat this for the second frame, and so on, until you've saved glow3.gif. You have now indexed all the frames to the same palette or created a global palette. You are now ready for the animation program.

Chapter 10 Animations

Creating the Glow Animation

Now it's time to do the actual animating. Before you open the animation program, you should figure out how the images will be shown. You want the animation to glow like a jittery neon light, so you need to determine the frame list.

Luckily, in this instance you can re-use the same three image files within a many-framed animation. This has a big payoff in efficiency, because each image is contained within the final GIF file once, and simply referred to repeatedly.

You want the neon light to be turned off—that's glow3.gif. Then you want to turn on the light brightly, but then go right to the medium glow so that you create a "flicker" effect—glow1.gif and glow2.gif. Finally, you want to turn off the light, then turn it back on quickly to give the effect the neon light is now working properly—glow3.gif and glow1.gif. The order for the frame list is glow3, glow1, glow2, glow3, and glow1.gif.

Now that you know how the frames will be placed, you can start up the animation program.

Mac Steps

As in the last technique, drag all of your images into the Frames window and organize them by selecting and dragging. glow1.gif and glow3.gif are used twice, so drag them in individually and arrange them in the proper order.

By clicking each frame while holding down the Shift key, you can select them all and set the delay options for the whole bunch. Click the Options menu and select Interframe Delay. Select any number, measured in 100ths of a second. Try making the delays between images irregular to make the animation look jittery.

Set the transparency color by selecting Transparency from the Options menu. Again, you want to tell it to use the first pixel to determine what the transparent color will be. Next, set the looping to 100 by selecting Loop from the Options menu. Select Save As from the File menu and you're finished.

PC Steps

After GIF Animator is loaded, you will want to load the frames one by one. Because GIF Animator loads the images from last to first, the frame list needs to be reversed. Open the last frame on the list first. Click the open button and load glow1.gif.

After the first frame has been loaded, you can add the other frames. Load the next image by clicking the Insert image button and adding the next frame on the list, glow3.gif.

Repeat this until all the other frames have been inserted; the order for loading the rest of the frames is glow2, glow1, and glow3.gif.

To set the timing and the removal of the background for the frames, click the Select All button at the top, and then click the Image Tab. Set the Undraw Method to "remove background."

Click Frame #1 (on the left) and then click the Image Tab. Set the Duration to 100. Now click Frame #3 and set the Duration to 10. Lastly, click Frame #5 and set the Duration to 300.

Now click the Animation Tab and make sure the Looping box is Checked and set to 1,000. Click the Save As button at the top and save the image as glow.gif. It's now ready to place on your Web page.

You will notice that the neon sign comes on, but flickers first. Then it stays on, making it look somewhat like a real neon sign. By changing the timing, you can change the effect of the animation. Play around with the timing, and see what you can come up with. This effect can really change a lot.

The Flashing Animation

To create a flashing effect with either the fade or the glow, just remove every second frame, keeping just the On/Off type frames. With the fade, use the full image, or the white background as the On/Off frames, and with the glow, use the non-glowing sign frame, and the glowing sign as the On/Off frames.

Chapter 10 Animations

The Moving Animation

In this technique, we take the word "HOME," cut up the image, move it piece by piece along a horizontal bar, and place each piece side by side to create a tickertape-like effect. This technique requires a lot of work in Photoshop, so let's begin.

Creating the Photoshop Images

First, create a new image (File➡New) and make it 120 pixels wide and 20 pixels high, RGB Color, with a white background. Now choose Select➡All, and then choose Select➡Save Selection. Click OK. (We are creating a long background for use in the animation program.)

Choose Image➡Mode➡Indexed Colors; set the Palette to Adaptive and set the Colors to 2. Now save it as a GIF and call it move_bak.gif.

Now you can move on to the animation program.

Mac Steps

Drag icon1b.gif into the frame seven times and make sure that on each the first pixel is transparent. Go to Effects and add a white color matte.

Repeat step one, only this time select Frame Position from the Options menu and displace the image by 20 pixels on the Y axis.

Repeat Step two five more times.

A ball rolls across the screen in seven frames. Now look at the following section and see how much more difficult this is on the PC. Ain't life grand?

PC Steps

First, you want to open the move_bak.gif; this will make a large background for you to work with. It will also be invisible. (That's because we created it to be transparent.)

Next, you want to load (use the Insert button) an old graphic that you created previously in the Graphics section (when you learned how to make icons). Load in one of the tiny bullet icons. We've loaded one from the CD-ROM called icon1b.gif.

Now click the Image tab, on the right, and set the Left alignment to 100. Insert the icon again, and set the Left alignment of that new frame to 80. (You are creating movement by changing the alignment of this icon.) Now insert another and set the Left alignment to 60. Insert another and set it to 40. Then again insert the icon1b.gif and set the Left alignment to 20. Finally, insert it again, but do not change the alignment.

You should now have seven frames, with the seventh frame being invisible. Frames one to six are aligned on the left, from 0 to 100 in increments of 20.

Click the first frame. Scroll down the frame list and Shift-click the sixth frame. Click the Image Tab. Set the Duration to 10 and set the Undraw Method to Remove background. Click Frame 7 and then click the Image tab. Set the Duration to 50.

Click the Animation Tab. Check the Looping box and set the looping to 1,000.

You can now save your animation (we called ours move.gif) and put it on your Web page.

This animation is rather simple, but it shows the effect of motion can be created by using a small image. This effect can be changed by timing or by making the background transparent image larger. You should now understand the basics of using motion "within" the animation program.

Conclusion

The purpose of this chapter was to teach you not only the basics of animation, but also the advanced techniques and the best way to create globally paletted, small-sized, fast-loading animations. This should be your goal with all animations because they can grow rather rapidly.

Remember, none of these techniques was meant to be written in stone, but rather to give you the idea of how things work and the knowledge to create animation properly. Experimentation is the key to learning.

With that in mind, the next chapter will teach you how to incorporate more advanced technologies such as Java, JavaScript, CGIs, and ActiveX components into your Web sites. In some cases, these could be used in conjunction with your newfound animation development skills to enhance the readability of your pages and navigability of your sites.

chapter

11

- → CGIs and Server-Side Scripting
- The Jabber about Java
- JavaScript and JScript
- → ActiveX

Beyond HTML: Making Web Sites That Think

The Web is changing right under your nose. It's becoming more interactive, more dynamic, and more useful. In addition to all of the more advanced layout tags we've discussed in previous chapters, Webmasters now must familiarize themselves with other techniques for making their pages eye-catching and easier to work with. Those functions simply cannot come from HTML commands alone, so thankfully the powers that be have granted us a number of frameworks to help us improve our Web site content and structure.

These frameworks come in the form of hot new technologies such as Java, JavaScript, ActiveX, VBScript, and Shockwave; as well as tried-and-true tools like CGI and other forms of server-side scripting. Incorporated into your site, each of these technologies can solve a specific problem for you, but each one comes with a price.

The purpose of this chapter is to introduce you to some of these new fully buzzword-compliant technologies and to help you better understand what the costs and benefits of using these tools will be.

CGIs and Server-Side Scripting

For years, the only tool Web designers had to make pages do anything more interactive than blink was Common Gateway Interface (CGI) scripting, which takes data inputted by Web users through forms, processes it, and returns the appropriate result. This frequently involves the long and drawn-out process of coding and compiling custom applications, which reside on the server. These code snippets were and are generally programmed in C or Perl.

As server products made their way to Macs and PCs, they were followed by libraries and support for CGI coding in languages such as Visual Basic, Visual C++, Frontier, and AppleScript. Perl still is probably the most popular language because its compilers are free, and because compared to C-based languages, it's pretty easy to learn. Perl is also available on all major computing platforms, which makes "porting" or translating programs written in Perl on one operating system to another possible.

CGIs process form data, which you learned about in Chapter 7. Most frequently CGIs process forms that send email to the server, order products from a Web site's catalog, search a company's database, or subscribe users to mailing lists. CGIs can also have much more subtle uses, such as in Web page access counters or ad banner generators.

Why Use CGIs?

CGIs have to be used in most situations when important information travels from a user's computer to the Web server. In most cases, Java applets eventually hand off resulting data to a CGI, although these days even the CGI itself might be a server-side Java applet.

Chapter 11 Beyond HTML: Making Web Sites That Think

The key advantage to consider when you're trying to decide if a CGI is right for an operation is compatibility. Because CGIs return standard HTML and because the POST method has been in use since the dawn of the Web, all browsers, no matter how old, are capable of interacting with your site.

The two potential pitfalls here are tied into the fact that CGIs execute on the server, not the client. Unless you have a high-speed Web server to play with, the more you rely on CGIs, the more problems you'll have when your site becomes heavily used.

First, running many contiguous processes, especially complex ones, on a server that is well-used will have you running to your computer reseller for more RAM in minutes. Second, CGIs always appear to be slow for wayward Web surfers, and heavy reliance on them can slow down your site, interrupting the flow of interactivity. Third, because you may not always have full control of the server where your Web site is hosted, dependence upon CGIs will expose you to accidental breakage by the system administrator and will possibly make your CGIs difficult to write and debug.

Working with CGIs

CGIs function on two basic principles: the POST and the GET. They are built into the original specifications for HTTP 1.0, and they are the portals through which CGIs work. When a CGI is invoked either by using information from a form or through the user clicking a direct link, it receives a great deal of information from the Web browser—this too was part of the genius that made HTTP such an extensible protocol. Why CERN created two methods for this we'll never understand. On the modern Web, POST and GET are essentially redundant, although there may still be some relevant differences.

POST

POST (the one we're more familiar with today) uses a form-based interface to enable virtually infinite numbers of input fields. As discussed earlier in Chapter 7, there are numerous INPUT types you can use in your forms to create customized outputs from your CGIs.

GET

GET was originally used in uncomplicated searches where only a single line was needed and the INPUT statement had to be self-contained. When you call a CGI directly by following a link or without any FORM input data, it is interpreted by the server as a GET action.

The test CGI (see Figure 11.1) simply returns the values sent by the client and interpreted by the server, and displays them with the explanations on the page. In this case, the input data came from a simple form that contained two text fields querying for a name and a birth date.

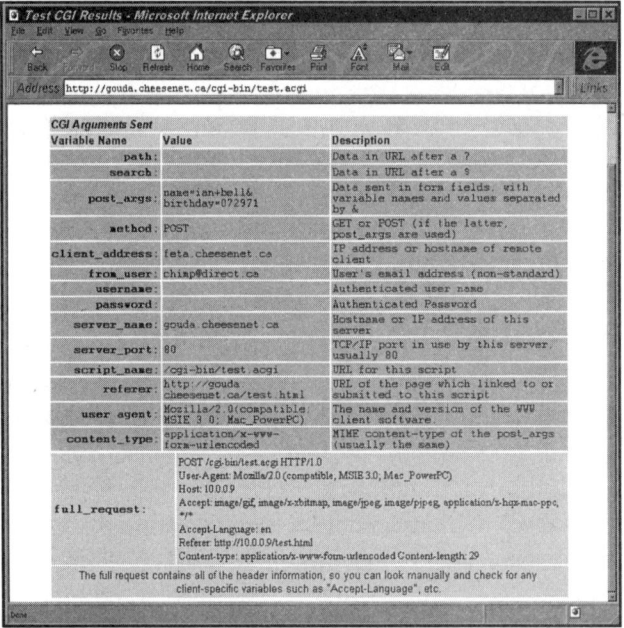

Figure 11.1

The test CGI as called through a form.

The resulting data also reflects who was using the server and the response data itself, as well as other useful information like the client's software and hostname. If you've ever looked at a Web server's log, you'll find the information it contains to be somewhat similar—this is because the client submits much of this information with every request it makes for a file. As you examine the types of information that you get with an HTTP request, you'll begin to get an idea of how this information can be used.

Chapter 11 Beyond HTML: Making Web Sites That Think

Perhaps you'd like to make a small CGI to track how many of the users on your Web site are using a given client type in real time, or maybe you want to take users from the ".ca" domain to a special page. More commonly, you may want to return the users to the referring document when they request a nonexistent file, replacing your "error.html" file with "error.cgi." All of this is possible without any user input, based purely on information that the client submits anyway. Aren't we lucky?

Creating Forms with CGIs

For our client, Rocco's Radios, we've been asked to implement some order forms that ultimately generate a message in Rocco's email box. This is a simple task once we've found a CGI we'd like to use. Because we're using Windows NT to host the Web site, we found a product called MAILTO at `http://www.net-shopper.co.uk/software/`. The freeware version has plenty of valuable features. We have also pointed you to several similar CGIs for other platforms on our Web site.

A MAILTO form (see Figure 11.2 and the following code) is easy to create. Obviously, the HTML code shows only the form and none of the formatting you see in the final result.

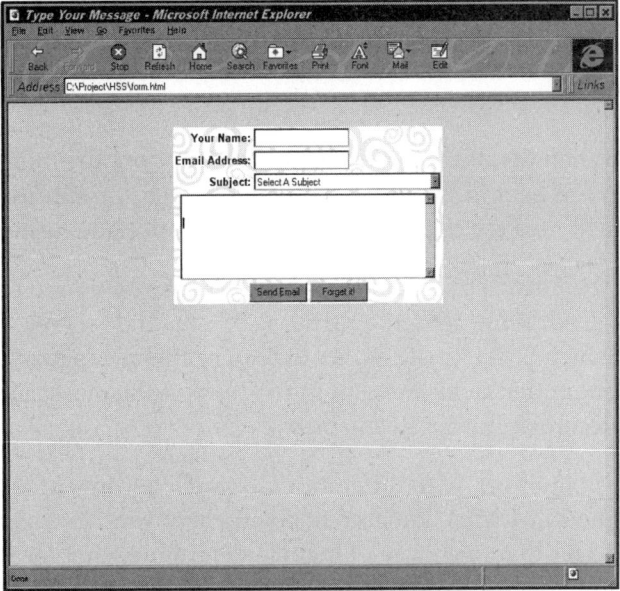

Figure 11.2

A standard MAILTO form.

From form.html:

```
<FORM ACTION="/cgi-bin/mailto.exe" METHOD="POST">
<INPUT TYPE="hidden" NAME="sendto" VALUE="rocco@studioskills.com">
<INPUT TYPE="hidden" NAME="server" VALUE="mail.studioskills.com">
<INPUT TYPE="hidden" NAME="resulturl" VALUE="/done.html">

Your Name:     <INPUT TYPE="text" SIZE="20" NAME="uname">

Email Address: <INPUT TYPE="text" SIZE="20" NAME="email">

Subject:
<SELECT NAME="subject" SIZE="1">
<OPTION>Select A Subject</OPTION>
    <OPTION>I'd like to find out more about a product.</OPTION>
    <OPTION>Can you take a special order?</OPTION>
    <OPTION>You're under arrest, pal.</OPTION>
    <OPTION>Comments about your WWW site.</OPTION>
    </SELECT>

<TEXTAREA NAME="message" ROWS="6" COLS="64" !WRAP="PHYSICAL">
</TEXTAREA>

<INPUT TYPE="submit" VALUE="Send Email">
<INPUT TYPE="button" VALUE="Forget it!">

</FORM>
```

When the user presses the SUBMIT button, the information he filled out is sent to the Web server, which calls /cgi-bin/mailto.exe. MAILTO will read the details sent and create a specially formatted message.

The form uses hidden fields to pass information to the CGI, such as "sendto" for determining the recipient, and "server" for determining which SMTP (mail) server to bounce the message off of. The rest of the submitted fields are sent in the body of the message and are organized according to variable names.

As you work with different CGIs you'll become accustomed to checking the READMEs that accompany them or reverse engineering the Web pages that make use of them to determine what form arguments you can pass to them. Because when form data is submitted it builds a (very long) URL, CGIs can be used as <IMG SRC=""> references or as regular

Chapter 11 Beyond HTML: Making Web Sites That Think

links. This is customarily how access counters and ad banners function. The examples on our Web site will give you valuable experience with such applications.

The Jabber about Java

The Java language, originally developed at Sun Microsystems during the early 1990s as a product called "Oak," is easily the focal point for most of the hype in Internet technology. If you believe half of what you read in magazines and Web sites, Java will be running your toaster, your automobile, and ultimately, your pets by the end of the century. By the way, it's also useful for making cool Web sites, which is somewhat appropriate because it's the only programming language we're aware of that has its own hip-looking mascot.

Java is a precompiled language similar to C++ in that it uses classes built from declarations. What this means is that you need a Java compiler and some programming dexterity before you can start building your own Java "applets," or programs. Java compilers are commercial software and are available from companies such as Sun, Symantec, Borland, Microsoft, Natural Intelligence, and a host of others. But you don't necessarily have to build your own applets to integrate Java's functionality into your page.

Why Use Java?

It is easy to pass information to Java from within Web documents. As the applet is downloaded from the server and executed, instructions contained in a simple HTML statement can control its functioning. The implications of this are significant because you can create generic applets and pass commands to them from HTML, without forcing Webmasters to learn complicated programming hierarchies, and without incurring any serious performance lags.

And there's more good news! Because Java is being revised slowly and carefully, the tools for creating Java applets from scratch may actually turn out to be simpler than some HTML editors. Several development kits exist today that require no programming on the part of the Webmaster to achieve some pretty interesting animation tricks and effects, such as "Ewan," from Sausage Software at http://www.sausage.com.

Java is supposed to be a cross-platform programming language. Unfortunately, it's still got some growing up to do before it propagates to every platform with 100% effectiveness.

The Java implementation on MacOS computers is, to say the least, still evolving. For the time being, Webmasters have to be careful not to rely too heavily on Java applets to anchor their interfaces. We had some problems with our example applet on MacOS machines running anything older than Netscape 3.01, and even then execution was slow. It's rather telling that even the JavaSoft home page at http://java.sun.com/ offers the Java version of its menu as an option, not as the default (see Figure 11.3). After you get to this menu, though, it's very functional.

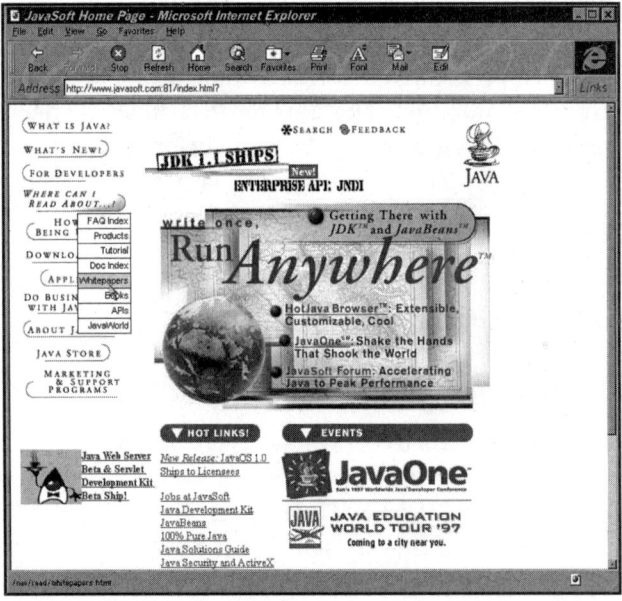

Figure 11.3

The Sun JavaSoft Web site.

As you roll over a menu item, the "button" alters and, for items with multiple subheadings, a pop-up menu appears, enabling you to select your destination from within it. This saves screen real estate, and the use of the rollover action makes the Web experience a great deal more like using traditional software. Now, we'll look at how to implement a similar applet ourselves.

Chapter 11 Beyond HTML: Making Web Sites That Think

Working with Java

Our sample applet, written by Nick Heinle, enables us to incorporate several different elements into menus on pages. "DYNIMG," as this applet is called, is a class that is downloaded when the page is viewed by a Java-capable browser. On Ian's sample site for Byte Computers, we use the applet to create several effects on a control panel contained in a frame that envelops the entire Web site to provide consistency (see Figure 11.4).

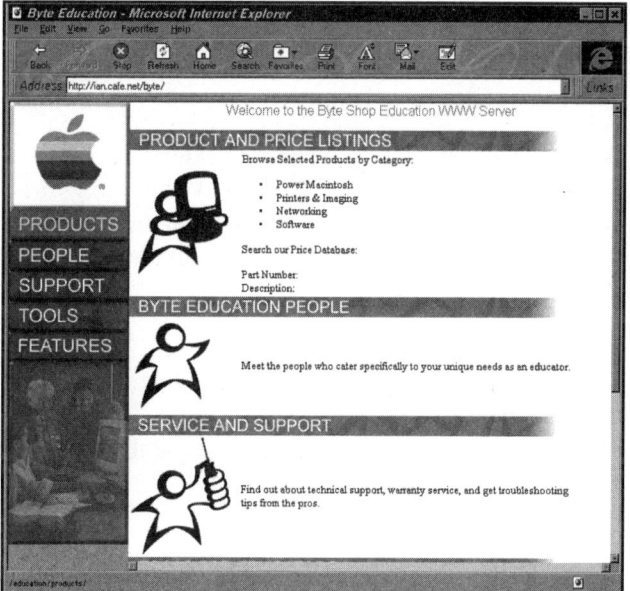

Figure 11.4

Byte Computers educational resources site.

The code that enables and controls this applet is as follows:

```
<APPLET CODE="dynimg.class" ALIGN="baseline" WIDTH="148" HEIGHT="35">
    <PARAM NAME="inactive_image" VALUE="prod.gif">
    <PARAM NAME="active_image" VALUE="prod2.gif">
    <PARAM NAME="active_sound" VALUE="bell1.au">
    <PARAM NAME="clicked_image" VALUE="prod3.gif">
    <PARAM NAME="clicked_sound" VALUE="bell2.au">
    <PARAM NAME="bgcolor" VALUE="#78B622">
    <PARAM NAME="url" VALUE="/education/products/">
    <PARAM NAME="target" VALUE="main">
```

```
            <A HREF="/education/products/" TARGET="main"><IMG SRC="prod.gif">
</A>
            </APPLET>
```

The applet code statement identifies the Java class we'll be using for this function so that it can be downloaded by the browser software. As the preceding code suggests, each image file in the control panel is executed as a separate applet. This applet needs instructions to be passed to it, accomplished by the use of <PARAM> tags: one for each file that the applet will use in the progression.

It's important to keep these files small, because they will each need to be loaded when the applet executes. You can incorporate both sound and image files into the buttons to achieve maximum effectiveness.

Just in case someone is viewing the Byte site without a Java-capable browser, we've included the usual <A HREF> and <IMG SRC> tags so that the applet is replaced by standard clickable images. We know that the old browsers will not understand (and will ignore) the <APPLET> and <PARAM> tags.

The meaning of each of the parameters is as follows:

Parameter	Function
INACTIVE_IMAGE	Image file to load and display until mouse activates the applet.
ACTIVE_IMAGE	Image file to load as mouse rolls over the button.
ACTIVE_SOUND	Sound file to load as mouse rolls over the button.
CLICKED_IMAGE	Image file to load when button is clicked.
CLICKED_SOUND	Sound file to load when button is clicked.
BGCOLOR	As in HTML, background color to use behind the image files.
URL	Document referenced by this applet (load on click).
TARGET	Target frame in which to load the referenced document.

Pretty simple, right? The Java class necessary for this function is available from Nick Heinle's contributions to the WebReference site at http://www.webreference.com/javascript.

Chapter 11 Beyond HTML: Making Web Sites That Think

We encourage you to explore the Web and discover the many sites we've listed in the appendix and on our site. There are many wonderful applets for you to make use of, without having to write your own code. As you learn more about what is possible, you'll be more prepared when you approach your first applet from scratch.

JavaScript and JScript

JavaScript and JScript have little to do with Java. The moniker was originally conceived at Netscape to propel JavaScript to the foreground amidst a swirl of hype about Sun's Java technology. Although Java and JavaScript are structured similarly, their implementations are altogether different.

JavaScript and JScript are roughly equivalent client-side programming languages as implemented by Netscape and Microsoft, respectively. They are excellent entry-level scripting languages, with most core functions being accessible to beginning programmers. You can sit down with a few commands and start piecing together the functions you need in a few hours. There is one caveat, though. When it comes to cross-platform compatibility, or even cross-browser compatibility, JavaScript and JScript are hit-and-miss.

Unfortunately, as the two languages are built around competing and evolving standards, more often than not, pages that make heavy use of JavaScript and JScript are announced by a plethora of error messages. Curiously, a reload of these broken pages sometimes seems to make these problems go away; however, not many users have learned this trick, and yet more of us make assumptions that any good error is a repeating error.

Why Use JavaScript and JScript?

Taking the previously stated considerations into account, once a standard is adopted these will likely be the predominant languages in use on the Web for the next few years—driven primarily by their ease of use. JavaScript and JScript are already creeping into your Web documents when you use their built-in event handlers, such as ONSUBMIT, ONCLICK, and ONBLUR.

The languages themselves enable you to quickly design dynamic pages that can be easily incorporated into your Web site, have very little impact on server performance or page loading times, and will be powerful once a baseline of reliability can be established. As Figure 11.5 shows, you can achieve some interesting effects in creating interactive interfaces even now.

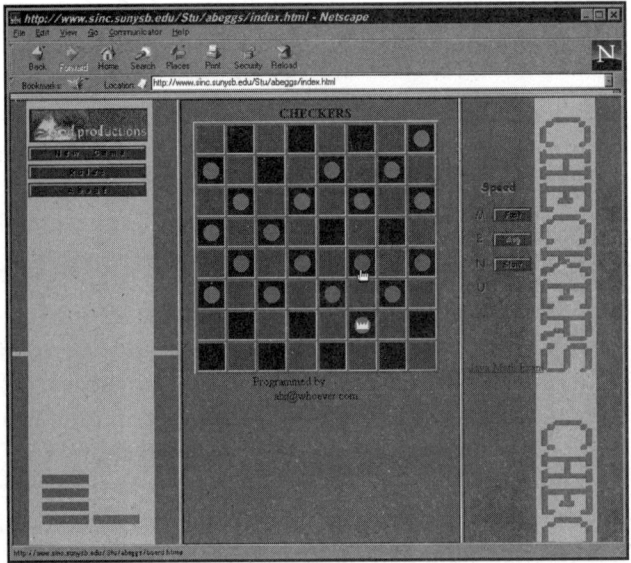

Figure 11.5

JavaScript outsmarts one of the authors.

Although it's great that we can play checkers, hangman, or tic-tac-toe with JavaScript, these scripting languages have far more interesting implications with regard to user interface design. JavaScript and JScript both enable you to do some fascinating work in tweaking the layout of your page or making your forms easier to work with.

Working with JavaScript and JScript

JavaScript and JScript are embedded into your Web pages either as event handlers within HTML tags (such as ONCLICK and ONMOUSEOVER in <INPUT> tags) or as statements and functions using the <SCRIPT> tag. The latter method conforms more to the traditional notion of the scripting language, and because we've already shown you a few of the HTML-based functions in action, this subsection will focus on the use of JavaScript within self-contained scripts. These are evaluated and can be run after the page loads. Functions are stored, but they are not executed until they are invoked by events in the page.

Chapter 11 Beyond HTML: Making Web Sites That Think

The next example shows you how to check a form to make sure that all of the fields are consistent with what the server expects to receive (before you waste any of the server's valuable CGI processing time). This also gives you some assurance that the data filled into the form fields at least looks like it's correct before the JavaScript hands the data off to the MAILTO CGI.

For this to work, some modifications must be made to the previous form.html file. We only have to modify one line in the form.html file that we used earlier in this chapter and add the script function near the end of the body of the message. The lines that follow represent additions that activate the script and enable it to do its work:

```
<FORM ACTION="/cgi-bin/mailto.exe" METHOD="POST" NAME="mail_form"
ENCTYPE = "multipart/form-data"
ONSUBMIT="return formValidate()">
```

The form now has a name that gives the script a way to reference it. ENCTYPE enables the script to parse the inputted data and grab each variable, and the onSubmit event handler invokes the script when the user clicks the form's Submit button. Subsequently, you can add the following lines of JavaScript at the end of the HTML file to make it all come together:

```
<SCRIPT LANGUAGE = "JavaScript">
<!-- this hides the script from old browsers
function formValidate()
{
        if (document.mail_form.email.value.indexOf("@") == -1 ||
        document.mail_form.email.value == "")
        {
        alert("Please use a proper email address.");
        return false;
        }

        if (document.mail_form.uname.value == "")
        {
        alert("Please enter your name.");
        return false;
        }
}
// end hiding from old browsers -->
</SCRIPT>
```

If it doesn't find the data it expects, the script displays an alert box (see Figure 11.6). Now you have some verification to ensure that the email address contains the @ character and that the person has entered a real name. Note the placement of the comment markers—they hide the JavaScript from old browsers so that the text of the script doesn't get laid out on the page for Netscape 1.1 users.

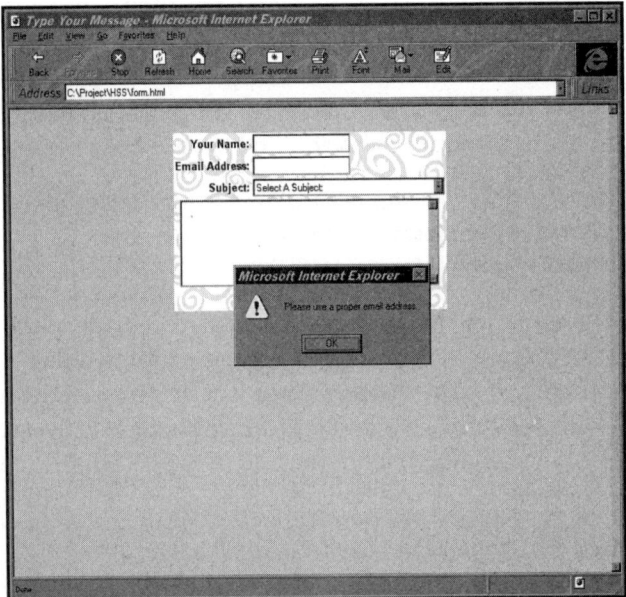

Figure 11.6
The Alert dialog box keeps users from leaving out information.

ActiveX

ActiveX (formerly known by the moniker OLE for Object Linking and Embedding) is a technology that has been a part of the Windows operating system for some time. It was only recently that this technology was adapted for use by the Web browser.

ActiveX is essentially a framework through which applications can share screen real estate, exchange data, and share workspace within the operating environment.

For example, you can run a Microsoft Excel document within a Netscape window, or you can operate a fully functional Windows 95 game within a frame on a Web site.

Chapter 11 Beyond HTML: Making Web Sites That Think

If you see a trend here, you're beginning to catch on. The one major drawback of ActiveX is the fact that for the foreseeable future it is directly married to the 32-bit Windows operating system. For as long as any platform is unable to run a Windows executable, it will be cut out of the ActiveX picture.

Sites that make use of ActiveX within the browser provide a peek into the future of network computing, providing true real-time applications sharing over great distances through the use of component-based software.

ActiveX components that you can use in your site are a lot harder to come by than their Java counterparts. On the whole, though, the classes you'll find are rather stunning because they come from commercially motivated producers like NCompass Labs of Vancouver, Canada. The spinning cube (see Figure 11.7) is a good example. It uses a control to load six images, one into each face of the cube, and it spins the cube on three axes. It is also controllable through left mouse-clicks, and resizable through right mouse-clicks.

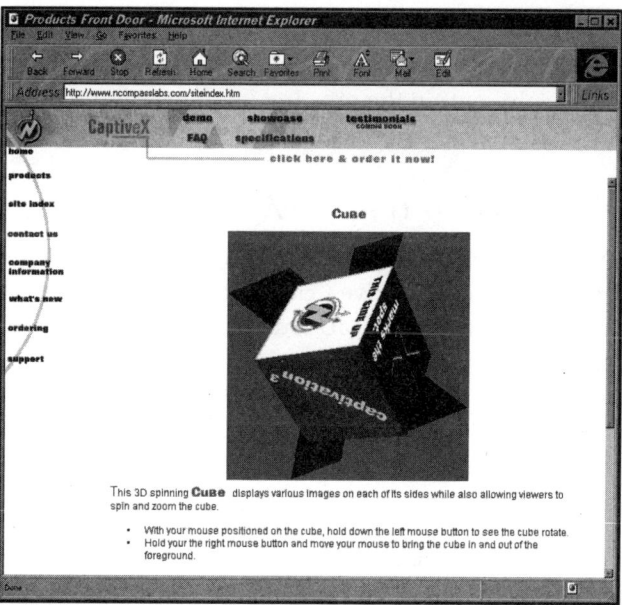

Figure 11.7

NCompass Labs spinning cube.

Why Use ActiveX?

If you're fortunate enough to have a predefined audience such as would occur with a software company that only made Windows software, or with a corporate intranet where the company had standardized on Windows 95, then using a component for ActiveX might be right for your site.

ActiveX is precompiled; and therefore, it executes significantly faster. The classes your clients will have to download are smaller in byte size than Java classes. In addition, the fact that ActiveX has less restricted security measures means greater flexibility in terms of what the components can accomplish.

In short, ActiveX is an excellent tool, but only if you can get away with using it. Support for ActiveX is incorporated into the Microsoft Internet Explorer Web browser and is a major component of Microsoft's strategy for Internet technologies. The plug-in that brings ActiveX to Netscape is available for evaluation from NCompass via their Web site at http://www.ncompasslabs.com/.

Given its tremendous potential and tainted by its platform dependency, it is highly likely that the use of ActiveX components in Web documents will evolve within the growing intranet marketplace, ultimately spinning out into the mainstream as other operating platforms catch up.

Working with ActiveX

Now that you've worked at putting Java applets into your Web pages, incorporating an ActiveX class into your Web page should seem like a piece of cake. The HTML code that makes the PowerPanels component work is similar to the structure of the HTML for the Java applet we covered earlier. Unfortunately, you can't implement this or many other components without purchasing the certified product from the developer, so what you're learning here is largely theory until you purchase a copy.

PowerPanels creates wipes and fades between a series of GIFs as its primary function (see Figure 11.8). Unfortunately, until we can animate this paper page, you'll have to take our word for it when we say that the effect is visually stunning. The HTML code, as with Java, works using the same structure as our Java applet:

Chapter 11 Beyond HTML: Making Web Sites That Think

```
<OBJECT ID="PowerPanels1" WIDTH=175 HEIGHT=175
   CLASSID="CLSID:039F8323-0FBF-11D0-B21E-00A02443D8EF"
   CODEBASE="../controls/npwrpnl2.cab#version=5,0,4,1">
   <PARAM NAME="_Version" VALUE="65536">
   <PARAM NAME="_ExtentX" VALUE="5027">
   <PARAM NAME="_ExtentY" VALUE="5027">
   <PARAM NAME="_StockProps" VALUE="0">
   <PARAM NAME="_LicenseKey" VALUE="This Control licensed to NCompass Labs
Inc. only. XJRXFTAOAVVVIPQI (c)1996 NCompass Labs Inc. Neither the Control
nor this text can be duplicated without license.">


</OBJECT>
```

Figure 11.8

NCompass Labs PowerPanels Control.

In the <OBJECT> tag several descriptors are used to identify the control. The ID= parameter of the <OBJECT> tag gives this particular object a "handle," or a special name so that when it is activated in future Web pages it will not need to reload all of the components. It also identifies the control so that if you need to interact with it using VBScript or even JavaScript you can call it by name.

The `CLASSID=` parameter represents the unique locator for this control within your Windows registry—it's like a URL that uniquely identifies where Windows can find the control on your computer. After it's been downloaded, the ActiveX component need not be downloaded again.

The `CODEBASE=` parameter is the location where your Web browser can find the ActiveX control and download it if it has never seen the control before. For instances where you see Web pages that do not identify a `CODEBASE=` parameter, rejoice! It is already installed on your computer by Windows 95.

Note the need for a LicenseKey field in the HTML code for this particular object. This prevents non-approved sites or users from making use of your components, and it gives NCompass a means of tracking components in the event that they spread due to piracy. Your license key is applied by NCompass when you purchase the product.

Obviously, the emphasis with ActiveX components can be placed on the integrity of developers' and providers' products. You can allow someone to use advanced functions on your Web site without exposing that component to unauthorized use and duplication.

It wasn't necessary to show you the entire code (more than 40 lines) that configured the ActiveX component because you won't be able to use it without purchasing the product. As with the Java applet, the parameters that are passed will be radically different from case to case. The PowerPanels Control is used, again like the Java applet, once for each animated square—which is, in the case of our example, twice.

Conclusion

You now have several more weapons in your arsenal for building highly advanced Web sites. More important, we hope that you've learned where these advanced techniques can be best applied. The last thing that anyone wants to see on the Web is a page that announces itself with a JavaScript runtime error, or crashes the browser because an applet failed to execute. As an effective designer, you want to tailor your site's services to the needs and limitations of your audience, not force users to endure errors and confusing, broken pages on their way to your valuable information.

Chapter 11 Beyond HTML: Making Web Sites That Think

You'll likely find yourself being a lot more liberal with your use of Java, ActiveX, and especially JavaScript a few months down the road from now, as the world catches up to these new standards. Unfortunately though, in making the Web a cleaner, more advanced technological frontier, we have to be careful not to saturate the limited bandwidth or to create pages that break whenever the client type strays in the slightest from what we expect (or hope for). It's wise to use these techniques with caution.

When in doubt, you can always fall back on CGIs. There is an extensive library of pre-built solutions out there and available for freeware use. The basic framework for coding your own CGIs on most platforms is so easy that it can be quickly enhanced by even a beginning programmer.

Whichever means you choose, we encourage you to make use of the collections and examples we've referenced on our Web site and CD-ROM. They will prove to be excellent resources as you further explore and develop these new arrows for your quiver.

The next chapter introduces you to your server, helping you to choose the right server options for your Web development and how to go about obtaining the right software for the job. We can't teach you how to use Unix in a single chapter, so if you're unfamiliar with one of the platforms we discuss, you should definitely allow that to influence your decision.

chapter 12

Working with Your Web Server

So you're now making a fortune building Web sites and your friendly Internet Service Provider, having run out of disk space and feeling the impact of your hugely popular sites on its performance monitor, is encouraging you to build your own Web server. What a fantastic problem to have!

There are many good reasons to establish your own Web server, but the primary one is self-determination. If you have explicit control over the machine, then you can allocate resources more effectively, keep better track of its activity, and make your own choices about where and how it should operate. An Internet Service Provider may be able to provide most of this information, but its agenda, not yours, is guiding the fates of your Web sites. This is why many companies (who might someday be your clients) prefer to operate their own servers.

 Comparing Platforms

Microsoft Internet Information Server for Windows NT

WebSTAR for MacOS

 Apache for Unix

Comparing Platforms

Let's face it: The best platform (or server operating system) to choose is the one you know. You're not going to be particularly effective administering a $30,000 Sun Microsystems SPARCstation if you've never seen a Unix prompt before, no matter how much faster the manual claims it'll go. There are certain subtle and not-so-subtle nuances you'll want to evaluate before you commit funds and effort to the running of your own Web server.

Figure 12.1 shows the clear lines along which most servers fall. You might want to take the advice of others, but be forewarned that your needs may be unique.

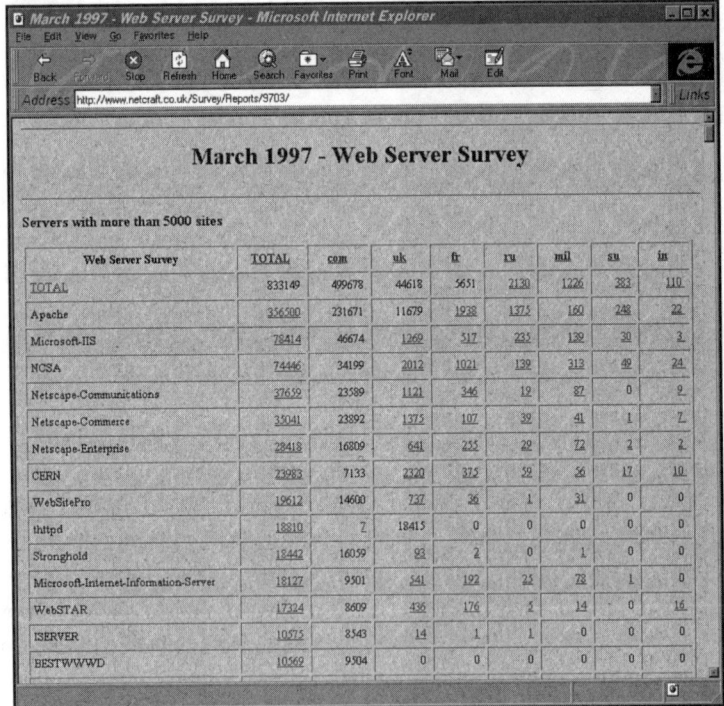

Figure 12.1

NetCraft U.K.'s server survey for March 1997.

The factors you should be considering, as with any other product, are performance, accessibility, extensibility, survivability, security, manageability, and cost.

Chapter 12 Working with Your Web Server

Performance

Can the machine and operating system successfully cope with the loads you are placing on it? Some platforms, as you will see, cope better with strict file request output than with CGI processing. Others have hang-ups when it comes to linking with databases, and so on. How much performance you need depends on whether you're serving four pages to a dedicated audience of three users or 2,300 pages to the world.

Accessibility

A major determining factor is the platform you use to author your sites. How is your workstation going to talk to your Web server? How well do you know how to communicate with the server's operating system?

Extensibility

Around each server product there has evolved a community of hard-working solutions providers that work as third parties to add functionality to each server through CGIs and APIs. What are the solutions you need? What is out there (both as freeware and as commercial product) for you to implement in your Web site? How much effort or expense is required to implement these solutions?

Survivability

Although this is a hotly contested and highly subjective category, influencing factors of the operating systems we'll discuss can affect your server's up time. Nobody likes to get up at 5:30 a.m. and power cycle their server. Some operating systems present more stable platforms than others, but often at the expense of increased complexity.

Security

How does your server software protect itself from unwanted intruders? Are there a plethora of daemons (in other jargon, server applications) that need patching? Are there monthly reports of loopholes being exploited by unfriendlies on your favorite operating system? Some people like to hack their way into servers and steal private files. As we'll see there's a dramatic difference among the platforms in how easy (if at all possible) this is.

Manageability

What is beyond your bounds? All of the other considerations mean nothing if you don't have the necessary knowledge to get the server up and keep it running. Does it require dedicated personnel to maintain it or can it run, virtually ignored, in your shoe closet beside your first pair of Vans? This is a major consideration if you want your focus to be on production and not maintenance.

Cost

How expensive will your foray into Internet serving be? Although you can influence all of the previously mentioned factors by throwing money at them, the baseline and recurrent costs of each platform are dramatically different.

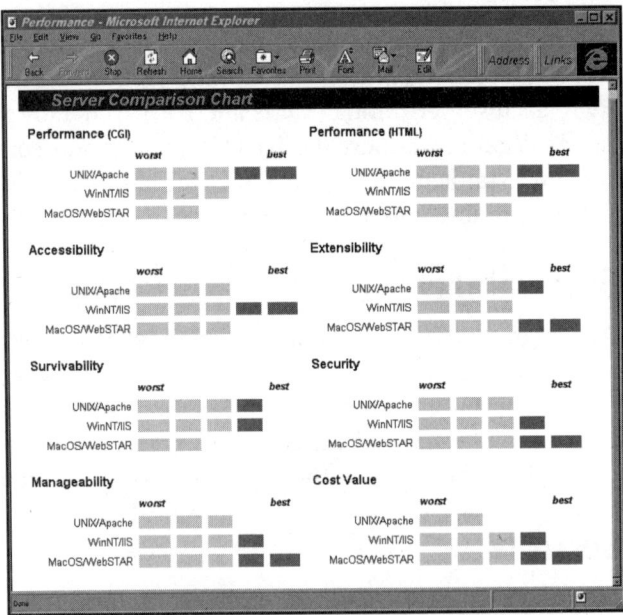

Figure 12.2

Window shopping for your server.

Figure 12.2 shows the different strengths and weaknesses of the various server platforms. This subjective measurement, based upon my real world experiences with the three major platforms, reveals no clear winner. It does, however, paint a good picture of Windows NT as a successful compromise.

Chapter 12 Working with Your Web Server

Microsoft Internet Information Server for Windows NT

Microsoft's Internet Information Server is the Web server platform of choice for the Microsoft Windows NT network operating system; it has experienced radical growth in recent months. The tight integration between OS and server reveals some tremendous performance advantages, and the graphical user interface linked to a powerful and well-designed engine gives you efficient access to the tools you'll need. Although the entire suite of tools that come with Microsoft BackOffice can be expensive, you'll get plenty of goodies to help build your site both today and as your needs grow down the road.

Features of IIS

The features of IIS and by extension Windows NT are as follows:

- **Server stability** is greatly improved with Windows NT 4.0 server, as are data throughput, memory management, and disk performance. Used in combination with fault tolerant hardware, NT represents a viable contender for bulletproof Internet service provision.

- **Multi-homing** represents a great advantage for IIS on the NT platform. Whereas Unix-based Web servers use a specific memory allocation for individual servers catering to multi-homed Web sites, NT assigns this memory dynamically. In essence, you get the most out of your physical memory, rather than assigning chunks of RAM to a specific site whether or not it's required. This, in addition to the ease with which you can serve up to 254 discrete Web sites from a single machine with one network card, makes NT the best multi-homing platform, period.

- **ISAPI**, a set of handles built into both the operating system and the Web server software, enables CGI authors to add high-speed functionality right into the server. Microsoft has demonstrated this ably by including some unique tools such as Active Server Pages with its product. Commercial third-party developers view this as an enabling technology around which they can build a great amount of value in added functions with incredible performance.

▶ **Dynamic Documents** take information from evolving databases and lay them out as Web pages each time the page is requested. Changes in the database are reflected in the Web documents. Usually dynamic documents are built from databases, constructing HTML from templates, replacing values based on user input. A tremendous advantage for Internet Information Server is its tight integration with Microsoft SQL and other ODBC database servers. Again, because all the tools you need come from Microsoft, you're ahead of the game.

▶ **Secure Sockets Layer (SSL)** is the key-certified means of securing communication between the server and the client. It's a valuable feature for commerce servers, and it is also included with Internet Information Server.

Connecting to the Server

Windows NT provides by far the greatest number of options for connecting over both local and wide area networks (LANs and WANs). If you're lucky enough to be on the same local area network as the NT server, you can talk to it over Windows networking or AppleTalk (assuming file sharing for Macintosh is installed and enabled). You can also perform remote administration of the server graphically, either via the Web or Windows Networking.

If you are connecting to the server remotely (from home, for instance) you have three basic options:

1. Using FTP you can connect to your server (with the IIS FTP server enabled) and access files using your regular account. From the end user's perspective, this is exactly the same as connecting to a Unix-based server.

2. Using the Microsoft FrontPage extensions for IIS, you have a tremendous range of possibilities for communicating with, and directly controlling, your Web server. If you like FrontPage, this is a great option. Getting this to work is as simple as installing FrontPage on an NT server that already has IIS running.

3. Using LMHOSTS is a very neat trick for getting file sharing-like access over an Internet connection to your NT Web server (if you're a Windows 95 user). In your WINDOWS directory (usually

Chapter 12 Working with Your Web Server

C:\WINDOWS) you should find two files: one is "LMHOSTS." and the other is "LMHOSTS.SAM". The second file is a sample that will help you in the event that you mess up on the first one. Figure 12.3 demonstrates how this file should look.

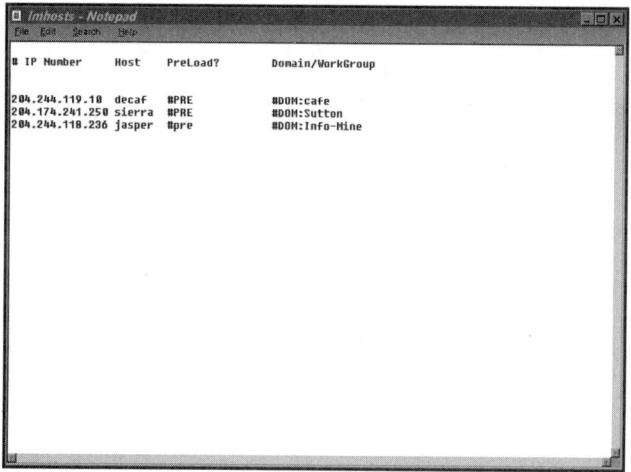

Figure 12.3

The LMHOSTS file.

Using the sample file as a guide, type in the IP address of your Web server (if you're using multiple IP addresses for multi-homing, choose the first number) and its name. Always add the <#PRE> tag so that the record is referenced and stored in memory, and add the Windows Networking domain (not the domain name) in which the server resides. Next, save the file (making sure it's named LMHOSTS and not LMHOSTS.TXT) and reboot your computer.

When you're back online, select Find Computer from the Start menu and type in the host's name exactly as you typed it in the LMHOSTS file. After a long delay, the server should appear in the results window as shown in Figure 12.4. Drag its icon to your desktop and you now have a shortcut to the server. With a decent, stable connection you will be able to drag files onto the server as if it was in the next room, albeit a tad slower.

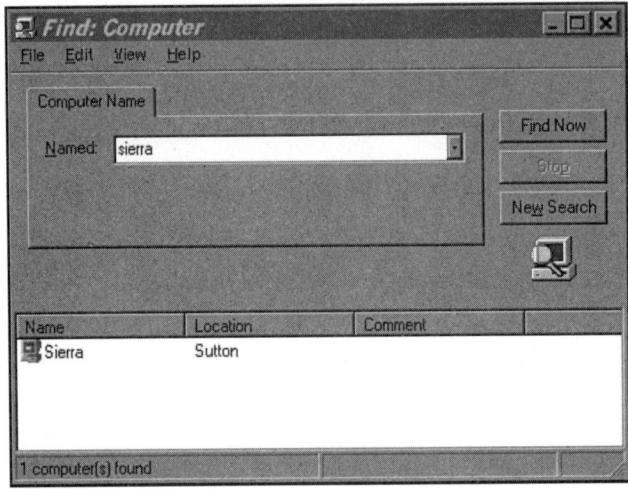

Figure 12.4

Using the Find Computer command.

Resources for IIS Administrators

The developer community is growing rapidly around IIS, but the technology is relatively new as compared to WebSTAR (nee MacHTTP) and Apache (basically a beefed-up version of the original CERN HTTPd). Third-party support still has a ways to go before it can catch up to the other platforms. As well, you'll be paying no small sum for most of the CGIs you use, unless they're from Microsoft (in this case, they are usually free). Following are some resources for your exploration of IIS.

The first place to visit is the Microsoft IIS Web site. It's an excellent example of the technologies we discuss in this book for both the server and the client. From this site, you'll learn about the tools Microsoft provides free with the server (as a part of the BackOffice suite) and get news and even evaluation copies.

http://www.microsoft.com/iis/default.asp

Jim Buyens has compiled some useful tools for Windows NT Server and IIS users, as well as some support documents that can be found at:

http://www.primenet.com/~buyensj/ntwebsrv.html

The people at Beverly Hills Software have worked very hard to provide an attractive and functional site that shows examples of IIS in action and provides a plethora of links to resources and developers around the Net:

http://www.bhs.com/ntwebsites/

WebSTAR for MacOS

WebSTAR is the platform of choice for the rest of us. At one point in the Web's evolution, it was the third most common Web server software in operation. Although this is no longer the case, WebSTAR is a viable, and indeed, vibrant platform that has experienced amazing growth, especially in situations where the dedicated personnel to support a Web server do not exist or where convenience supersedes the need for performance. WebSTAR, in its latest incarnation, is no slouch, although some of its limitations are trickled-down from the limitations of the MacOS, it is a very nice piece of software that is firmly rooted in the Mac's emphasis on ease of use.

Given the instability of recent MacOS revisions, especially with regard to their networking software OpenTransport, the prospective server administrator should be warned that extensions and control panels (even ones originating from Apple) present a whole minefield of potential problems.

Experienced MacOS users have already had to deal with these, though, and therefore the concern is relatively minor. Inexperienced users should turn to tools such as Conflict Catcher to help them diagnose conflicts and problems. Although Unix users must be diligent about reading the latest security alerts, MacOS Webmasters must be as diligent (if not more so) about OS updates, extensions patches, and bug reports.

Features of WebSTAR

WebSTAR's success is largely due to its emphasis on features rather than the MacOS' performance, as the Macintosh was clearly conceived as a single-user machine rather than a server platform and suffers significant performance degradation as a result:

- **Third-party support** for WebSTAR is perhaps the strongest of any of the server software products. A large and friendly community has grown around the software since its inception as MacHTTP. The collective efforts of a few hundred developers and individuals have contributed volumes of added value to the server product. The fact that many of this software is free (or at least shareware) is a nice bonus, too.

- It's been said that hacking your way into a Macintosh is like hacking your way into a fridge—there simply are no points of entry. **Security** on the MacOS is very solid, for the simple reason that the operating system was never intended for network computing. Whereas Unix servers have scores of daemons to be uninstalled before you begin, the MacOS has none. Since late 1995, a contest offering $10,000 USD to anyone who could edit a file on a WebSTAR server has yielded no claimants.

- The **Plug-ins API** is WebSTAR's answer to ISAPI. It's a simple framework that gives developers streamlined access to the server in their CGI software. The plug-ins load at startup and remain in memory all the time. They bypass the CGI framework, and therefore, experience significant performance gains by providing services like server-side includes and redirection.

- **Multi-homing** is supported through third-party applications such as HomeDoor; it is, however, not fully transparent and requires you to reveal the host server's "real" hostname. This is a limitation imposed by OpenTransport, Apple's networking protocol.

- **SSL** is available as part of the WebSTAR 2.0 package, as with IIS. The **Java Virtual Machine** enables the execution of server-side Java applets and is included with WebSTAR 2.0, along with many other bells and whistles such as:

    - Built-in imagemap handling

      Built-in forms to SMTP (email) handling

    - Expanded command set for server-side includes (enables you to add headers, and so on to outbound data)

    - Built-in support for "page-at-a-time" byte streaming of Acrobat PDF files

Chapter 12 Working with Your Web Server

▶ Full conformance to HTTP 1.1 specifications

▶ The **cost** of the WebSTAR server software is remarkably low, and it can be run competently on any PowerPC Mac over 100mHz with about 32 MB RAM. Taking into account the total cost of implementation on other platforms, the WebSTAR/Mac combination comes in at a substantially lower price.

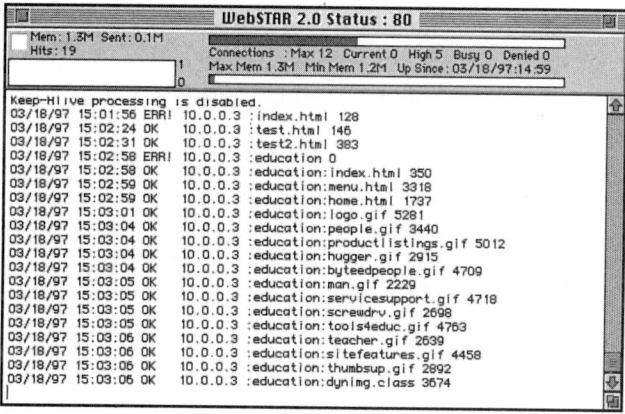

Figure 12.5

The famous WebSTAR status window.

Finally, perhaps the nicest feature of WebSTAR is its scrolling status window, which enables you to monitor the activity of your server in real-time by watching the various clients viewing pages on your site. Apart from having definite emotional appeal, this feature enables you to debug CGIs, find errors on the site, and observe how the server handles different types of loads with different memory and cache settings, and so on.

Connecting to the Server

Although Macs prefer to talk with other Macs, there's nothing to prevent you from creating your files on a Mac and uploading them to the server for testing:

1. **AppleShare** is perhaps your simplest option if you have a Mac as your workstation. If this is the case, you can do everything, including managing the server, over your existing AppleTalk network. WebSTAR ships with its remote administration application for you to install on other machines on your network.

2. If you're using **Windows 95** to author your Web site, a product called COPStalk will solve your connectivity problems. It enables PC users to connect to AppleShare/AppleTalk devices and file servers, and it represents the easiest way to talk to your server. The software is available from http://www.copstalk.com/.

3. Using **FTP** to access your server is an option available through another piece of software called "NetPresenz," written by Peter Lewis, one of the premier designers of Macintosh Internet software. NetPresenz makes use of your already existing file sharing accounts and privileges to ease setup and administration. NetPresenz is shareware and is available from http://www.stairways.com/.

Resources for WebSTAR Administrators

The "us and them" mindset that pervades the Mac community can work in your favor here. The strength of the support from freeware/shareware developers is surprising even to veteran Mac users, and the wide range of options for enhancing your server is definitely a big part of the appeal of MacOS-based Web serving.

The best place to start your research is of course at the home of Star-Nine, the creators of WebSTAR 2.0. They provide a wealth of information and many resources to get you up and running:

http://www.starnine.com/

Another good source is Ian (your humble author) Bell's own Web site for Macintosh Webmasters, in operation at various sites since 1993:

http://www.byteshop.com/ian/tools

Apache for Unix

As you saw in Figure 12.1, Apache is clearly the most popular Web server on the Internet: a signifier that Unix is still very much alive and well and keeping things running. The appeal of the Apache/Unix option for the Webmaster is raw horsepower and stability. Given that both the operating system and, in many cases, the hardware platforms are designed purely for network computing, it's no surprise that this combination is chosen for most high-end Web serving environments.

Chapter 12 Working with Your Web Server

Apache is maintained by an organization, not a company. As a result, it is freeware, and it is maintained by committee. The work that they have done along Apache's rapid growth track has been amazing, and the degree to which this software has been embraced by Webmasters bears testimony to its quality and strength.

It is not a viable platform for the inexperienced or the faint of heart, mind you—maintaining a Unix server and its various daemons is a full-time occupation. The risk of not keeping up with the latest security patches and fixes is very hazardous, and the complexity of the operating system ensures that many trees will be sacrificed to the publishing gods in order to educate the novice administrator.

As with most of us, however, you'll likely be maintaining your own little cubbyhole on someone else's Apache server. Therefore, you should read this section to gain a better understanding of what you're up against.

Features of Apache for Unix

Author's biases aside, why would you want to run Unix and Apache? The answer is simple: performance. If you want to configure a machine that is relatively bullet-proof and probably faster than a cluster of small-to-medium-sized Web sites will ever need, here's the ticket. It's also extremely scaleable, so if Sony ever beats down your door offering a lucrative contract, you're ready. The notable features of the Unix/Apache solution are as follows:

- Compatibility is usually a major headache with Unix applications—not so much with Apache. It will compile on almost any platform available, from FreeBSD to Linux to Solaris, although it does encounter several different problems on each.

- Compliance with all of the latest standards is important, too. HTTP 1.1 features are already integrated into recent Apache releases. Also, Apache uses a Server Side Includes framework similar to that of WebSTAR.

- Multi-homing is achieved through a combination of a server handler called "InetD" and Apache. Unfortunately, it still requires the allocation of separate server processes and thus memory allocations for virtual servers (which is inefficient use of resources, though very fast).

- Proxying, a feature not native to any of the non-Unix servers, is also an optional feature with Apache. Proxying enables the Web server to act as a medium between a secure local network and the Internet at large, caching frequently requested files, and providing a secure curtain for users.

- Built-in support for browser-based environment variables enables you to write different HTML pages for each browser type and let Apache determine which ones are appropriate and serve them out accordingly. This is a valuable feature that other platforms can only acheive through the use of CGIs.

- Security is always a concern, but several steps are taken to lower risk, such as having the capability to run CGIs under user accounts other than the one that starts the server. This enables you to give CGI user accounts highly restricted privileges.

Connecting to Your Unix HTTP Server

Although there are a wide range of highly complex connectivity options, realistically your only portal to your files is likely to be server access via FTP. Because the FTP daemon already exists on the server, you don't need to download it from anywhere. What you do need to get a hold of is an FTP client.

MacOS

If you're on the MacOS platform we recommend a program, again by Peter Lewis, called Anarchie. It is a simple application that incorporates the increasingly obscure Archie FTP server search protocol with a really good FTP connection interface. It's available at http://www.stairways.com/.

Figure 12.6 displays the simple Anarchie connect window pane. Just fill in where you want to go and who you are and you're away! Clicking the Get Listing radio button will always show you the files in the current directory before you begin work. The easiest way to place your files is to drag them from the desktop into the directory listing.

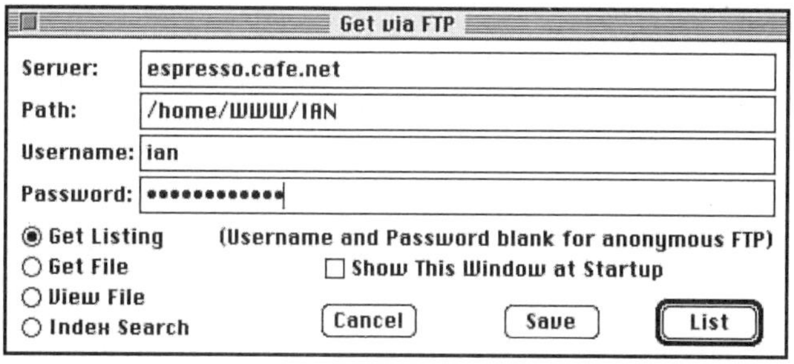
Get via FTP
Server:
espresso.cafe.net
Path:
/home/WWW/IAN
Username:
ian
Password:
Get Listing
(Username and Password blank for anonymous FTP)
Get File
Show This Window at Startup
View File
Index Search
Cancel
Save
List

Figure 12.6

The Anarchie connect window.

Windows 95/NT

If you're using Windows 95, you should ignore the built-in FTP client and head directly for a program called WS_FTP from IpSwitch. This is an elegant yet powerful application that enables you to perform many useful Unix tasks on the remote host, in addition to file transfer and remote editing. It's available at `http://www.ipswitch.com/`.

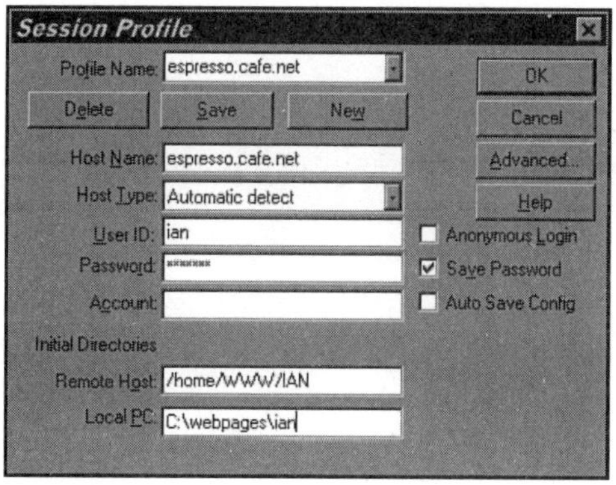
Session Profile
Profile Name:
espresso.cafe.net
Delete
Save
New
OK
Cancel
Host Name:
espresso.cafe.net
Advanced...
Host Type:
Automatic detect
Help
User ID:
ian
Anonymous Login
Password:
Save Password
Account:
Auto Save Config
Initial Directories
Remote Host:
/home/WWW/IAN
Local PC:
C:\webpages\ian

Figure 12.7

The WS_FTP connect window.

WS_FTP is an easy tool to use, and it enables you to specify both remote and local directories, which is convenient for frequent visits. Just enter the pertinent data and away you go. After you're connected, it's as easy as using the arrow keys to move files back and forth.

Resources for Unix/Apache Administrators

The organizational infrastructure that surrounds this highly popular product is, as you'd expect, very large. Although it's contributed to mostly by nonprofit groups and individuals, the support you'll find is excellent.

The starting point for getting to know Apache is of course its home Web site. It contains all of the product information, security alerts, and latest downloads for the software. You'll probably want to bookmark this for frequent visits:

http://www.apache.org/

You can also check out a weekly newsletter and Web site with lots of Apache-specific information, tools, documentation, and links:

http://www.apacheweek.com/

A great example of what a dedicated individual can bring to the Internet, Matt's Script Archive, is definitely a great starting point for exploring the possibilities of your Apache server:

http://www.worldwidemart.com/scripts/

Conclusion

We've presented three options to you—each representing the leaders of the major hardware platforms. There is a much wider range of products out there, and as the tides of popularity for one product wane, another is inevitably stepping up to take its place. A good server administrator always monitors the environment surrounding software that he implements and maintains a keen eye for any advantages to be gained through change.

Chapter 12 Working with Your Web Server

No one product will be perfect for you. Performance comparisons are not included in this book because they are highly subjective and rarely reflect real world use. In our experience, Windows NT using Internet Information Server has represented a good compromise between ease of maintenance and setup, reliability, and cost.

You may, however, have unique needs and desires that lead you toward a different product. Our best advice is to learn to sort through the hype to get to the real meat: Ask the question, and then search for the best possible answer.

If, after surfing your way through all of the resources we suggested, you're still confused, join some of the organizational mailing lists, and read newsgroups in the `comp.sys.infosystems.www` hierarchy to get a sense for how the users feel about the various platforms.

index

Symbols

% (percent signs), form encoding, 138
& (ampersands), form encoding, 138
* (asterisks), form input passwords, 142
+ (plus signs)
    font size, 46-47
    form encoding, 138
– (minus signs), font size, 46-47
3D text, 199-202
    see also shadow effects

A

<A> tag, 63-68, 266
    HREF attribute, 64-66
    NAME attribute, 66-68
    TARGET attribute (frames), 170-171
Acetex Corporation Web site, 2, 16
ACTION attribute, <FORM> tag, 136
actions (Photoshop), 211-215
    animated GIFs, 244
    Button mode, 211-212
    copying, 214
    Default mode, 211
    editing, 214
    recording, 214
ActiveX, 270-274
    advantages, 272
    forms, 137
    incorporating ActiveX classes, 272-274
    obtaining, 272
Adobe Photoshop, *see* Photoshop 4.0
AIFF files, *see* audio
alert boxes, 270
ALIGN attribute
    <COL> tag, 131
    <COLGROUP> tag, 128-129
    <FRAME> tag, 168-169
    <HR> tag, 56
    <IMAGE> tag, 71-72
    <INPUT> tag, 148-149
    <P> tag, 52-53
    <TABLE> tag, 93-94
    <TD> tag, 113-114
    <TR> tag, 108
alignment
    frames, 168-169
    horizontal rules, 56
    images, 71-72
        forms, 148-149

paragraph text, 52-53
tables, 93-94
  cells, 113-115
  columns, 128-129, 131
ALINK attribute, <BODY> tag, 43-44
alpha channel mapping, transparent GIFs, 186
ALT attribute
  <AREA> tag (imagemaps), 80
  <IMAGE> tag, 75
alternate text
  imagemaps, 80
  images, 75
ampersands (&), form encoding, 138
Anarchie program, 290
anchors, 63-64, 66-68
  visual (icons), 191
  see also links
animated GIFs, 229-231
  backgrounds, 243
  fade animations, 243-250
    assembling animation, 247-250
    creating images (Photoshop), 243-247
    global palettes, 245-246
    Macintosh (GifBuilder), 247-248
    PC (GIF Animator), 249-250
  file size, 237-239
  flashing animations, 254
  GIF Animator (PC), 232, 234-237
    backgrounds, 243
    changing animation parameters, 236
    duration (timing), 242
    fade animations, 249-250
    glowing animations, 254
    Loop command, 237
    moving animations, 255-256
  GIF Construction Set (PC), 232, 234-237
    backgrounds, 243
    Control command, 242
    Delay (timing), 242
    global palette, 234-235
    inserting control options, 236-237

GifBuilder (Mac), 231-234
  Effects menu, 234
  fade animations, 247-248
  Frame Position, 233
  glowing animations, 253
  Interframe Delay, 233
  Loop command, 233
  moving animations, 255
  Options menu, 232-233
glowing animations, 250-254
  assembling animation, 253-254
  creating images (Photoshop), 250-252
  Macintosh (GifBuilder), 253
  PC (GIF Animator), 254
moving animations, 255-256
  assembling animation, 255-256
  creating images (Photoshop), 255
  Macintosh (GifBuilder), 255
  PC (GIF Animator), 255-256
palettes, 240
  creating global palettes, 240-242
  timing, 242
anti-aliasing, transparent GIFs, 185-186
Apache for Unix server, 288-292
  Apache Web site, 292
  connecting to, 290-292
  resources, 292
Apple's 20th Anniversary Mac Web site, 10
<APPLET> tag (Java applets), 265-267
<AREA> tag, imagemaps, 78-80
asterisks (*), form input passwords, 142
attributes
  ACTION, <FORM> tag, 136
  ALIGN
    <COL> tag, 131
    <COLGROUP> tag, 128-129
    <FRAME> tag, 168-169
    <HR> tag, 56
    <INPUT> tag, 148-149
    <P> tag, 52-53
    <TABLE> tag, 93-94
    <TD> tag, 113-114
    <TR> tag, 108

ALINK, <BODY> tag, 43-44
ALT
  <AREA> tag, 80
  <IMAGE> tag, 75
AUTOPLAY, <EMBED> tag, 89
BACKGROUND
  <BODY> tag, 31-39
  <TABLE> tag (Explorer), 105-106
  <TD> tag (Explorer), 124-125
BGCOLOR
  <BODY> tag, 39-42, 189
  <TABLE> tag, 94
  <TD> tag, 115-116
  <TR> tag, 110-111
BGPROPERTIES, <BODY> tag, 42
BORDER
  <IMAGE> tag, 72-73
  <TABLE> tag, 95-96
BORDERCOLOR (Explorer)
  <TABLE> tag, 104-105
  <TD> tag, 123-124
  <TR> tag, 112-113
CELLPADDING, <TABLE> tag, 96
CELLSPACING, <TABLE> tag, 97
CHECKED, <INPUT> tag, 152
CLASS, <AREA> tag (imagemaps), 80
CLEAR, <BR> tags, 54-55
COLOR
  <FONT> tag, 47-50
  <HR> tag (Explorer), 56-57
COLS
  <FRAMESET> tag, 162
  <TEXTAREA> tag, 154-155
COLSPAN, <TD> tag, 116-119
CONTENT, <META> tag, 29-30
CONTROLLER, <EMBED> tag, 89
CONTROLS, <IMG> tag, 88
COORDS, <AREA> tag, 79
DYNSRC, <IMG> tag, 87
ENCTYPE, <FORM> tag, 138
FACE
  <BASEFONT> tag (Explorer), 46
  <FONT> tag, 51
FRAME, <TABLE> tag (Explorer), 97-99
FRAMEBORDER
  <FRAME> tag, 167
  <FRAMESET> tag, 164
FRAMESPACING, <FRAMESET> tag, 164-165

Index

HEIGHT
  <EMBED> *tag, 85*
  <IFRAME> *tag, 172*
  <IMAGE> *tag, 73-74*
  <TABLE> *tag, 101-104*
  <TD> *tag, 120-122*
HREF
  <AREA> *tag, 79*
  <A> *tag, 64-68, 77*
HSPACE
  <IMAGE> *tag, 72-73*
  <IMG> *tag, 194, 209-211*
HTTP-EQUIV, <META> *tag, 28-29*
  Refresh command, 30-31
ID, <AREA> tag (imagemaps), 80
ISMAP, <IMAGE> *tag, 77*
LEFTMARGIN, <BODY> *tag, 42-43*
LINK, <BODY> *tag, 43-44*
LOOP
  <EMBED> *tag, 89*
  <IMG> *tag, 87*
  <BGSOUND> *tag, 83-84*
  <EMBED> *tag, 84*
LOWSRC, <IMAGE> tag (Netscape), 74-75
MARGINHEIGHT, <FRAME> *tag, 167*
MARGINWIDTH, <FRAME> *tag, 168*
METHOD, <FORM> *tag, 136-137*
MULTIPLE, <SELECT> *tag, 153-154*
NAME
  <A> *tag, 66-68*
  <FRAME> *tag, 167*
  <INPUT> *tag, 139*
  <MAP> *tag, 78*
  <SELECT> *tag, 153*
NOHREF, <AREA> *tag, 79*
NORESIZE, <FRAME> *tag, 169*
NOSHADE, <HR> *tag, 56-57*
NOTAB, <AREA> tag (imagemaps), 80
NOWRAP
  <TD> *tag, 119-120*
  <TR> *tag, 111*
ONBLUR, <INPUT> *tag, 150-152*
ONCHANGE, <INPUT> *tag, 150-152*
ONCLICK, <INPUT> *tag, 150-152*

ONFOCUS, <INPUT> *tag, 150-152*
ONSUBMIT, <FORM> *tag, 137*
ROWS
  <FRAMESET> *tag, 162-163*
  <TEXTAREA> *tag, 154-155*
ROWSPAN, <TD> *tag, 116-119*
RULES, <TABLE> *tag (Explorer), 99-100*
SCROLLING
  <FRAME> *tag, 169*
  <FRAMESET> *tag, 165-166*
SELECTED, <OPTION> *tag, 153*
SHAPE, <AREA> *tag, 79*
SIZE
  <FONT> *tag, 46-47*
  <HR> *tag, 56*
  <SELECT> *tag, 153*
SPAN, <COLGROUP> *tag, 129-130*
SRC
  <BGSOUND> *tag, 83-84*
  <FRAME> *tag, 166-167*
  <IMG> *tag, 70*
START
  <IMG> *tag, 87-88*
  <OL> *tag, 62*
TAB, <AREA> tag (imagemaps), 80
TARGET
  <AREA> *tag (imagemaps), 79*
  <A> *tag, 170-171*
  <FORM> *tag, 137*
TEXT, <BODY> *tag, 43-44*
TITLE, <AREA> tag (imagemaps), 80
TOPMARGIN, <BODY> *tag, 42-43*
TYPE
  <OL> *tag, 60-61*
  <INPUT> *tag, 140-152*
USEMAP (<IMAGE> *tag), 77-80*
  <AREA> *tag (hot spots), 78-80*
  <MAP> *tag, 78*
VALIGN
  <TABLE> *tag, 94*
  <TD> *tag, 114-115*
  <TR> *tag, 109*
VALUE
  <INPUT> *tag, 139-140*
  <OPTION> *tag, 153*
VLINK, <BODY> *tag, 43-44*

VSPACE
  <IMAGE> *tag, 72-73*
  <IMG> *tag, 194, 210-211*
WIDTH
  <EMBED> *tag, 85*
  <HR> *tag, 56*
  <IFRAME> *tag, 172*
  <IMAGE> *tag, 73-74*
  <TABLE> *tag, 101-104*
  <TD> *tag, 120-122*
WRAP=, <TEXTAREA> tag (Netscape), 156
.AU files, *see* audio
audience, 5-6
audio, 83-85
  backgrounds (<BGSOUND> tag), 83-84
  embedded (<EMBED> tag), 84-85
author's (Ian Bell) Web site, 288
AUTOPLAY attribute,
  <EMBED> tag (video), 89
AVIs, *see* video

B

<B> tag, 58
BACKGROUND attribute, 31-39
  <TABLE> tag (Explorer), 105-106
  <TD> tag (Explorer), 124-125
  tiling
    horizontal, 32-34
    small images, 36-38
    texture, 38-39
    vertical, 34-36
backgrounds
  animated GIFs, 243
  audio (<BGSOUND> tag), 83-84
  BGPROPERTIES attribute, <BODY> tag, 42
  color, 39-42
    muting, 181-182
  creating graphics, 175-184
    blurring, 181
    filling in selections, 180
    layers, 178
    line guides, 178
    muting backgrounds, 181-182
    Photoshop preferences, 176

preparing images for the Web,
   182-184
   textures, 177
tables, 105-106
   cells, 115-116
   color, 94
tiling
   horizontal, 32-34
   small images, 36-38
   table cells, 123-125
   tables, 105-106
   texture, 38-39
   vertical, 34-36
bandwidth (connection speed), 5-6
<BASEFONT> tag (Explorer), 46-47
   FACE attribute, 46
beveled text, 199-202
Beverly Hills Software Web site, 285
BGCOLOR attribute
   <BODY> tag, 189
   <TABLE> tag, 94
   <TD> tag, 115-116
   <TR> tag, 110-111
<BGSOUND> tag, 83-84
blending layers (Photoshop 4.0), 216-217
blocking pages, 18-22
   graphics, 20-21
   HTML templates, 21-22
   laying out pages on paper, 20
blurring graphics (Photoshop), 181, 198-201, 219-220
BMPs (bit maps), *see* **tiling (backgrounds)**
body sections, 31-44
   backgrounds, 31-39
      horizontal tiling, 32-34
      small image tiling, 36-38
      texture tiling, 38-39
      vertical tiling, 34-36
   color, 39-42
      hex numbering, 41-42
      RGB values, 39-40
   links, 43-44
   margins (LEFTMARGIN/ TOPMARGIN attributes), 42-43
   text (TEXT attribute), 43-44

<BODY> tag, 26, 31
   BACKGROUND attribute, 31-39
      horizontal tiling, 32-34
      small image tiling, 36-38
      texture tiling, 38-39
      vertical tiling, 34-36
   BGCOLOR attribute, 39-42, 189
      hex numbering, 41-42
      RGB values, 39-40
   BGPROPERTIES attribute (Explorer), 42
   LEFTMARGIN/TOPMARGIN attributes (Explorer), 42-43
   LINK attribute, 43-44
   TEXT attribute, 43-44
bold text, 58
BORDER attribute
   <IMAGE> tag, 72-73
   <TABLE> tag, 95-96
BORDERCOLOR attributes
   <TABLE> tag (Explorer), 104-105
   <TD> tag (Explorer), 123-124
   <TR> tag (Explorer), 112-113
borders
   frames, 164, 167
   images, 72-73
   tables, 95-96
      color, 104-105
bots, 28
   <META> tag
      CONTENT attribute, 29-30
      HTTP-EQUIV attribute, 28-29
bottom-aligning images, 71
boxes
   alert boxes, 270
   checkboxes, forms, 143-144
   text boxes (<TEXTAREA> tag)
      forms, 154-155
      WRAP= attribute (Netscape), 156
**
 tag, 53-55**
   CLEAR attribute, 54-55
   transparent GIF spacing, 209-210
**breaks (
 tag), 53-55**
browsers
   browser-specific sites, 7-9
   non-frame browsers, 170
   see also Internet Explorer; Netscape Navigator

bullets, 191-194
Button mode (Photoshop), 211-212
buttons, form input, 145-146
   CHECKED attribute, 152
   radio buttons, 144-145
   reset buttons, 147-148
   submit buttons, 147
Byte Computers Web site, 265

C

c|net Web site, 18-19
CELLPADDING attribute, <TABLE> tag, 96
cells, tables, 113-125
   alignment, 113-115
   backgrounds
      color, 115-116
      pattern (Explorer), 124-125
   border color (Explorer), 123-124
   column span, 116-119
   graphical tables, 206-208
   headers/footers, 125-127
   height, 120-122
   padding, 96
   row span, 116-119
   spacing, 97
   text wrap, 119-120
   width, 120-122
CELLSPACING attribute, <TABLE> tag, 97
center-aligning images, 71
CGI (Common Gateway Interface), 258-263
   advantages, 258-259
   forms, 136, 261-263
   GET method, 259-261
   imagemaps, 77
   POST method, 259
checkboxes, form input, 143-144
CHECKED attribute, <INPUT> tag, 152
circles, imagemap hot spots, 79
CLASS attribute, <AREA> tag (imagemaps), 80
CLASSID= parameter, <OBJECT> tag, 274
CLEAR attribute, <BR> tags, 54-55

Index

client-side imagemaps, 75-77
  USEMAP attribute, 77-80
  versus server-side, 76-77
  see also imagemaps
CODEBASE= parameter, <OBJECT> tag, 274
<COL> tag, 127, 130-132
  ALIGN attribute, 131
<COLGROUP> tag, 127-129
  ALIGN attribute, 128-129
  SPAN attribute, 129-130
color
  backgrounds, 39-42
    hex numbering, 41-42
    muting, 181-182
    RGB values, 39-40
    table cells, 115-116
  bit depth, 221-223
  fonts, 47-50
  horizontal rules (Explorer), 56-57
  image borders, 72
  links, 43-44
  reducing palette, 221-223
  tables
    backgrounds, 94, 124-125
    borders (Explorer), 104-105, 112-113
    cell background, 115-116
    cell borders (Explorer), 123-124
    row backgrounds, 110-111
  text, 43-44, 47-50
COLOR attribute, <FONT> tag, 47-50
COLS attribute
  <FRAMESET> tag, 162
  <TEXTAREA> tag, 154-155
COLSPAN attribute, <TD> tag, 116-119
columns
  form text boxes, 154-155
  frames, 162
  tables, 116-119, 127-132
    <COL> tag, 130-132
    <COLGROUP> tag, 127-130
    COLSPAN attribute, <TD> tag, 116-119
Common Gateway Interface, see CGI
compressing GIFs, 182
CompuServe GIFs, see GIFs

CONTENT attribute, <META> tag, 29-30
CONTROLLER attribute, <EMBED> tag, 89
controls (ActiveX), 270-274
  forms, 137
CONTROLS attribute, <IMG> tag, 88
COORDS attribute, <AREA> tag, 79
copying actions (Photoshop), 214-215

D-E

data cells, tables, see cells, tables
<DD> tag, 62-63
definition lists, 62-63
deleting layers (Photoshop 4.0), 216
depth, Web sites, 16
dithering images (Photoshop), 182-183
<DL> tag, 62-63
<DT> tag, 62-63
DYNSRC attribute, <IMG> tag, 87

e-mail, hyperlinks, 65-66
<EMBED> tag
  audio, 84-85
  video, 88-89
encoding forms (ENCTYPE attribute, <FORM> tag), 138
Explorer, see Internet Explorer

F

FACE attribute
  <BASEFONT> tag (Explorer), 46
  <FONT> tag, 51
fade animations, 243-250
  assembling animation, 247-250
    Macintosh (GifBuilder), 247-248
    PC (GIF Animator), 249-250
  creating images (Photoshop), 243-247
    creating global palettes, 245-246
  global palettes, 245-246
file size, animated GIFs, 237-239

flashing animations, 254
focus (ONFOCUS attribute, <INPUT> tag), 150-152
<FONT> tag, 45-51
  COLOR attribute, 47-50
  FACE attribute, 51
  SIZE attribute, 46-47
footers, tables, 125-127
<FORM> tag, 135-138
  ACTION attribute, 136
  ENCTYPE attribute, 138
  GET/POST options, 136-137
  METHOD attribute, 136-137
  ONSubmit attribute, 137
  TARGET attribute, 137
formatting text, 58
forms, 133-138
  CGI, 136, 258-263
    advantages, 258-259
    creating forms, 261-263
    GET method, 259-261
    POST method, 259
  encoding, 138
  frames, 137
  input, 138-152
    button input type, 145-146
    checkbox input type, 143-144
    CHECKED attribute, 152
    image type, 148-150
    ONFOCUS/ONBLUR/ONCHANGE/ONCLICK events, 150-152
    password input type, 142
    radio input type, 144-145
    reset input type, 147-148
    submit input type, 147
    text input type, 140-142
    type names, 139
    values, 139-140
  processing, 136-137
    hidden input type, 149-154
  scripts/ActiveX controls, 137
  selection lists, 153-154
  text boxes, 154-155
FRAME attribute, <TABLE> tag (Explorer), 97-99
<FRAME> tag, 166-169
  ALIGN attribute, 168-169
  FRAMEBORDER attribute, 167
  MARGINHEIGHT attribute, 167
  MARGINWIDTH attribute, 168
  NAME attribute, 167
  NORESIZE attribute, 169
  SCROLLING attribute, 169
  SRC attribute, 166-167

FRAMEBORDER attribute
  <FRAME> tag, 167
  <FRAMESET> tag, 164
frames, 157-166
  alignment, 168-169
  borders, 164, 167
  columns, 162
  forms, 137
  inline frames, 171-172
  margin height/width, 167-168
  names, 167
    targets, 170-171
  nesting, 161
  non-frame browsers, 170
  preventing resizing, 169
  rows, 162-163
  scrollbars, 165-166, 169
  spacing, 164-165
  tables, 97-99
  URLs, 166-167
<FRAMESET> tag, 160-166
  COLS attribute, 162
  FRAMEBORDER attribute, 164
  FRAMESPACING attribute, 164-165
  <NOFRAMES> tag, 170
  ROWS attribute, 162-163
  SCROLLING attribute, 165-166
FRAMESPACING attribute,
  <FRAMESET> tag, 164-165
FrontPage site maps, 16
FTP hyperlinks, 65

G

Gaussian Blur shadow, graphics, 198, 201, 219-220
GET method (forms)
  CGI, 259-261
  <FORM> tag, 136-137
GIF Animator, 232, 234-237
  backgrounds, 243
  changing animation parameters, 236
  duration (timing), 242
  fade animations, 249-250
  glowing animations, 254
  Loop command, 237
  moving animations, 255-256
  Web site, 232

GIF Construction Set, 232, 234-237
  Control command
    backgrounds, 243
    Delay (timing), 242
  global palette, 234-235
  inserting control options, 236-237
  Web site, 232
GIF89a plug-in, 186-190
GifBuilder (Mac), animated GIFs, 231-234
  Effects menu, 234
  fade animations, 247-248
  Frame Position, 233
  glowing animations, 253
  Interframe Delay, 233
  Loop command, 233
  moving animations, 255
  Options menu, 232-233
GIFs (Graphics Interchange Format)
  animations, *see* animated GIFs
  backgrounds, *see* tiling (backgrounds)
  compression, 182
  inline images, 70
  transparent GIFs, 185-190, 201
    alpha channel mapping, 186
    anti-aliasing, 185-186
    creating, 187-190
    GIF89a plug-in, 186-187
    spacing, 208-210
  see also graphics
global palettes, GIF animation, 234-235, 240
  creating, 240-242
    Custom option, 241
    fade animations, 245-246
    indexing colors, 240
glowing animations, 250-254
  assembling animation, 253-254
    Macintosh (GifBuilder), 253
    PC (GIF Animator), 254
  creating images (Photoshop), 250-252
gopher site hyperlinks, 65
graphics, 175
  aligning images, 71-72
  alternate text, 75

animations, *see* animated GIFs
backgrounds, 175-184
  blurring, 181
  filling in selections, 180
  layers, 178
  line guides, 178
  muting backgrounds, 181-182
  Photoshop preferences, 176
  preparing images for Web, 182-184
  textures, 177
borders, 72-73
color, bit depth, 221-223
dithering (Photoshop), 182-183
grids, 204-205
halos, correcting, 187-188
height, 73-74
icons, 191-195
  creating, 191-194
  sizing/spacing, 194-195
imagemaps, 75-82
  <AREA> tag (hot spots), 78-80
  client-side versus server-side, 76-77
  coordinates, 80-82
  ISMAP attribute (server-side), 77
  <MAP> tag, 78
  USEMAP attribute (client-side), 77-80
inline images, 69-71
low-resolution images, 74-75
page blocking, 20-21
photographs, 223-226
resizing, 220-221
shadow effects, 218-220
  blurring, 219-220
  layers, 218
small image tiling, 36-38
tables (graphical tables), 202-208
  creating image, 202-206
  HTML, 206-208
text (graphical text), 195-202
  beveled text, 199-202
transparent GIFs, 185-190, 201
  alpha channel mapping, 186
  anti-aliasing, 185-186
  creating, 187-190

Index

GIF89a plug-in, 186-187
spacing, 208-210
video, 85-89
   <EMBED> tag, 88-89
   <IMG> tag, 86-88
width, 73-74
see also Photoshop 4.0
Graphics Interchange Format,
see **GIFs**

H

halos (graphics), correcting,
187-188
head sections (<HEAD> tag),
26-31
  <META> tag, 28-31
    CONTENT attribute, 29-30
    HTTP-EQUIV attribute, 28-29
    Refresh command, 30-31
    search engines, 28
<HEAD> tag, 26
  see also head sections
headers, tables, 125-127
height
  frames
    inline frames, 172
    margins, 167
  images, 73-74
  tables, 101-104
    cells, 120-122
HEIGHT attribute
  <EMBED> tag, 85
  <IFRAME> tag, 172
  <IMAGE> tag, 73-74
  <TABLE> tag, 101-104
  <TD> tag, 120-122
hex color numbering
  page backgrounds, 41-42
  table backgrounds, 94
    rows, 110-111
    cells, 115-116
  see also color
horizontal
  rules (<HR> tag), 56-57
  spacing, see HSPACE attribute
  tiling, 32-34
hot spots, imagemaps, 78-80
  coordinates, 80-82
  see also imagemaps
HotBot search engine, 28
  <META> tag
    CONTENT attribute, 29-30
    HTTP-EQUIV attribute, 28-29

<HR> tag, 56-57
HREF attribute
  <A> tag, 64-66
    anchors, 66-68
    imagemaps, 77
  <AREA> tag (imagemaps), 79
HSPACE attribute
  <IMAGE> tag, 72-73
  <IMG> tag
    icon spacing, 194
    transparent GIFs, 209-211
<HTML> tag, 25-26
HTML (HyperText Markup
Language) tags, 25-26
  <A>, see <A> tag
  <APPLET>, 265-267
  <AREA>, 78-80
  <B>, 58
  <BASEFONT>, 46-47
  <BGSOUND>, 83-84
  <BODY>, see <BODY> tag

, 53-55, 209-210
  <COL>, 127, 130-132
  <COLGROUP>, 127-130
  <DD>, 62-63
  <DL>, 62-63
  <DT>, 62-63
  <EMBED>, 84-85, 88-89
  <FONT>, see <FONT> tag
  <FORM>, see <FORM> tag
  <FRAME>, see <FRAME> tag
  <FRAMESET>, see <FRAMESET>
    tag
  <HEAD>, 26
  <HR>, 56-57
  <HTML>, 25-26
  <I>, 58
  <IFRAME>, 171-172
  <IMAGE>, see <IMAGE> tag
  <IMG>, 70, 86-88
  <INPUT>, see <INPUT> tag
  <LI>, 59-60
  <META>, 28-31
  <NOFRAMES>, 170
  <OBJECT>, 273-274
  <OL>, 59-61
  <OPTION>, 153-154
  <P>, 52-53
  <PARAM>, 265-267
  <SCRIPT>, 268-270
  <SELECT>, 152-153
  <TABLE>, see <TABLE> tag
  <TBODY>, 125-127

  <TD>, see <TD> tag
  <TEXTAREA>, 154-155
  <TITLE>, 27
  <TFOOT>, 125-127
  <THEAD>, 125-127
  <TR>, 207-208
  <TR>, see <TR> tag
  <U>, 58
  <UL>, 59-61
HTTP (HyperText Transport
Protocol) servers, see **servers**
(Web)
HTTP-EQUIV attribute, <META>
tag, 28-29
  Refresh command, 30-31
hyperlinks, 63-68
  anchors, 66-68
  color, 43-44
  FTP sites, 65
  gopher sites, 65
  imagemaps, 79
  mailto: option, 65-66
  newsgroups, 65
  Telnet servers, 65
  URLs (Uniform Resource
    Locators), 64-65
HyperText Markup Language,
see **HTML tags**
HyperText Transport Protocol
(HTTP) servers, see **servers**

I

<I> tag, 58
icons, 191-195
  creating, 191-194
  shadow effects, 193
  sizing/spacing, 194-195
  tiling, backgrounds, 36-38
ID attribute, <AREA> tag
(imagemaps), 80
<IFRAME> tag, 171-172
<IMAGE> tag, 71-75
  ALIGN attribute, 71-72
  ALT attribute, 75
  BORDER attribute, 72-73
  HEIGHT attribute, 73-74
  HSPACE attribute, 72-73
  ISMAP attribute, 77
  LOWSRC attribute (Netscape),
    74-75
  USEMAP attribute, 77-78
  VSPACE attribute, 72-73
  WIDTH attribute, 73-74

imagemaps, 75-82
  client-side
    USEMAP *attribute, 77-80*
    versus server-side, 76-77
  hot spots (<AREA> tag), 78-80
    coordinates, 80-82
  <MAP> *tag, 78*
  server-side
    ISMAP *attribute, 77*
    versus client-side, 76-77
images
  aligning, 71-72
    forms, 148-149
  alternate text, 75
  animations, *see* animated GIFs
  borders, 72-73
  color, bit depth, 221-223
  dithering (Photoshop), 182-183
  form input, 148-150
  graphical tables, 202-208
    creating images, 202-206
    HTML, 206-208
  height, 73-74
  inline images, 69-71
  low-resolution images, 74-75
  resizing, 220-221
  video, 85-89
    <EMBED> *tag, 88-89*
    <IMG> *tag, 86-88*
  width, 73-74
  see also graphics; Photoshop 4.0
<IMG> *tag, 70*
  HSPACE attribute
    icon spacing, 194
    transparent GIFs, 209-211
  SRC attribute, Java pages, 266
  video, 86-88
  VSPACE attribute
    icon spacing, 194
    transparent GIFs, 210-211
indexes
  imagemaps, *see* imagemaps
  search engines, 28
    CONTENT *attribute,* <META> *tag, 29-30*
    HTTP-EQUIV *attribute,* <META> *tag, 28-29*

inline
  frames, 171-172
  images, 69-71
  video, 85-89
    <EMBED> *tag, 88-89*
    <IMG> *tag, 86-88*
  see also images
<INPUT> tag, 135, 138-152
  ALIGN attribute, 148-149
  CHECKED attribute, 152
  NAME attribute, 139
  ONBLUR attribute, 150-152
  ONCHANGE attribute, 150-152
  ONCLICK attribute, 150-152
  ONFOCUS attribute, 150-152
  TYPE attribute, 140-152
    button, 145-146
    checkbox, 143-144
    image, 148-150
    password, 142
    radio, 144-145
    reset, 147-148
    submit, 147
    text, 140-142
  VALUE attribute, 139-140
interactive sites
  flow, 16-17
  objectives, 3-5
Internet
  bandwidth, 5-6
  search engines, 28
    CONTENT *attribute,* <META> *tag, 29-30*
    HTTP-EQUIV *attribute,* <META> *tag, 28-29*
Internet Explorer, 7-9
  ActiveX, 272
  <BASEFONT> tag FACE attribute, 46
  <BODY> tag,
    BGPROPERTIES *attribute, 42*
    LEFTMARGIN/TOPMARGIN *attributes, 42-43*
  browser-specific sites, 7-9
  <HR> tag COLOR attribute, 56-57
  <TABLE> tag
    BACKGROUND *attribute, 105-106*
    BORDERCOLOR *attributes, 104-105*

    FRAME *attribute, 97-99*
    RULES *attribute, 99-100*
  <TD> tag
    BACKGROUND *attribute, 124-125*
    BORDERCOLOR *attributes, 123-124*
  <TR> tag BORDERCOLOR attributes, 112-113
Internet Information Server, 281-285
  connecting to, 282-283
  features, 281-282
  resources, 284-285
IpSwitch Web site, 291
ISMAP attribute, <IMAGE> tag, 77
italic text, 58

J-K

Java, 263-267
  advantages, 263-264
  Macintosh, 264
  sample applet, 265-267
JavaScript, 267-270
  adding to pages, 268-270
  advantages, 267-268
  form button events, 150-152
JavaSoft Web site, 264
JPEG (Joint Photographic Experts Group) graphics
  inline images, 70
  see also graphics
JScript, 267-270
  adding to pages, 268-270
  advantages, 267-268

L

layering graphics (Photoshop), 215-217
  background graphics, 178
  blending, 216-217
  deleting, 216
  graphical tables, 203
  graphical text, 196-197
  Layers palette, 196
  moving, 216
  scanned photographs, 223-226
  shadow effects, 218
  transparency, 201, 215

Index

left-aligning images, 71
LEFTMARGIN attribute, <BODY> tag, 42-43
<LI> tag, 59-60
line breaks (
 tag), 53-55
  CLEAR attribute, 54-55
links, 63-68
  anchors, 66-68
  color, 43-44
  FTP sites, 65
  gopher sites, 65
  imagemaps, 79
  mailto: option, 65-66
  newsgroups, 65
  Telnet servers, 65
  URLs (Uniform Resource Locators), 64-65
lists, 59-63
  definition lists, 62-63
  ordered lists, 59-61
  selection lists, forms, 153
  unordered lists, 59-61
LOOP attribute
  <IMG> tag, 87
  <BGSOUND> tag, 83-84
  <EMBED> tag, 84
  video, 89
Loop command, GIF animation
  GifBuilder program (Macintosh), 233
  GIF Animator (PC), 237
LOWSRC attribute, <IMAGE> tag (Netscape), 74-75
Lycos search engine, 28
  <META> tag
    CONTENT attribute, 29-30
    HTTP-EQUIV attribute, 28-29

M

Macintosh
  Apache for Unix server, connecting to, 290
  GifBuilder program, 231-234
    Effects menu, 234
    fade animations, 247-248
    Frame Position, 233
    Interframe Delay, 233
    glowing animations, 253
    Loop command, 233
    moving animations, 255
  Java, 264

WebSTAR server, 285-288
  connecting to, 287-288
  features, 285-287
  resources, 288
Magellan search engine, 28
  <META> tag
    CONTENT attribute, 29-30
    HTTP-EQUIV attribute, 28-29
MAILTO form software, 261-263
  Web site, 261
mailto: option, hyperlinks, 65-66
<MAP> tag, 78
MapEdit software, 82
Mapper Web site, 82
mapping
  imagemaps, see imagemaps
  site maps, 13-18
    entry/exit points, 17
    flow of interactivity, 16-17
    resource points, 18
MARGINHEIGHT attribute, <FRAME> tag, 167
margins, frames, 167-168
  LEFTMARGIN/TOPMARGIN attribute, <BODY> tag, 42-43
MARGINWIDTH attribute, <FRAME> tag, 168
<META> tag, 28-31
  CONTENT attribute, 29-30
  HTTP-EQUIV attribute, 28-29
    Refresh command, 30-31
  search engines, 28
METHOD attribute, <FORM> tag, 136-137
Microsoft
  GIF Animator, see GIF Animator
  Internet Information Server, 281-285
    connecting to, 282-283
    features, 281-282
    resources, 284-285
.MID files, see audio
middle-aligning images, 71
minus signs (–), font size, 46-47
modem speed, 5-6
Motion blur shadow, graphics (Photoshop), 198, 219
movies, see video
moving animations, 255-256

assembling animation, 255-256
  Macintosh (GifBuilder), 255
  PC (GIF Animator), 255-256
  creating images (Photoshop), 255
MPEGs, see video
MULTIPLE attribute, <SELECT> tag, 153-154
muting background color, 181-182

N

NAME attribute
  <A> tag, 66-68
  <FRAME> tag, 167
  <INPUT> tag, 139
  <MAP> tag, 78
  <SELECT> tag, 153
NCompass Labs (ActiveX), 271-274
nested frames, 161
NetCraft U.K. server survey, 278
Netscape Navigator, 7-9
  ActiveX, 272
  browser-specific sites, 7-9
  <IMAGE> tag
    HSPACE/VSPACE attributes, 72
    LOWSRC attribute, 74-75
  <TEXTAREA> tag WRAP= attribute, 156
newsgroup hyperlinks, 65
<NOFRAMES> tag, 170
NOHREF attribute, <AREA> tag, 79
NORESIZE attribute, <FRAME> tag, 169
NOSHADE attribute, <HR> tag, 56-57
NOTAB attribute, <AREA> tag (imagemaps), 80
NOWRAP attribute
  <TD> tag, 119-120
  <TR> tag, 111

O

Object Linking and Embedding (OLE), see ActiveX
<OBJECT> tag, 273-274
  ActiveX controls, 273-274
  CLASSID= parameter, 274
  CODEBASE= parameter, 274

\<OL\> tag, 59-62
    START attribute, 62
    TYPE attribute, 60-61
OLE (Object Linking and Embedding), *see* ActiveX
ONBLUR attribute, \<INPUT\> tag, 150-152
ONCHANGE attribute, \<INPUT\> tag, 150-152
ONCLICK attribute, \<INPUT\> tag, 150-152
ONFOCUS attribute, \<INPUT\> tag, 150-152
ONSUBMIT attribute, \<FORM\> tag, 137
operating systems, 6-9
\<OPTION\> tag, 153-154
    see also \<SELECT\> tag
ordered lists, 59-61
Over The Moon Web site, 4

P

\<P\> tag, 52-53
page blocking, 18-22
    graphics, 20-21
    HTML templates, 21-22
    laying out on paper, 20
pagination, 52-58
    formatting text, 58
    horizontal rules (\<HR\> tag), 56-57
    line breaks (\<BR\> tag), 53-55
        CLEAR *attribute,* 54-55
    paragraphs, 52-53
palettes
    GIF animation, 234-235, 240
        creating, 240-242
        fade animations, 245-246
    reducing (image colors), 221-223
paragraphs, 52-53
\<PARAM\> tag, 265-267
passwords, form input, 142
percent signs (%), form encoding, 138
photographs, scanned, 223-226
Photoshop 4.0, 211-223
    actions, 211-215
        animated GIFs, 244
        Button mode, 211-212
        copying, 214-215
        Default mode, 211

editing, 214
recording, 214
Actions palette, 211-212
animated GIFs
    fade animations, 243-247
    glowing animations, 250-252
    moving animations, 255
backgrounds, 176-184
    blurring, 181
    filling in selections, 180
    layers, 178
    line guides, 178
    muting backgrounds, 181-182
    preferences, 176
    preparing images for Web, 182-184
    textures, 177
bit depth, colors, 221-223
Brushes palette, 224
dialog boxes
    Fill, 190
    Image Size, 221
    Indexed Color, 183, 222
    New, 177
    Offset, 193
    Texturizer, 177
    Type Tool, 189, 196
dithering images, 182-183
global palettes, animated GIFs, 245-246
Gradient tool, 192, 200
graphical tables, 202-208
    creating image, 202-206
    HTML, 206-208
graphical text, 195-202
    beveled text, 199-202
grids, 204-205
icons, creating, 191-194
Lasso tool, 202
layers, 215-217
    background graphics, 178
    blending, 216-217
    deleting, 216
    graphical tables, 203
    graphical text, 196-197
    moving, 216
    scanned photographs, 223-226
    shadow effects, 218
    transparency, 201, 215
Layers palette, 196, 215
Marquee tool, 192

resizing images, 220-221
scanned photographs, 223-226
shadow effects, 218-220
    blurring, 181, 219-220
    icons, 193
    layers, 218
transparent GIFs, 185-190
    alpha channel mapping, 186
    anti-aliasing, 185-186
    creating, 187-190
    GIF89a plug-in, 186-187
zooming, 177
pictures, *see* graphics; photographs
planning Web sites, 1-2
    audience
        bandwidth (connection speed), 5-6
        demographics, 9-10
        platform, 6-9
    objectives, 2-5
        informative sites, 2-3
        interactive sites, 3-5
    page blocking, 18-22
        graphics, 20-21
        HTML templates, 21-22
        laying out on paper, 20
    site maps, 13-18
        entry/exit points, 17
        flow of interactivity, 16-17
        resource points, 18
    surveying content, 10-11
        competition sites, 11
platforms, 6-9
plus signs (+)
    font size, 46-47
    form encoding, 138
polygons, imagemap hot spots, 79
POST method
    CGI, 259
    \<FORM\> tag, 136-137

Q-R

QuickTime movies, *see* video

Radial blur shadow, graphics (Photoshop), 199, 219
radio buttons, form input, 144-145
    CHECKED attribute, 152
.RAM files, *see* audio

Index

rectangles, imagemap hot spots, 79
Refresh command (<META> tag), 30-31
reset buttons, forms, 147-148
resizing
   frames, preventing, 169
   images, 73-74, 220-221
resolution, images, 74-75
RGB color values
   backgrounds, 39-40
   text color, 47-50
right-aligning images, 71
Rocco's Radios Web site
   animated GIFs, 238-239
   browsers, 8-9
   CGI, 261-263
   interactivity, 4
   site map, 14
   site objective, 3
rows
   forms, 154-155
   frames, 162-163
   tables, 106-113
      alignment, 108-109
      background color, 110-111
      border color (Explorer), 112-113
      number of rows (row span), 116-119
      text wrap, 111
ROWS attribute
   <FRAMESET> tag, 162-163
   <TEXTAREA> tag, 154-155
ROWSPAN attribute, <TD> tag, 116-119
rules
   horizontal rules (<HR> tag), 56-57
   tables, 99-100, 127
RULES attribute, <TABLE> tag (Explorer), 99-100

S

Sausage Software Web site, 263
scanned photographs, 223-226
<SCRIPT> tag, 268-270
scripts
   forms, 137
   JavaScript, 267-270
      adding to pages, 268-270
      advantages, 267-268
   JScript, 267-270
      adding to pages, 268-270
      advantages, 267-268
SCROLLING attribute (scrollbars)
   <FRAME> tag, 169
   <FRAMESET> tag, 165-166
search engines, 28
   <META> tag
      CONTENT attribute, 29-30
      HTTP-EQUIV attribute, 28-29
<SELECT> tag, 152-153
   MULTIPLE attribute, 153-154
   NAME attribute, 153-154
   SIZE attribute, 153
   see also <OPTION> tag
SELECTED attribute, <OPTION> tag, 153
selection lists, forms, 153
server-side imagemaps, 75-77
   ISMAP attribute, 77
   versus client-side, 76-77
   see also imagemaps
servers (Web), 277
   Apache for Unix, 288-292
      connecting to, 290-292
      resources, 292
   comparisons, 280
      NetCraft U.K. server survey, 278
   Microsoft Internet Information Server, 281-285
      connecting to, 282-283
      features, 281-282
      resources, 284-285
   WebSTAR (Macintosh), 285-288
      connecting to, 287-288
      features, 285-287
      resources, 288
shadow effects (Photoshop), 218-220
   blurring, 198-199, 201, 219-220
   icons, 193
   layers, 218
SHAPE attribute, <AREA> tag, 79
site maps, 13-18
   entry/exit points, 17
   flow of interactivity, 16-17
   resource points, 18
   see also Web sites
SIZE attribute
   <FONT> tag, 46-47
   <HR> tag, 56
   <SELECT> tag, 153
slide shows, Refresh command (<META> tag), 30-31
software
   MAILTO form software, 261-263
   Photoshop, see Photoshop 4.0
   Sausage Software Web site, 263
sound, 83-85
   backgrounds (<BGSOUND> tag), 83-84
   embedded (<EMBED> tag), 84-85
spacing, see HSPACE attribute; VSPACE attribute
SPAN attribute, <COLGROUP> tag, 129-130
spiders, 28
   <META> tag
      CONTENT attribute, 29-30
      HTTP-EQUIV attribute, 28-29
SRC attribute
   <BGSOUND> tag, 83-84
   <FRAME> tag, 166-167
   <IMG> tag, 70
   Java pages, 266
SRC image input type, forms, 148-149
Star-Nine Web site, 288
START attribute
   <IMG> tag, 87-88
   <OL> tag, 62
submit buttons, forms, 147

T

TAB attribute, <AREA> tag (imagemaps), 80
<TABLE> tag, 92-106
   ALIGN attribute, 93-94
   BACKGROUND attribute (Explorer), 105-106
   BGCOLOR attribute, 94
   BORDER attribute, 95-96
   BORDERCOLOR attributes (Explorer), 104-105
   CELLPADDING attribute, 96
   CELLSPACING attribute, 97
   FRAME attribute (Explorer), 97-99

graphical tables, 206-208
HEIGHT attribute, 101-104
RULES attribute, 99-100, 127
VALIGN attribute, 94
WIDTH attribute, 101-104
tables, 91-92
  alignment, 93-94
  backgrounds, 105-106
    color, 94
  borders, 95-96
    color (Explorer), 104-105
  cells, 113-125
    alignment, 113-115
    background, 115-116, 124-125
    border color (Explorer), 123-124
    column span, 116-119
    height, 120-122
    padding, 96
    row span, 116-119
    spacing, 97
    text wrap, 119-120
    width, 120-122
  columns, 127-132
    <COL> tag, 130-132
    <COLGROUP> tag, 127-130
    COLSPAN attribute, <TD> tag, 116-119
  footers, 125-127
  frames (Explorer), 97-99
  graphical tables, 202-208
    creating image, 202-206
    HTML, 206-208
  headers, 125-127
  height, 101-104
  rows, 106-113
    alignment, 108, 109
    background color, 110-111
    border color (Explorer), 112-113
    text wrap, 111
  rules (Explorer), 99-100
  width, 101-104
tags (HTML), 25-26
  <A>, 63-68, 266
    HREF attribute, 64-66
    NAME attribute, 66-68
    TARGET attribute, 170-171
  <APPLET>, 265-267
  <AREA>, 78-80
  <B>, 58
  <BASEFONT>, 46-47

  <BGSOUND>, 83-84
  <BODY>, 26, 31
    BACKGROUND attribute, 31-39
    BGCOLOR attribute, 39-42, 189
    BGPROPERTIES attribute (Explorer), 42
    LEFTMARGIN/TOPMARGIN attributes (Explorer), 42-43
    LINK attribute, 43-44
    TEXT attribute, 43-44

, 53-55
    CLEAR attribute, 54-55
    transparent GIF spacing, 209-210
  <COL>, 127, 130-132
    ALIGN attribute, 131
  <COLGROUP>, 127-129
    ALIGN attribute, 128-129
    SPAN attribute, 129-130
  <DD>, 62-63
  <DL>, 62-63
  <DT>, 62-63
  <EMBED>
    audio, 84-85
    video, 88-89
  <FONT>, 45-51
    COLOR attribute, 47-50
    FACE attribute, 51
    SIZE attribute, 46-47
  <FORM>, 135-138
    ACTION attribute, 136
    ENCTYPE attribute, 138
    GET/POST options, 136-137
    METHOD attribute, 136-137
    ONSUBMIT attribute, 137
    TARGET attribute, 137
  <FRAME>, 166-169
    ALIGN attribute, 168-169
    FRAMEBORDER attribute, 167
    MARGINHEIGHT attribute, 167
    MARGINWIDTH attribute, 168
    NAME attribute, 167
    NORESIZE attribute, 169
    SCROLLING attribute, 169
    SRC attribute, 166-167
  <FRAMESET>, 160-166
    COLS attribute, 162
    FRAMEBORDER attribute, 164
    FRAMESPACING attribute, 164-165
    <NOFRAMES> tag, 170

    ROWS attribute, 162-163
    SCROLLING attribute, 165-166
  <HEAD>, 26
    see also head sections
  <HR>, 56-57
  <HTML>, 25-26
  <I>, 58
  <IFRAME>, 171-172
  <IMAGE>, 71-75
    ALIGN attribute, 71-72
    ALT attribute, 75
    BORDER attribute, 72-73
    HEIGHT attribute, 73-74
    HSPACE attribute, 72-73
    ISMAP attribute, 77
    LOWSRC attribute (Netscape), 74-75
    USEMAP attribute, 77-78
    VSPACE attribute, 72-73
    WIDTH attribute, 73-74
  <IMG>, 70
    HSPACE attribute, 194, 209-211
    Java pages, 266
    video, 86-88
    VSPACE attribute, 194, 210-211
  <INPUT>, 135, 138-152
    ALIGN attribute, 148-149
    NAME attribute, 139
    TYPE attribute, 140-152
    VALUE attribute, 139-140
    CHECKED attribute, 152
    ONBLUR attribute, 150-152
    ONCHANGE attribute, 150-152
    ONCLICK attribute, 150-152
    ONFOCUS attribute, 150-152
  <LI>, 59-60
  <MAP>, 78
  <META>, 28-31
    CONTENT attribute, 29-30
    HTTP-EQUIV attribute, 28-29
    Refresh command, 30-31
    search engines, 28
  <NOFRAMES>, 170
  <OBJECT>
    ActiveX controls, 273-274
    CLASSID= parameter, 274
    CODEBASE= parameter, 274
  <OL>, 59-62
    START attribute, 62
    TYPE attribute, 60-61

Index

<OPTION>, 153-154
  see also <SELECT> tag
<P>, 52-53
<PARAM>, 265-267
<SCRIPT>, 268-270
<SELECT>, 152-154
  MULTIPLE attribute, 153-154
  NAME attribute, 153-154
  SIZE attribute, 153
<TABLE>, see <TABLE> tag
<TBODY>, 125-127
<TD>, 93, 113-125
  ALIGN attribute, 113-114
  BACKGROUND attribute
    (Explorer), 124-125
  BGCOLOR attribute, 115-116
  BORDERCOLOR attribute
    (Explorer), 123-124
  COLSPAN attribute, 116-119
  graphical tables, 207-208
  HEIGHT attribute, 120-122
  NOWRAP attribute, 119-120
  ROWSPAN attribute, 116-119
  VALIGN attribute, 114-115
  WIDTH attribute, 120-122
<TEXTAREA>
  forms, 154-155
  WRAP attribute (Netscape), 156
<TFOOT>, 125-127
<THEAD>, 125-127
<TITLE>, 27
<TR>, 106-113
  ALIGN attribute, 108
  BGCOLOR attribute, 110-111
  BORDERCOLOR attribute
    (Explorer), 112-113
  graphical tables, 207-208
  NOWRAP attribute, 111
  VALIGN attribute, 109
<U>, 58
<UL>, 59-61
TARGET attribute
  <AREA> tag (imagemaps), 79
  <A> tag, frames, 170-171
  <FORM> tag, 137
<TBODY> tag, 125-127
<TD> tag, 93, 113-125
  ALIGN attribute, 113-114
  BACKGROUND attribute
    (Explorer), 124-125
  BGCOLOR attribute, 115-116
  BORDERCOLOR attribute
    (Explorer), 123-124

COLSPAN attribute, 116-119
graphical tables, 207-208
HEIGHT attribute, 120-122
NOWRAP attribute, 119-120
ROWSPAN attribute, 116-119
VALIGN attribute, 114-115
WIDTH attribute, 120-122
Telnet hyperlinks, 65
templates (HTML), 21-22
text
  aligning
    images, 71-72
    paragraphs, 52-53
  color, 43-44, 47-50
  font, 45-51
    color, 47-50
    face, 51
    size, 46-47
  formatting, 58
  forms
    input, 140-142
    selection lists, 153-154
    text boxes, 154-155
  graphical text, 195-202
    beveled text, 199-202
  horizontal rules (<HR> tag),
    56-57
  line breaks (
 tag), 53-55
    CLEAR attribute, 54-55
  lists, see lists
  paragraphs, 52-53
  tables, see tables
  wrapping
    tables (NOWRAP attribute), 111,
      119-120
    <TEXTAREA> tag, WRAP=
      attribute (Netscape), 156
**<TEXTAREA> tag, forms,
  154-156**
  WRAP= attribute (Netscape),
    156
**textures, background tiling,
  38-39**
  creating graphics, 177
<TFOOT> tag, 125-127
<THEAD> tag, 125-127
tiling (backgrounds), 32-39
  horizontal, 32-34
  small images, 36-38
  tables (Explorer), 105-106
    cells, 124-125
  texture, 38-39

vertical, 34-36, 176-182
  blurring, 181
  filling in selections, 180
  layers, 178
  line guides, 178
  muting backgrounds, 181-182
  preparing images for Web,
    182-184
  textures, 177
**TITLE attribute, <AREA> tag
  (imagemaps), 80**
<TITLE> tag, 27
top-aligning images, 71
**TOPMARGIN attribute, <BODY> tag,
  42-43**
<TR> tag, 106-113
  ALIGN attribute, 108
  BGCOLOR attribute, 110-111
  BORDERCOLOR attribute
    (Explorer), 112-113
  graphical tables, 207-208
  NOWRAP attribute, 111
  VALIGN attribute, 109
**transparency, layers
  (Photoshop), 215**
transparent GIFs, 185-190, 201
  alpha channel mapping, 186
  anti-aliasing, 185-186
  creating, 187-190
  GIF89a plug-in, 186-187
  spacing, 208-210
TYPE attribute
  <OL> tag, 60-61
  <INPUT> tag, 140-152
    button, 145-146
    checkbox, 143-144
    image, 148-150
    password, 142
    radio, 144-145
    reset, 147-148
    submit, 147
    text, 140-142

U

<U> tag, 58
<UL> tag, 59-61
underlining text, 58
**Uniform Resource Locators,
  see URLs**
**Unix, Apache for Unix server,
  288-292**
  connecting to, 290-292
  resources, 292

unordered lists, 59-61
URLs (Uniform Resource Locators)
    CGI, 262-263
    forms
        image files, 148-149
        processing programs, 136
    frames, 166-167
    hyperlinks, 64-65
    inline images, 70
USEMAP attribute, <IMAGE> tag, 77-80
    <AREA> tag (hot spots), 78-80
    <MAP> tag, 78
Usenet newsgroup hyperlinks, 65
users, planning for
    bandwidth (connection speed), 5-6
    demographics, 9-10
    platform, 6-9

V

VALIGN attribute
    <TABLE> tag, 94
    <TD> tag, 114-115
    <TR> tag, 109
VALUE attribute
    <INPUT> tag, 139-140
    <OPTION> tag, 153
vertical
    spacing, *see* VSPACE attribute
    tiling, backgrounds, 34-36, 176-182
        blurring, 181
        filling in selections, 180
        layers, 178
        line guides, 178
        muting backgrounds, 181-182
        preparing images for Web, 182-184
        textures, 177
video, 85-89
    <EMBED> tag, 88-89
    <IMG> tag, 86-88
Virtual Reality Markup Language, *see* VRML
VLINK attribute, <BODY> tag, 43-44

VRML (Virtual Reality Markup Language), 85-89
    <EMBED> tag, 88-89
    <IMG> tag, 86-88
VSPACE attribute
    <IMAGE> tag, 72-73
    <IMG> tag
        icon spacing, 194
        transparent GIFs, 210-211

W

.WAV files, *see* audio
Web pages
    body sections (<BODY> tag), 31-44
        backgrounds, see backgrounds
        links, 43-44
        margins, 42-43
        text, 43-44
    head sections (<HEAD> tag), 26-31
        <META> tag, 28-31
        search engines, 28
    incorporating ActiveX classes, 272-274
Web servers, 277
    Apache for Unix, 288-292
        connecting to, 290-292
        resources, 292
    comparisons, 278, 280
        NetCraft U.K. server survey, 278
    Microsoft Internet Information Server, 281-285
        connecting to, 282-283
        features, 281-282
        resources, 284-285
    WebSTAR (Macintosh), 285-288
        connecting to, 287-288
        features, 285-287
        resources, 288
Web sites
    Acetex Corporation, 2, 16
    Alchemy Mindwork GIF Construction Set, 232
    Apache, 292
    Apple's 20th Anniversary Mac, 10
    author's (Ian Bell), 288
    Beverly Hills Software, 285

Byte Computers, 265
c|net, 18-19
depth, 16
hyperlinks, 64-65
IpSwitch, 291
JavaSoft, 264
MAILTO form software, 261-263
MapEdit, 82
Mapper, 82
Microsoft GIF Animator, 232
NCompass Labs, 271, 273
Over The Moon, 4
planning, 1-2
    objectives, 2-5
    page blocking, 18-22
    site maps, 13-18
    surveying content, 10-11
Rocco's Radios
    animated GIFs, 238-239
    browsers, 8-9
    CGI, 261-263
    interactivity, 4
    site map, 14
    site objective, 3
Sausage Software, 263
Star-Nine, 288
WebReference, 266
width, 16
WebReference Web site, 266
WebSTAR server (Macintosh), 285-288
    connecting to, 287-288
    features, 285-287
    resources, 288
width
    frames
        inline frames, 172
        margins, 168
    images, 73-74
    tables, 101-104
        cells, 120-122
    Web sites, 16
WIDTH attribute
    <EMBED> tag, 85
    <HR> tag, 56
    <IFRAME> tag, 172
    <IMAGE> tag, 73-74
    <TABLE> tag, 101-104
    <TD> tag, 120-122

Index

windows, *see* **frames**
Windows 95/NT
   connecting to Apache for
     Unix server, 291-292
   Microsoft Internet
     Information Server, 281-285
World Wide Web (WWW)
   search engines, 28
     CONTENT attribute, <META>
      tag, 29-30
     HTTP-EQUIV attribute, <META>
      tag, 28-29
   see also Web pages; Web
     servers; Web sites
wrap
   tables (NOWRAP attribute)
     rows, 111
     cells, 119-120
   <TEXTAREA> tag, WRAP=
     attribute (Netscape), 156
WS_FTP program, 291-292

X-Y-Z

Yahoo! search engine, 28
   <META> tag
     CONTENT *attribute, 29-30*
     HTTP-EQUIV *attribute, 28-29*

What's on the CD-ROM

Unless otherwise noted, the software programs on this CD-ROM are shareware, freeware, or trial versions designed to demonstrate the major features of a commercial product.

If you try this software and find it useful, you are requested to register and purchase it as discussed in this documentation or in the About screen of the application. The publisher of this book has not paid the registration fee for this shareware; the cost of this book does not cover the cost of the shareware.

Effects

Auto F/X Coporation

Photo/Graphic Edges™ demo

Typo/Graphic Eges™ demo

Fonts

FontHead Design

Snyder Fonts

SynFonts by Synstelien Design

Vintage Type

Software

Adobe Acrobat Reader 3.0

Bare Bones Software

BBEdit 4.0 demo

BBEdit 4.0 Lite

clip2gif

DeBabelizer Lite® LE

DeBabelizer® Toolbox 1.6.5 demo

Eye Candy 3.0 demo

GifBuilder

GIFConverter

GIFmation™

Mapper

PageSpinner

PhotoGIF™

ProJPEG ™